REHEARSALS OF MANHOOD

Rehearsals of Manhood

ATHENIAN DRAMA AS SOCIAL PRACTICE

John J. Winkler

PRINCETON UNIVERSITY PRESS
PRINCETON & OXFORD

Published by Princeton University Press
41 William Street, Princeton, New Jersey 08540
99 Banbury Road, Oxford OX2 6JX

press.princeton.edu

Library of Congress Cataloging-in-Publication Data

Names: Winkler, John J., author.
Title: Rehearsals of manhood : Athenian drama as social practice / John J. Winkler.
Description: Princeton : Princeton University Press, 2023. | Includes bibliographical references and index.
Identifiers: LCCN 2022013089 (print) | LCCN 2022013090 (ebook) | ISBN 9780691206486 (hardback) | ISBN 9780691213729 (ebook)
Subjects: LCSH: Greek drama—History and criticism. | Masculinity in literature. | Men in literature. | Literature and society—Greece—Athens—History—To 1500. | Theater—Greece—Athens—History—To 500. | Athens (Greece)—Intellectual life. | BISAC: DRAMA / Ancient & Classical | HISTORY / Ancient / Greece
Classification: LCC PA3136 .W56 2023 (print) | LCC PA3136 (ebook) | DDC 882/.0109351—dc23/eng/20220531
LC record available at https://lccn.loc.gov/2022013089
LC ebook record available at https://lccn.loc.gov/2022013090

British Library Cataloging-in-Publication Data is available

Editorial: Rob Tempio and Chloe Coy
Production Editorial: Natalie Baan
Jacket Design: Heather Hansen
Production: Erin Suydam
Publicity: Charlotte Coyne and Alyssa Sanford
Copyeditor: Hank Southgate

Jacket image: Apulian red-figure bell-krater. NM47.5, Nicholson Collection, Chau Chak Wing Museum, The University of Sydney. Donated by the Classical Association 1946.

This book has been composed in Miller

Printed on acid-free paper. ∞

Printed in the United States of America

10 9 8 7 6 5 4 3 2 1

To

David Andrew Braaten

for a ten-year fantastic voyage

CONTENTS

LIST OF ILLUSTRATIONS

Color Plates (following page 116)

FOREWORD

David M. Halperin

JOHN J. WINKLER, the author of this book, died on April 25, 1990. He was forty-six years old. At the time of his death, due to complications caused by AIDS, he left *Rehearsals of Manhood* virtually complete. The manuscript required only minor alterations—stylistic, bibliographical, organizational—most of them of a cosmetic nature.

I began editing the manuscript for publication in 1990, but various upheavals in my personal and professional life prevented me from finishing the work. As time passed and my sense of closeness to the book and its argument faded, the task of completing it became more daunting. Also, the amount of editing necessary to do justice to its achievement increased: after all, I wanted the book to remain timely and to maintain its relation to relevant work in classical scholarship, including new work that had appeared since the author's death. Just at that moment, however, my own relation to the field of classical scholarship, which had always been marginal, became even more tenuous, and I began to lose confidence in my ability to see the project through. Fortunately, in 2014, Kirk Ormand came to my aid and offered to help me complete the work during a year when we were both on leave from teaching. Together we have been able to bring this project to a successful, though extremely belated, conclusion.

In his afterword at the end of this volume, Kirk explains the nature of the revisions to the manuscript that he considered necessary in order to bring the book up to date and to address the developments in classical scholarship that have taken place over the three decades separating the book's composition from its publication. In this foreword, I describe how the book came into being, how it differs from earlier versions (both published and unpublished), and the nature of the editorial alterations that Kirk and I have made in the course of producing the current and now definitive text for publication.

When he wasn't being an author, John J. Winkler referred to himself, and was universally known to his acquaintances, as Jack Winkler. He even published an early essay under that name.[1] So that is how I shall refer to him here.

1. Winkler 1981.

Rehearsals of Manhood grew out of a long article that Jack published in 1985 in *Representations*, the flagship journal of The New Historicism, based at Berkeley and distributed by the University of California Press. The article was entitled "The Ephebes' Song: *Tragôidia* and *Polis*."[2] It offered a new theory of the origins and the social meanings of Greek tragedy. Jack was convinced that he had come up with a truly original interpretation of Greek tragedy, and his confidence in the rightness of his approach to the topic only grew with time. Nonetheless, he had to concede that his initial presentation of that approach provoked a certain amount of skepticism, some of it understandable, from various quarters. He ultimately came to be dissatisfied with the way he had laid out his argument in the *Representations* article, and, in any case, he wanted to develop it into a more extended study.

Jack initially reformulated his interpretation in the form of a revised version of his 1985 article. The new article appeared, still bearing the same title, in a collection of scholarly essays called *Nothing to Do with Dionysos? Athenian Drama in Its Social Context*, which Jack coedited with Froma Zeitlin.[3] The collection was published in February 1990, not long before Jack's death. The second version of "The Ephebes' Song" addressed some of the criticisms that had been leveled at the earlier article; it omitted a good deal of material from that article and added a number of qualifications along with much new original evidence and many new arguments. It reads like an intermediate draft of *Rehearsals of Manhood*, laying out as it does, in incomplete form, the arguments deployed in the first half of the book. Anyone who takes the trouble to compare the revised article of 1990 with the present volume will find nearly all of it reproduced here, though parceled out and distributed among the introduction, chapter 1, chapter 2, and appendix I. Most of that material had figured to some extent in the original 1985 article on "The Ephebes' Song"; it is striking, in retrospect, to find already present there many of the insights elaborated in this book.

Meanwhile, in September 1988, Jack delivered The Martin Classical Lectures at Oberlin College. On that occasion, he presented a more developed, and further revised, formulation of his approach to Classical Athenian drama. The lecture series consisted of four talks, which now correspond to the four chapters of this book. Individual lectures from the series were also delivered elsewhere. Two of them were revised for publication. A version of the first Martin Classical Lecture appeared in the Spring 1989 issue of the new *Stanford Humanities Review* under the title "Women in Armor Men in Drag: The Poetics of Manhood in Athenian Drama."[4] A version of the second Martin Classical Lecture appeared posthumously in 1990 in a special issue of the feminist journal *differences*, based at the Pembroke Center for Teaching and Research on Women at Brown University, under the title "Phallos Politikos:

2. Winkler 1985.
3. Winkler 1990b.
4. Winkler 1989.

Representing the Body Politic in Athens."[5] This book incorporates the published versions of the first two Martin Classical Lectures, combining them with material from the 1990 version of "The Ephebes' Song" to form the first two chapters of *Rehearsals of Manhood.*

That, then, is the editorial background the reader will need to bear in mind in order to understand the textual basis for the first half of *Rehearsals of Manhood.* In order to account for the state of the remainder of the book, I need to explain the circumstances under which the final draft of it took shape.

In July 1989, Jack Winkler, already quite ill, confronted a sudden, particularly grave medical crisis. It seemed possible that he might not survive. When I visited him in his hospital room at Stanford, he asked me whether I was prepared to take charge of *Rehearsals of Manhood* and to complete it for publication. The book already existed at the time in the form of an entire draft, but it suffered—or so Jack felt—from significant omissions.

I answered that I was prepared to undertake the task of completing the book. I did so with the full knowledge that Jack had not asked me to do it because either of us thought that I was qualified to be his understudy by virtue of some special expertise in the field of Attic drama. In fact, I have virtually no such expertise—unlike, in that respect, Kirk Ormand, whose collaboration in the editing of this book has therefore been particularly beneficial to it. Rather, Jack turned the manuscript over to me because he knew I was willing, indeed eager, to see his work completed in the spirit in which he had composed it.

Jack and I had, for several years, been working closely together on a number of related projects. With Froma Zeitlin, we coedited an anthology of essays, by various classical scholars, devoted to the history of sexuality; it appeared in 1990 under the title *Before Sexuality: The Construction of Erotic Experience in the Ancient Greek World.*[6] Jack received an advance copy of the book two days before he died. Jack and I had also encouraged each other to produce collections of our own essays on sex and gender in the ancient Greek world; the two resulting volumes both appeared about the same time, in late 1989.[7] In addition, I happened to land a Fellowship at the Stanford Humanities Center, and so I spent fifteen months, from June 1987 until August 1988, at Stanford, the university where Jack taught, during the period when he was working most intensely on *Rehearsals of Manhood* (along with a number of other projects: it was an extraordinarily productive period in his scholarly career). I later attended several of the Martin Classical Lectures when Jack delivered them at Oberlin College in September 1988, so I was able to watch

5. Winkler 1990c.

6. Halperin, Winkler, and Zeitlin 1990.

7. Winkler 1990a, Halperin 1990b.

him present *Rehearsals of Manhood* in condensed oral form, and I heard him respond to questions about his project. Jack and I had talked at length about some of the ideas contained in his manuscript. Jack was therefore confident that I understood much of what he wanted to accomplish in his book and that I was in sympathy with his goals and methods.

As it happened, my editorial duties proved to be quite light. Jack survived the medical crisis of July 1989 and regained some of his strength. Susan Stephens, his friend and colleague, first at Yale and then at Stanford, urged him to avail himself of her assistance to put *Rehearsals of Manhood* into final form. She procured the enthusiastic and able assistance of Kathy Veit, a dissertation student of Jack's. Under Jack's direction, the two of them produced, a few weeks before Jack's death the following April, a manuscript that combined the material he had already published, or was about to publish, with the unpublished texts of the Martin Classical Lectures. Jack pronounced himself satisfied with the result, even though it fell short of his hopes for the project. Susan Stephens conveyed to me the completed manuscript on June 28, 1990, newly reformatted, on which she had done some preliminary editorial work—for example, she had, as she put it, patched together an introduction "by appropriating some paragraphs" from the end of what had been chapter 1.[8] That manuscript represents the most finished version of *Rehearsals of Manhood* that Jack left us. It has served as the basis for this book.

Jack's illness and impending death forced him to scale down his ambitions for *Rehearsals of Manhood*, on which he had once set great hopes. After all, before his health began to fail, he had thought he was within reach of producing a definitive, if admittedly speculative and hypothetical, reinterpretation of Classical Greek drama. That would indeed have been a remarkable achievement. Jack wanted to complete it on a suitable scale, with all the range, the complexity, and the broad documentary support that such a project required in order to be successful. Anyone who consults—as I urge every reader of this book to do—the original 1985 version of "The Ephebes' Song" will notice the author's characteristic determination, from the very start, to nail down every detail of the argument to the greatest possible extent, his resolve to anchor fully and convincingly every point of interpretation in the ancient sources and to situate his claims in the context of centuries of classical scholarship. Jack originally planned a book of five chapters, each of them on the scale of "The Ephebes' Song," taking full account of all the surviving literary, pictorial, archaeological, and comparative evidence.

8. I quote from Susan Stephens's cover letter to me of June 28, 1990.

In July 1989, Jack was still intent on assembling a wide array of sources to support his interpretation. Weak as he was at the time, he continued to reflect on the shape of his argument, to come up with new ideas about additional material he might include and about places in the book where it might go. During our interview, he gave me a list of instructions to carry out in order to bring the book to completion. Some time later, when his health had temporarily improved and he was back at work on the book, I got out that list and went over it with him, but he just shrugged it off: he indicated that he would have to settle for sketching out some general lines of interpretation, rather than trying to prove his case definitively, based on a complete survey of the evidence, as he had originally intended to do. "Other people will have to fill in the details," he said. Implicit in that remark, along with a sense of resignation, was Jack's enduring conviction that he was right about Greek tragedy and that future scholarship would provide independent support for his argument, extending it both in its broadest outlines and in many of its finer dimensions.

Despite his diminished hopes, Jack was able, as it turned out, to complete, on his own, much of the to-do list he gave me in July 1989. Kirk and I have in fact made a careful comparison of the final manuscript with all previously published versions as well as with that list. When we came across an argument, a paragraph, a sentence, or even a word from one of Jack's publications that did not make it into the final manuscript, we weighed Jack's final wishes, as I have been able to reconstruct them, against an understanding of what Jack thought he was ultimately in a position to accomplish at the time he was forced to abandon his work on the project. I have altered the manuscript when I judged it necessary in order to realize his final intentions or where I thought I was in a position to supply material that Jack would have wished to include, if he had had the energy to do so. I have taken courage from the injunction Jack gave me during our somber meeting in July 1989. Jack was then too ill to correct the page proofs of his essay collection, *The Constraints of Desire*, and I was doing it for him. I had some questions about the text that I wished to refer to him. He told me, simply, "Use your own authority."

I have used it. I did not need to do so extensively in editing the first two chapters of *Rehearsals of Manhood*, inasmuch as Jack had completed the work for publication and had reconciled, sometimes with the help of Susan Stephens, the material from the published versions of "The Ephebes' Song" with the material from the two published versions of the Martin Classical Lectures. Chapters 3 and 4, however, were never published; they represent elaborations of the last two Martin Classical Lectures. The versions of them contained in the final manuscript that Susan Stephens passed on to me were highly polished and beautifully written, but in places they still reflected the circumstances of oral delivery. For example, sometimes the antecedents of pronouns were not immediately clear; phrases connecting one part of an argument to another in what was plainly intended to be a single, integrated sequence were missing;

ideas were introduced but not developed until later; the cadence of a final paragraph seemed incomplete. These problems would not have bothered the members of a live audience, whose understanding would be guided by Jack's vocal cues, but they did make the written text harder for readers to follow and, sometimes, less persuasive. I have therefore freely altered Jack's prose and reorganized his argument in places, making explicit what was merely implicit or unclear. I have not changed Jack's meaning, so far as I know, but I have expanded it.

My first impulse, on returning to the manuscript of *Rehearsals of Manhood* more than twenty years after I last worked on it, was very different. I wanted to preserve for posterity every single one of Jack's *ipsissima verba*. Then I found that already in 1991, when I was much closer to the text and to the spirit of my final understanding with Jack than I am now, I had allowed myself, where necessary, a great deal of freedom to alter his sentences and to add others, so as to bring out his emphasis or to underscore theoretical or methodological points in his argument. It is therefore too late, and it would be disloyal, to try and restore the posthumous 1990 manuscript, if the goal is to be true to Jack's final wishes. For what Jack wanted most of all was to leave behind him a book that would read well and be successful on its own terms. And he relied on me to do whatever I felt was necessary to achieve those ends. So I have continued to take a free hand with text. But I have also tried to preserve Jack's distinctive voice. When, in 1991, I showed David Braaten, Jack's surviving boyfriend, the partially edited version of chapter 4 that I had produced, I was gratified that David identified, as Jack's own, some phrases I had written, and he ascribed to me what Jack had actually written himself. The memory of that reassuring verdict has emboldened me to resume my prior editorial practice. It is in that spirit that Kirk and I have completed the editing of chapters 3 and 4 of *Rehearsals of Manhood*. We have not attempted to indicate in the text which additions or alterations are ours (with the exception of certain footnotes that Kirk has added, in order to point out the various ways in which recent scholarship has confirmed—or, much more rarely, contested—Jack's hypotheses). This is a reading text, not a critical edition. I have deposited the typescript that Susan Stephens and Kathy Veit produced (it bears my handwritten annotations from the early 1990s, but I ultimately decided not to incorporate many of those emendations in the final text) in the Department of Special Collections and University Archives of the Stanford University Libraries, where it has been added to the existing collection entitled "Winkler (John J.) papers" (SC1451). That is where those who are interested in such textual questions can consult it.

Let me now say a few words about the intellectual evolution of Jack Winkler's approach to Greek tragedy during the years he worked on *Rehearsals of Manhood*. As I mentioned, Jack eventually became dissatisfied with the way he had made his case, in the first version of "The Ephebes' Song," for his new interpretation of Greek tragedy. His original, abiding discovery, first announced in that 1985 article, was that Classical Greek plays made more sense when they could be seen in relation to certain gendered practices of contemporary Athenian social life—when they could be viewed, in particular, as "rehearsals of manhood." In other words, Jack believed that Classical Greek drama had a special relevance to the initiation of young men into manhood and, specifically, into their future social identity as warriors. He wanted to anchor our understanding of Greek drama in a larger "cultural poetics of manhood," in a systematic set of formal elements specific to the social practices of gender in Classical Greece, that underlay Greek attitudes and behavior in general and generated the shape, themes, and organization (physical, political, ritual, social, semiotic, visual) of the Attic dramatic festivals in particular. He thought at first that such an approach could provide a new key to understanding Greek tragedy, and he was excited to uncover a wide range of evidence that combined, he believed, to support his hypothesis. That evidence is what he laid out in preliminary form in his 1985 article.

Jack later came to feel, however, that his initial presentation of his interpretation in that article had been too hasty and had inadvertently prejudiced classical scholars against it. For example, he thought he might have been unwise to present his contribution as a new account of the *origins* of Greek tragedy—a longstanding, highly contested, and necessarily speculative topic in classical scholarship—rather than as a study of "the recoverable [and therefore more concrete, verifiable] social meanings of the [dramatic] festival" in its own day.[9] By attempting to intervene in the controversy over tragic origins, he had needlessly stepped on the toes of many intellectual and scholarly stakeholders in that disputed subject area and had raised all sorts of specialized and speculative questions that he could not adequately address—and that were not germane, in any case, to the core of his thesis. All the same, this book does offer the reader, or so Jack continued to maintain, possible insights into Greek drama's "early days" and "early character": it presents a theory about where the choruses of Greek plays may have come from, even if it now focuses more on the social meanings of the dramatic festivals themselves and of ancient theatrical performances in their own historical moment.

Beyond that, Jack came to believe that the way he originally pitched his argument had misled his readers in at least three ways.

First, on Jack's view, Greek tragedy made special reference to young Athenian men of citizen status, about eighteen to twenty years of age, who were undergoing military training in order to prepare themselves for the task of warfare. Jack saw the City Dionysia, the chief dramatic festival at Athens, as "a social event focused precisely" on such young men: it was a civic ceremony in which the city's future warriors, and young men in general, were put on

9. Winkler 1990b: 20n.

display and made the center of public attention—a special moment when their behavior (and the behavior of young men like them) was scrutinized, tested, and celebrated . . . or shown to be disastrous.[10] Jack called these young men "ephebes." Although Jack intended the word "ephebe" in an informal and non-technical sense, to refer to young citizen men on the verge of manhood who were training to be warriors, his use of the word rekindled an old debate in classical scholarship about the origins and exact date of the formal institutionalization of the ephebate (the collective military training of young citizen males) at Athens—a question that Jack sought to avoid in later elaborations of his argument, because he thought it represented a distraction from the point he wished to emphasize.

Indeed, much of the controversy among classicists that followed the 1985 publication of "The Ephebes' Song" was taken up with the perennial and largely irrelevant debate about the date of the formal institution of the ephebate at Athens. In chapter 42 of the *Constitution of the Athenians*, composed during the latter half of the fourth century BCE, Aristotle (or one of his students) describes a two-year transitional period in the lives of young Athenian men of citizen status; these young men, called ephebes, train as soldiers, patrolling the borders of Attika, and in their second year perform a drill in the theater before an assembly of the people. The veracity of the testimony of the Aristotelian text to the existence of the institution of the ephebate is not much disputed; rather, the question scholars have pursued is at what exact date in time did the institution described in the fourth-century text begin and when did it assume the complete form that the author of the *Constitution of the Athenians* specifies.

I call this debate largely irrelevant, because it makes little difference to Jack's argument whether in fact all the young men of citizen status at Athens were expected to take part in universal, compulsory, state-supported, formally institutionalized two-year military training during the period in the fifth century BCE when the great dramatic poets were having their plays performed. Whether or not the ephebate already existed in a formal sense at that time, after all, some young men were still being educated, and some militia training, whether public or private, would have been necessary to prepare them for military duty. It doesn't matter to Jack's argument whether such young men were "ephebes" in a formal, official sense, no more than it matters whether they were referred to by that name. So there was ultimately no need for him to insist on identifying them by means of that specific label. In the end, Jack decided that his loose use of the term "ephebe" tended to sidetrack classical scholars from his central focus on Greek plays as "rehearsals of manhood." He chose accordingly to soft-pedal the ephebic identity of the young warriors-to-be, though he still employed the term because he liked the way

10. Winkler 1985: 29.

"ephebe" designates at once a transitional age-class (or life-stage) and a transitional military status. He used "ephebe" interchangeably, however, with "young warrior," a less formal, more descriptive formula that is not freighted with the same historical baggage.

Second, Jack proposed to interpret the word *tragōidos* (tragic chorister, member of the chorus of a tragedy) to mean "billy goat singer." Though derived from *tragos*, the word for "billy goat," *tragōidos*, Jack suggested, referred more specifically to the bleating (we would say breaking) of the male voice in adolescence. That claim also elicited skepticism from classicists and led them to argue about the meaning of the word instead of about the significance of its possible relation to male adolescence. Jack's etymology of *tragōidos* was admittedly speculative, and he did not insist on it. Still, to call tragedy "The Ephebes' Song" seemed to place greater weight on that speculative etymology, and to give it more definitional importance, than Jack had intended. In *Rehearsals of Manhood*, accordingly, this etymological argument, which Jack continued to develop, has been removed from the main text and placed in an appendix (appendix I). It now focuses less insistently on the breaking of the male adolescent voice in favor of a more general emphasis on puberty as a transitional social status for young men.

Finally, the 1985 article's discussion of ephebic themes in Attic tragedy is extraordinarily ingenious; it is, in my view, still worth consulting.[11] Jack omitted it from the revised version of the article because it elicited the complaint from literary authorities on Greek drama that Jack's approach ignored the thematic complexity of the extant texts and tended simplistically to reduce that complexity to military propaganda—as if there were nothing more to Greek tragedy than a West Point graduation skit, as Jack at one point called it. Jack saw his approach as providing an enhanced understanding of Greek tragedy, not an exhaustive one, let alone a philistine simplification of the extant dramas. At the same time, he did intend to champion a social approach to understanding Greek drama at the expense of a purely aesthetic approach. In the end, he decided to downplay the significance of ephebic themes in the plays (which he had once hoped to make the focus of a separate, fifth chapter), so as to avoid giving the false impression that his social reinterpretation of Greek drama should be taken principally as literary criticism of the texts of the surviving plays rather than as a reconstruction of the social meanings of their performances. And he disclaimed any intention to provide a full aesthetic or literary consideration of the plays' texts—or "scripts," as he now preferred to call them—let alone any attempt to derive his interpretation of Athenian drama as a social practice from a reading of those texts or from an analysis of their themes.

11. See Winkler 1985: 32–38.

For all those reasons, Jack came to jettison what he later called his "relentless and univocal . . . emphasis on the isolated figure of the ephebe."[12] He gave greater prominence in his final argument to the role and social function of the audience at the dramatic festivals. Nonetheless, in the 1990 revision of "The Ephebes' Song," he spent a good deal of time and effort assessing how different historical understandings of "ephebe" affected his argument. He wanted to confront the objections that his use of "ephebe" had elicited. One result is that the revised article, though important for its clarification of Jack's earlier intentions, may strike today's reader as overly defensive—and as grappling too closely with a now-outdated controversy. In any case, the portions of it that deal with the ephebate have done their work. In later elaborations of his argument, accordingly, Jack omitted some of those defensive gestures and came to rely on what he regarded as the three indisputable facts supporting his thesis: "like the individual poles which form a tepee, no one of [them] can stand alone," or so he continued to insist in the 1990 version of "The Ephebes' Song" (reprising a motif from his 1985 article), "but their coincidence forms a structure which is far stronger than its simple components."[13]

Here is how Jack went on to describe those "three crucial facts about performances in the theater of Dionysos" in a passage omitted from this book but alluded to in the introduction.

1. The chorus members for tragedy are represented on the Pronomos Vase as young men with fully grown bodies and curls of sideburn creeping down their cheeks, but no beards. They are, iconographically speaking, ephebes—young adult (or late adolescent) males represented in their athletic prime. Their portrayal is in systematic opposition to that of the three actors on the same vase who are represented as older men with beards.
2. The distinctive and regular formation of the chorus for tragic dancing was rectangular, by rank and file. This stands in systematic contrast to the circular dancing of dithyrambs at the same festival (performed by the age groups above and below the ephebes—men and boys).
3. The eighteen- to twenty-year-old male citizens, who underwent military training and civic training in the ephebate, as the institution is known from the fourth century BCE, displayed at the beginning of their second year their hoplite military maneuvers and close-order drill in front of the assembled citizen body. They did so not on exercise fields outside the city but in the orchestra of the theater of Dionysos ([Aristotle], *Ath. Pol.* 42.4).[14]

12. Winkler 1990b: 20n.
13. Winkler 1990b: 21. Cf. Winkler 1985: 26.
14. Winkler 1990b: 22.

And here is how Jack specified the differences between the earlier and later versions of "The Ephebes' Song" in a headnote to the later version: "For readers familiar with that [earlier] version the changes here consist principally of a new preface, which X-rays the argument [referring to the three points quoted above]; a fuller discussion of the ephebate . . . ; the omissions of the sections on ephebic themes in tragic scripts, on Peisistratos, and on satyr-plays; and somewhat fuller notes throughout."[15]

Jack then went on, in the same headnote, to distinguish the argument of "The Ephebes' Song" from the "expanded study" that he intended to bring out in the form of *Rehearsals of Manhood*. One of the new book's aims, he wrote, would be to "try to remedy" the "defects" in his previous work on the topic. The projected book would put "the figure of the ephebe, defined more in terms of status than of birthdays, into the larger web of social meanings and practices concerning Mediterranean *andragathiē*, manly excellence. It will deal also with comedy, costume, military dancing, quasi-dramatic performances at private symposiums, courtroom trials, melodrama, and Aristotle's *Poetics*."[16] We have retained this language (with some expansions and alterations) in the introduction. For it describes the book you are now holding, to the degree that Jack was able to finish it.

Anyone who knew Jack Winkler knew that he was constantly rethinking and revising his ideas, finding new material and new interpretative angles on it, as well as new parallels from other fields of study. His reflections on Attic drama continued to change as his ideas fermented and as he found new inspiration in unexpected sources. The book that emerged from that dynamic process, *Rehearsals of Manhood*, is nonetheless rooted in its time and place. It is indebted to feminist and cultural anthropology, to structuralism, to The New Historicism, to semiotics, to postcolonial theory, to radical democratic politics, and to the work of Michel Foucault, whom Jack knew personally. Jack intended it as a contribution to women's studies and the history of sexuality at least as much as to the discipline of classics. Jack strongly identified with the field of cultural anthropology—not surprisingly, in a period when the bible of The New Historicism was Clifford Geertz's *The Interpretation of Cultures*. He was versed in ethnographies of modern Greece and the contemporary Mediterranean world. He was particularly fascinated by the advances in feminist anthropology, with which he was familiar most immediately from the work of

15. Winkler 1990b: 20n.
16. Winkler 1990b: 20n.

his sister, Cathy Winkler. The final manuscript of *Rehearsals of Manhood* bore the subtitle, "An Anthropological Account of Athenian Drama."[17]

Even as he championed those intellectual and social commitments, Jack was mildly perturbed by the possibility that the passage of time might make his anthropological approach to Greek tragedy seem quaint, a mere culture-bound artifact of its own historical epoch—an anthropological curiosity in its own right. He raised that possibility himself in *The Constraints of Desire* (similarly subtitled "The Anthropology of Sex and Gender in Ancient Greece"), denying that he wanted to make anthropology into the one and only valid approach to studying the societies of the ancient Mediterranean world: "There is no magic phrase, such as 'Anthropology!,' that will guarantee success to our hermeneutic project, any more than earlier slogans worked to unlock all secrets."[18] In my editing, I have tried accordingly both to freshen up the conceptual vocabulary and to make clear its relation to the intellectual currents of its own time. I have always thought that the kind of scholarly work that retains its value longest is that which is most fully and richly immersed in the preoccupations of its own age.

Let me return one last time to the summer of 1989. When I visited Jack in his hospital room, I told him that I had formed the intention of endowing a charitable foundation in his memory. I asked him whether he wanted it to be attached to an existing institution and what purpose he would like it to serve. Jack decided that it should not be part of any university or professional association but should rather be independent and self-sustaining. He also decided that its purpose would be to award an annual prize in his name to the best unpublished paper by a North American undergraduate or graduate student in a risky or marginal field of classical studies. He figured that students of the classics were already rewarded by the profession for pursuing safe, accepted, conventional, or reputable topics. He proposed that a prize be created to *encourage* students to do *whatever* the profession of classical studies as a whole specifically *discouraged* them from doing.

In the summer of 1990, accordingly, a few months after Jack's death, I set about the process of establishing The John J. Winkler Memorial Trust as a private, charitable foundation under US federal tax code. The first competition for The John J. Winkler Memorial Prize took place in the spring of

17. In the headnote to Winkler 1990b, the subtitle of the book was announced as "Athenian Drama and the Poetics of Manhood": Winkler 1990b: 20n. I have had to alter that subtitle, which might actually have been my own composition, or suggestion, so as to avoid the repetition of "manhood" in the title and subtitle of the book.

18. Winkler 1990a: 98.

1991. The winner, selected anonymously by a jury composed that year of the members of the Trust's Advisory Board, was Kirk Ormand, one of Jack's last graduate students at Stanford, who had submitted a feminist study of the figure of Ariadne in Catullus 64. Since then, the Trust has awarded the Winkler Prize to forty-six students (graduate and undergraduate) in classics and other fields. The annual competition for the Prize is now conducted by Kirk, whom I have appointed to the Trust's Advisory Board; the Trust's finances remain under my control. Kirk is currently the senior member of the Classics Department at Oberlin College, where I first acquired my love of ancient Greek literature and culture as an undergraduate, and where Jack delivered The Martin Classical Lectures in the fall of 1988. Each year, through Kirk's good graces, the winner of the Winkler Prize is invited to present the winning paper as The John J. Winkler Memorial Lecture at Oberlin College. It is therefore more than appropriate that *Rehearsals of Manhood* should at last see the light of day as a new addition to The Martin Classical Lectures, published through joint arrangement between Oberlin College and Princeton University Press. Royalties from its sale will go in their entirety to The John J. Winkler Memorial Trust.

I wish to thank Susan Stephens and Kathy Veit for the hard work that went into preparing the final draft of Jack's manuscript many years ago. I also wish to thank Maud Gleason who, in the winter of 1991–92, offered me her home and her encouragement, providing me with a most welcome environment, one especially conducive to preparing Jack's manuscript for publication, thereby enabling me to make significant progress on the editing of it. I am grateful to David A. Braaten for his help, his support, and his understanding. I would like to acknowledge the assistance of various students and colleagues over the years who have aided me with some aspect of this work, particularly my late friend and fellow Stanford graduate student David Sullivan, who worked on the bibliography and scholarly references in the manuscript. Christian Axelgard at the University of Michigan furnished ingenious, expert help in identifying vases, updating the scholarship on them, and tracking down their whereabouts, complete with illustrations. Kirk and I have also benefited from the generous and learned advice provided by Kathryn Topper and by Dimitrios Yatromanolakis.

Kirk and I owe a considerable debt to David Konstan and to the second, anonymous reviewer of the manuscript for Princeton University Press. We thank them in particular for their substantial, learned, rigorous, engaged, and sympathetic critiques of the final manuscript. The published version silently incorporates a number of their corrections and suggestions. Kirk and I are grateful to Rob Tempio at the Press for his patient, deft, and considerate guidance of this entire project, to his colleagues Matt Rohal and Chloe Coy for their valuable help and advice with the preparation of the manuscript, to Natalie Baan for overseeing its production, to Dimitri Karetnikov and David Campbell for expert assistance with the illustrations and the catalogue copy, and to Hank Southgate for his scrupulous and rigorous but flexible, sympathetic, and eagle-eyed copyediting.

It will be evident that my debt to Kirk Ormand is immense, far greater than I can easily express, but that is no reason not to record my gratitude to him here, however inadequately.

I wish to thank the Wissenschaftskolleg zu Berlin / the Institute for Advanced Study in Berlin for giving me a yearlong residential Fellowship in 2014–15, during which I returned to editing *Rehearsals of Manhood* and was able at long last to complete the bulk of the work on it (along with this foreword). I am grateful to the University of Michigan for providing the salary support that allowed me to accept that Fellowship as well as for a grant that provided a publication subvention to offset the costs of including so many images in this volume. Kirk and I owe a special debt of gratitude to Olivia Moore, a Financial Specialist at the College of Literature, Science, and the Arts at the University of Michigan, who strenuously and uncomplainingly negotiated with far-flung museums and the University's Procurement Services in order to arrange payment for permissions to reproduce the visual material contained in this book. I wish to thank the Wissenschaftskolleg, in addition, for giving Kirk Ormand two guest residencies during the period of my Fellowship, in November 2014 and May 2015, which made it possible for the two of us to work together on this project under ideal conditions. The scholarship and conversation of Luca Giuliani, Rektor of the Wissenschaftskolleg at the time, provided inspiration and assistance to us in assessing the dubious value of vase-painting for reconstructing the scripts of Attic drama. I also wish to thank William Marx, my fellow Fellow at the Wissenschaftskolleg, for his help, his criticisms, and his encouragement.

Kirk wishes, similarly, to thank the Wissenschaftskolleg for the two guest residencies. He also thanks Oberlin College for two sabbatical leaves during which he had time to work on this project, and for a Powers travel grant, which allowed him to work in Berlin and Athens on various aspects of this book. The American School of Classical Studies in Athens also deserves our gratitude for Kirk's use of the splendid Blegen Library and other facilities. Kirk and I offer thanks as well to Oberlin alumnus Tom Cooper for his continued support of the Oberlin Classics Department, and for providing substantial material assistance toward the production of this volume.

REHEARSALS OF MANHOOD

Introduction

INVESTIGATORS OF TRAGEDY'S early days have for quite some time been stuck in an impasse, recycling constantly and inconclusively the same few bits of ancient information. Comedy seems, if anything, in a worse condition, so far as accounts of its emergence are concerned: with less anecdotal evidence, and with scripts later by half a century, its early days and development are even more of a mystery and equally the object—or victim—of far-fetched speculation about ritual, myth, and the seasons. The average skeptic (and I count myself one) would rightly doubt that anything new, much less true, could be said about such subjects. Nevertheless, the present book does try to offer an original approach to the old question of where tragic choruses came from—or, as I would prefer to put it, what they were doing in the life of the city. Part of the novelty of this approach lies in considering Athenian drama in the social context of its original performance at the festivals of Dionysos (the rural Dionysia, the Lenaia, and the City Dionysia) and in noticing the untranslatable cultural differences between the Athenian theater and ours.[1]

The following chapters suggest that, in a large sense, Athenian dramatic festivals were the occasion for elaborate symbolic play on themes of proper and improper civic behavior on the part of men, predicated on the assumption

1. [This aspect of Winkler's work anticipates some of the excellent studies in recent years on the cultural production of tragedy in the Greek world. In particular, D. Carter 2011b includes a number of essays dealing with the finances and social organization of the Athenian tragic festivals and their relation to fifth-century Athenian government and society. See especially Wilson 2011 and D. Carter 2011a. Wilson 2007a provides numerous essays on what Greek documentary sources (especially inscriptions) tell us about dramatic festivals in Athens and elsewhere. Wilson 2000 offers a comprehensive account of the Athenian institution of the *khorēgia* (private financial sponsorship of the costs of training and preparing a chorus for performance at a dramatic festival), especially as a vehicle for aristocratic competition within the democratic *polis*. Marx 2012 emphasizes the untranslatable cultural differences between Greek tragedy and modern tragedy and argues for the radical alterity of Greek drama, in ways often aligned with Winkler's general approach.]

that the principal component of proper male citizenship was military. At those festivals, just as at private symposia, such play with embodied definitions of good and bad masculinity occurred in both serious and facetious formats: tragedy and comedy alike were built on contrasts of behavior (and physique) represented in terms of the taut and the slack. A central reference point for these representations—the notional targets of their lessons (*paideia*) about the trials of manhood (*andreia*)—were the young men of the city.[2] These young men were also the choral performers of tragedy at least, and perhaps of comedy as well.

It is therefore with the young men of the Athenian *polis*, or city-state, that this study begins. It looks in particular at the figure of the *ephebe*, defined in terms of status (rather than in terms of birthdays or formal institutions) as a young, propertied, Athenian citizen male on the border between boyhood and manhood who is training to prepare himself for warfare as a *hoplite*, or heavy-armed foot-soldier in an infantry phalanx. It puts the ephebe into the larger web of social meanings and practices concerning *andragathiē*, or manly excellence, in Mediterranean societies. It then reaches out to touch on such subjects as tragedy, comedy, costume, military dancing, quasi-dramatic performances at private symposia, courtroom trials, melodrama, and Aristotle's *Poetics*.

If I may be allowed just one small attempt to elicit the skeptical reader's benevolence: I hereby acknowledge that each of the pieces of evidence I am about to assemble could, taken one by one, be construed in ways other than I have construed it here. Some of them are late, some are incomplete, most are relatively small and either ambiguous or inconclusive. Most have to do with performance and social context rather than with the dramas themselves. Indeed, it is because of these very features of the evidence, and especially because of our fetishizing of the "dramas themselves" and the Text, that no one has noticed the coherence that I am about to trace.

To arrive at the fuller cultural understanding of Athenian drama on offer here requires as thick a description as possible, and (to speak frankly) the overall persuasiveness of the present argument rests not on any one irresistible fact but on the ensemble of many details. My ideal reader, therefore, will be of two minds. On one level, they will check the weight and accuracy of each fact or interpretation to see how far it contributes to a reasonable and believable picture of what was once a living practice. On that level, the final judgment may have to be "Not Proven." But on another level, I expect the serious reader not to be content with a merely skeptical attitude to all this suggestive material but to take responsibility for explaining what the aggregate of the evidence assembled

2. See Rosen and Sluiter 2003 for a collection of essays exploring how the concept of *andreia* functioned in Greek and Roman society. Bassi 2003 is particularly helpful for the diachronic analysis of the term, as it developed from a concept of military valor to a democratic ideal in other spheres of social life.

here does mean. To make these readerly activities possible, I have laid out some of the significant evidence about Athenian fighting, dance training, and citizenship—topics usually slighted in accounts of Athenian drama.[3]

The subject treated here would traditionally be labeled "the origin of Greek tragedy." But the word "origin" seems to me to claim much too much, suggesting as it does something primal—whether seminal or oval—before which there was nothing. Founding events do, of course, occur; the more usual social operation, however, is not to create but to adapt whatever is at hand. In hopes of avoiding the typical mystification that often attends discussions of origins, I would prefer to say that the hypothesis advanced here is about the early character of Attic tragedy (and comedy) rather than their absolute Beginning.

From the early days of tragedy to its later and more fully represented period, the character of its scripts changed in marked ways. That is an aesthetic history, which has been told many times on its own terms. But such a history, if it is to avoid being a Rorschach fantasy of the modern interpreter, needs to be founded on a concrete knowledge of dramatic performance—particularly on the shared and usually unspoken presuppositions of the composers, performers, and audience. This book, therefore, does not aim at a general interpretation of tragedy *based on* the surviving scripts. Rather, it tries to reconstruct from the facts of festival performance the framework of understanding that the audience originally brought to its viewing of the plays.

In other words, this study advances a hypothesis about performance and its social meanings, not primarily a hypothesis about the scripts that we call tragedies. The relation of those thirty-two extant scripts to the social and physical performance as I describe it is rather like that of a clay sculpture to the wire frame on which it is built up. The visible surface of the sculpture conceals the enabling framework at its core, and X-raying the core (the speculative enterprise undertaken here) may not be essential to some kinds of aesthetic appreciation of the surface. But what I am trying to do with Attic drama could not be accurately characterized as aesthetic appreciation. My goal is rather to explore, to reconstruct if you will, *the social meanings of the material and physical components* of its original production.

To change the artistic metaphor, you might say that I am concerned not with the individual paintings in a museum but with the question of how they were originally framed and hung and lit, and who was admitted to view them; only after I have advanced some answers to that question will I go on to ask,

3. [Of these three topics, the last has received considerable attention in the past three decades, though often focusing (as Winkler does not) on the texts of the tragedies themselves as evidence for citizenship and democratic discourse. See, among other works, D. Carter 2011b, 2008, Wilson 2007a, Meier 1993, and numerous articles on individual authors and specific plays. Of particular interest (and influenced by Winkler) are the essays by Pozzi, Mitchell-Boyask, Segal, Goff, Katz, Tyrrell, and Zweig in Padilla 1999.]

quite tentatively: by what criteria were some awarded prizes? In the case of tragedy, those criteria of original appreciation, I shall try to maintain, have much more to do with Attic *andragathiē*, the poetics of manhood, and the ethics of citizen-soldiery than they do with such abstract philosophical issues as fate and freedom. The world of values, choices, and social possibilities inhabited by Medeia, Xerxes, Deianeira, and Orestes is a world centered on the primary social role assigned to aristocratic soldiers, on whose *andragathiē* the survival and welfare of all people depend and in terms of which the reciprocal duties of all classes are defined or, in some cases, challenged. What we may learn from such a study is, as it were, how to light and hang the tragic pictures so that we are likely to be viewing them from the proper angle and thus can better estimate what the original audience was intended to notice.

The suggestion that the performance of tragedy had a military aspect, related (perhaps distantly) to the physical and moral training of young men, is based on the coincidence of three facts: the rectangular formation of tragic choruses, the identity of the choristers as young men, and the account given in chapter 42 of Aristotle's *Constitution of the Athenians*, which describes the institutionalized ephebate of the later fourth century BCE. Enrolled when they had reached their eighteenth birthday, the ephebes spent two years in training—the first year learning the use of weapons while stationed in Peiraieus (the port of Athens), the second on guard duty at the border forts of Attika. At the beginning of their second year, an assembly of all citizens was held and the ephebes displayed their ability to march and maneuver in close formation as a hoplite phalanx. Now the interesting fact about this performance, which was a kind of first-year graduation ceremony at which the young warriors received from the state a shield and a spear, is that it took place not on some marching field or parade ground outside the city but in the theater of Dionysos—in the same orchestral area where select groups of ephebes (if I may so call them) danced as the tragic chorus, in rectangular formation, performing what I would describe as an aesthetically elevated version of close-order drill.

Together these three facts suggest that there was an analogy between the movement and personnel of the tragic choruses and the movement and personnel of the ephebate on parade. The very persons (or rather a representative selection of them) who marched in rectangular rank and file in the orchestra as second-year cadets, performing for the assembled citizenry, also marched and danced in rectangular formation at the City Dionysia, though on that occasion they did so wearing masks and costumes.

Supporting this perception, but in the second rank, is the audience's character as a civic assembly—not a fortuitous gathering of "theatergoers" but a quasi-official gathering of (male) citizens, who were seated in tribal order, one tribe per wedge of tiered seats.[4] (This was evidently the seating arrangement

4. On the question of the presence of citizen women in the audience, see chapter 2, n. 75.

used for the *Ekklēsia*, the Athenian Popular Assembly, when it met for official business on the Pnyx.) The more prominent citizens sat toward the front, with a special section reserved for the members of the *Boulē*, the Council. The layout of the auditorium thus displayed the organization of the body politic in terms both of tribal equality and of social hierarchy. Further, the entire festival had a civic-military aura, suggesting that *polis* and *tragōidia* in Athens were not so distant from each other as the modern understandings of "politics" and "tragedy" would imply.[5]

Readers of this book will find the evidence for the military meanings of Athenian tragic performance and for the audience's identity as a civic collective laid out, respectively, in chapters 1 and 2. Following them, in chapter 3, is a hypothesis about how the ethics of citizen-soldiery and the social drama of masculine risk-taking might be related to the plots of tragedy. In the final chapter, chapter 4, I try to show that some oddities in Aristotle's *Poetics*, long neglected if not repressed by modern readers, make sense when they are viewed in the light of the evidence presented in the previous chapters. The result, I hope, will be both a consistent and a plausible interpretation of Athenian drama as a social practice preoccupied specifically with rehearsals of manhood.

5. [Winkler's observations here have gained indirect support from evidence for theatrical practices elsewhere in ancient Greece. Chaniotis 2007 points out that theaters in Makedonia, Kaunos, and Samos had markings for seating by tribe. See below, chapter 2, n. 76.]

CHAPTER ONE

Hippokleides Dances

MILITARY TRAINING AND OTHER DRAMAS OF MASCULINE DISPLAY

IN THE EARLY part of the sixth century BCE, Kleisthenes, the wealthy tyrant of Sikyon, decided that his daughter Agariste would have as her husband the finest man that could be found in all of greater Greece.[1] His method for locating this best man was to announce at the Olympic competition that any Greek who thought himself worthy to be Kleisthenes' son-in-law should appear within the next sixty days at Sikyon to undergo a yearlong scrutiny. The initial self-selection produced, as we might expect, a group of contenders, thirteen all told, whose wealth was extensive, whose blood was blue, and who thought very well of themselves—as Herodotos puts it in telling this tale, each one was "swelled up" (*exōgkōmenoi*, 6.126.3) with himself and his fatherland.

Kleisthenes put the suitors through their paces like a horse-trainer looking for a superb stud. He made them run and wrestle, of course (6.126.3). But, above all, he tested their manly excellence (*andragathiē*), their temperament (*orgē*), their education (*paideusis*), and their individual character or personal style (*tropos*), both in private interviews and in the assembled group. The gymnasium was an important site for some of this testing, particularly for the younger men (6.128.1), but the real theater of excellence was the banquet hall, where Kleisthenes entertained the suitors lavishly for the year, all the while calculating the measure of their manhood.

Toward the end of this process, the two Athenians in the group had risen to seem in Kleisthenes' eyes the cream of the cream of the cream. Of them,

1. For analyses of this passage in terms of larger social politics, see Kurke 2011: 412–26; Ormand 2014: 226–35.

he was inclined to favor the wealthy and handsome (*ploutōi kai eidei propherōn*, 6.127.4) Hippokleides, both for his manly excellence (*andragathiē*) and for his descent from the Kypselids of Korinth. The day finally arrived when Kleisthenes would declare his choice. A hundred cattle were barbecued for the suitors and for all the people of Sikyon, and as the banquet progressed a spirit of contest came over the suitors and they strove to outdo one another in displays of musical and poetic ability. Wine was flowing freely, and at the culmination of this rivalry Hippokleides did more than sing or recite: while the *aulos*-player droned an exotic tune, he danced. Pleased with himself, and not noticing Kleisthenes' wrinkled brow, Hippokleides called for a table and, standing on it, he performed first some Spartan steps, then he showed off some Athenian moves, and finally he put his head on the table and gesticulated with his legs (literally, he moved his legs like arms: *ekheironomēse*, 6.129.3).

The conclusion of the story is well known. Kleisthenes was disgusted at the dancing but held his anger until Hippokleides did his headstand, at which point he declared out loud, "Son of Teisander, you have danced away your marriage." To which the dancer replied, in words that became proverbial, *ou phrontis Hippokleidēi* (6.129.4): "Hippokleides has no worries"—or (in contemporary English) "Hippokleides could care less."

Let us back up from this famous conclusion and return to the crucial moment when Hippokleides is dancing upside down on a table with his legs moving like arms. To know what that gesture meant, to take the specific measure of its apparent shamelessness (*anaideiē*), we will have to establish around Hippokleides some frames of reference, schemas of cultural evaluation that were operative in the Greek *poleis* (or "city-states") of the sixth and fifth centuries. For Hippokleides' dancing was not a simple act of drunkenness. It was a rather more complex miscalculation of what would best display his manliness in a forum that was both competitive and festive. In later chapters, I will recur to other features of Hippokleides' performance: the Mediterranean encouragement of cockiness in men, the political and social restraints on that problematic behavior, and the community occasions—trials, games, theater—at which the poetics of manhood were represented in all their complexity.

At this juncture, I will simply sketch the two sides from which Hippokleides' behavior could be evaluated, since he is located at a sort of cultural balance point where an idealized military manhood momentarily risks tipping over into its opposite. So let us leave Hippokleides holding his balance until we can return to him with a fuller understanding of the premises concerning masculine performance on which he and Kleisthenes were operating. As part of that framing, I will also offer a performance-based hypothesis about the early character—not the origin—of Athenian tragedy.

A Duel on the Border: The Trick of the Black Goatskin

A second story will focus the issue. In the old days of the kings, a dispute arose between Attika and Boiotia over the control of a village in the hill country that forms the natural boundary between them.[2] Border squabbles, of course, were endemic in a culture that is aptly described as not only face-to-face but scowling, and it is not surprising to find disagreement too over the name of the hamlet, which is variously given as Melainai, Oinoē, Panakton, and Eleutherai.[3] An agreement was reached to settle the issue by single combat between Xanthos, king of Boiotia, and Melanthos, who had been promised the kingship of Attika if he won the fight. As Melanthos strode forward, he either saw or claimed to see behind Xanthos an apparition of a beardless man wearing a black goatskin over his shoulders. He shouted out to Xanthos that it was unfair for him to bring a helper to fight what was agreed to be a single combat; as Xanthos turned to look behind him, Melanthos struck with his spear and killed him.[4]

There is a curious fact about the use of this story, which will set up the parameters of my hypothesis. In the cycle of Athenian festivals, the tale of Melanthos' trick or deception (*apatē*) served as the etiology for the Apatouria, a very

2. Connor 1988: 16: "Apart from the anomalous seizure of Messenia by the Spartans, territorial acquisition . . . appears primarily in the change of sovereignty over marginal border lands. Each state retains control over its main agricultural land."

3. Melainai and Oinoē are demes, Panakton a fort, Eleutherai a village: Chandler 1926. The history of actual fighting over these settlements on both sides of Mount Kithairon is surveyed by Brelich 1961: 53–59. On border-fighting in general, see Aristotle, *Politics* 7.10.1330a14–25. "Oropos has often been in dispute, for it is situated in the border country between Attika and Boiotia" (Strabo 9.1.22). See Ober 1985: 191–207, who provides a systematic overview of the border fortification system in Attika in the fourth century BCE; he argues that there was no organized system of border fortifications before the middle of the fifth century (191–92) and that ephebic training at border fortifications began after the Peloponnesian War (90–95). On the fortress at Panakton, see Munn 1996: 52–53, who found fragmentary ephebic dedications there dating to the Lykourgan period in the 330s, and Munn 2010, with bibliography, who argues that the fortress, built in the mid-fifth century, disrupted centuries of shared grazing in the area by Athenians and Boiotians (but he disputes the view advanced by Ober 1985: 195 that the fortress was part of a border defense system).

4. A similar Butch Cassidy trick in a territory dispute between two kings is recorded by Plutarch, *Qu. Gr.* 13 (294B–C). Hyperokhos, king of the Inakhians, advancing to the field was accompanied by his dog; his opponent Phemios, king of the Ainianians, objected to the dog as a second combatant; while Hyperokhos was shooing his dog away and had his back turned, Phemios hit him with a stone and killed him, thus winning for his people possession of the country. A less violent trick solved another border dispute between Athens and Boiotia over the region called Sida. Epaminondas during the debate reached out and plucked a pomegranate, a plant growing profusely in that area, and asked the Athenians what they called it. "*Rhoa*," they said. "But we call this a *sida*," he replied, thus winning the day (Agatharkhides, *Eurōpiaka* = Ath. 14.650F–651A = *FGrHist* 86 F 8).

old kinship celebration in the fourth month of the Attic year (the month called *Pyanopsiōn*, roughly September–October).[5] On the three days of this festival, the phratries (or "clans") recognized boys and girls born in the preceding year with sacrifices to Zeus Phratrios and Athena Phratria and also acknowledged the coming manhood (*hēbē*) of sixteen-year-old boys with a sacrifice called the *koureion*, held on the day Koureōtis. The latter words were etymologized either by reference to *kouros*, youth/young man, or to *kourā*, cutting the hair: once it was cut, the hair was dedicated to Artemis,[6] who was one of the several goddesses known as Kourotrophos, because she watched over the nurture and successful growth (*trophē*) of youngsters to adulthood.

The Apatouria was thus a clan festival at which birth and adolescence were acknowledged. But it seems also to have been overlaid with themes pertaining to slightly older males, *kouroi* in a different sense. *Kouroi* in Homer are young warriors, not the sixteen-year-olds featured at the Apatouria. The later word for young men in the prime of life, on the threshold of adulthood, was not *kouroi* but *ephēboi*, "ephebes," literally those at (*ep'*) their youthful prime (*hēbē*). In addition to denoting the ideal youth at the first flowering of his adult vigor (a flexible usage not bound to birthdays), "ephebe" also came to be the specific designation in the fourth century for the eighteen- to twenty-year-old citizens who were in training to be *hoplitai*, "hoplites" (heavy-armed soldiers), learning to fight in a phalanx against the hoplites of other cities.[7] This training began, after their enrollment as eighteen-year-olds in the register of tribe and deme, in the third month of the Attic year (*Boēdromiōn*), the month before *Pyanopsiōn*.

The Apatourian phratry induction at sixteen had natural analogies to the *polis* (city-state) induction at eighteen, at which civic-military duties were paramount.[8] The sixteen-year-old is registered with and celebrated by his clan as one able to succeed his father, to maintain the line of the *oikos* (household) by begetting his own children; the eighteen-year-old is registered with and acknowledged by the *polis*, through his enrollment in a tribe and deme, as one able to start taking his place in the closed ranks of adult male citizens, who

5. Deubner 1932: 232–34; Parke 1977: 88–92.

6. Scholiast to Ar., *Akh.* 146; Hesykhios, s.v. *Koureōtis*. The young men having their locks cut also honored Herakles (whose divine consort was Hēbē) by a special libation and shared cup: Hesykhios, s.v. *Oinistēria*; Pamphilos, quoted in Ath. 11.494F. Eustathios (582.20) accepted the derivation of *kouros* from *keirō*; in regard to this etymological discussion, which I will not enter into, perhaps it should be emphasized that *keir-* is not simply "cut a lock" or "trim" but "crop closely."

7. Krentz 1985 and 2002.

8. On the relation of the phratry's enrollment at age sixteen (*hēbē* proper) to the deme's enrollment at age eighteen (technically described as *epi dietes hēbēsai*, "having reached one's *hēbē* for two years"), see Labarbe 1953; Pélékidis 1962: 52–70; Golden 1979: 25–38.

collectively administered the commonwealth and defended its territory and its *oikoi* by force of arms.

The slide between these two transitional life-stages[9] may be illustrated by the particular myth-historical figure who is represented as a young warrior cutting his hair—that is, both as a *kouros/ephēbos* ready for battle and as one who cuts his hair like a sixteen-year-old at the Apatouria. He is Parthenopaios, one of the Seven against Thebes, portrayed on seven Attic vases (all dated to about 500–470 BCE). On some he is a beardless warrior, on others bearded.[10] Aiskhylos chooses to describe him in terms of age- and beard-class as an ephebe (without of course employing that term): "a man-boy man [*andropais anēr*], the down is just now creeping along his cheeks as his youthful beauty grows and the hair there thickens" (*Seven against Thebes* 533–35).

The Ephebate in Athens

A reason for the association of the tale of Melanthos with the Apatouria was discerned by Pierre Vidal-Naquet, using the young warrior as its focus. But before looking at what he dubbed the "black hunter," we must briefly dip our toes in the swirling waters of historical controversy. Concern for the registry and training of young citizen-soldiers must have been as old as the quasi-democratic city and the hoplite phalanx. The seventh-century revolution in military tactics through which the older heroic soloists and horsemen were replaced by shield-to-shield masses of heavily armed infantry is connected by most analysts—as cause and/or effect—with the social revolution in which citizen rights in the *polis* were extended to a larger land-owning but not aristocratic class.[11] Not all eligible citizens need have been trained as hoplites, just enough to man the ranks, but membership in the interdependent fighting team must have been regulated in regards to both capability and eligibility. One cannot send unskilled or unknown men to fight in the close formation of a hoplite phalanx: one would not trust one's own safety in battle to men in the same line who might be untrained fools or Thebans.

Yet there is neither plentiful nor solid testimony to the existence of ephebic military training in Athens—training that is both citywide and

9. Ceccarelli 1998 speculatively associates the life-stage transition at the Apatouria with an armed dance called the *pyrrhikē* (on which see the section of this chapter entitled *Paideia/Andreia*, below).

10. Kunisch 1974: plate 8.

11. Detienne 1968; Snodgrass 1965; Greenhalgh 1973, esp. chs. 4 and 7; Cartledge 1977, esp. 21–24; Salmon 1977. Latacz 1977 gives an excellent analysis of the phalanx formation in Homer, which sometimes assumed a close and quasi-hoplitic order for defensive purposes (esp. 55–65). In the past thirty years, a great deal of work has been published on the rise of the *polis*; for good discussions of this development, especially in relation to the development of the hoplite phalanx, see Snodgrass 1993b; Raaflaub 1993 and 1997.

compulsory—before the 330s. The inscriptions that begin to appear from that time are usually related to an "enactment concerning the ephebes" (*nomos peri tōn ephēbōn*) said to have been proposed by one Epikrates.[12] Since the earliest, certainly dated inscription concerning an ephebic class is from the year 334/3,[13] Epikrates' proposal must have been passed in 335/4 at the latest. The move can be plausibly related to the Athenian defeat at Khaironeia (338)—it could have been an attempt to bolster the city's military strength and confidence—as well as to the wider Lykourgan program of renewing the physical and cultural institutions of Athens.

On the history of the ephebate in Athens, three positions have been taken, spanning the field of possibilities: the Lykourgan ephebate was a wholly new creation;[14] it was a codification of existing practices;[15] or (as Pélékidis maintains) it was nothing new at all, having existed virtually unchanged since before the fifth century.[16]

Let us introduce some distinctions to sort out this issue. First, we should distinguish the linguistic development of such age-designating words as *kouros* and *hēbē* from the institutional development leading from archaic warrior training to the fourth-century ephebate. Just as the noun *ephēbos* is a later coinage[17] than *kouros*, so the organization of the Athenian ephebate as it is

12. "There is another Epikrates whom Lykourgos mentions in his speech *On the Financial Administration*, saying that a bronze statue of him was erected on account of his enactment concerning the ephebes; they say he possessed an estate of six hundred talents" (Harpokration, s.v. *Epikratēs*). Davies 1971: record 4909 on p. 182; Humphries 1985, n. 13.

13. Reinmuth 1971 claimed to have found an earlier inscription, but its dating has been challenged by Lewis 1973 and Mitchel 1975.

14. The existence of an earlier ephebate was denied briefly but with his customary authority by U. von Wilamowitz-Moellendorff 1893: I.193–94; his objection is answered by Loraux 1986; also by Bryant 1907. (On the peculiar cultural authority of Wilamowitz, see Nimis 1984.) Sommerstein 2010: 48–49 endorses Wilamowitz's view and argues that the ephebate as a formal institution was a "revolutionary innovation" of the 330s.

15. Mitchel 1964, esp. n. 34: "Aristotle's description contains many elements which were already ancient. . . . In fact the ephebeia, as it is known from Aristotle and the contemporary inscriptions, is but a temporary phase in an institution which had ancient precedents and one which later, beginning with the oligarchic revolution of 322/1, underwent many further changes." Mitchel suggests that the ephebate was organized by tribes, as were most things military. Other defenders of an earlier ephebate in some form are Lofberg 1925; Pleket 1965; Gauthier 1976; Ridley 1979. McCulloch and Cameron 1980 see a reference to soldiers of ephebic age in the prologue of Aiskhylos' *Seven against Thebes*.

16. Pélékidis 1962: 9 and 52: "If the ephebate is attested before 336/5, one has no right to suppose that it is a different ephebate from the one we know"; "The ephebate before the fifth century—a period in which it must have had a form more or less close to that which we know for the fourth century."

17. First in Xen., *Kyr.* 1.2.4, describing the Persian disposition of soldier-citizens into four distinct groups: boys, ephebes, grown men, and those beyond the years of campaigning. The ephebes alone sleep away from their homes in common quarters (except for those

known in the fourth century was undoubtedly different from whatever earlier measures had been taken to train future hoplite-citizens. Both of these fields, linguistic and institutional, show changes—more recoverable for the words than for the practices—and those changes may be interrelated. Second, we should mark off, as separate from the shifts either of vocabulary or of social organization, the cluster of themes and propositions that underlies both of them. These themes show much less variation over the years and should be regarded as the framework of social concern within which the developments of both language and practice took place. Principal among those themes are the son's ability to defend himself and his father's *oikos* against challenges, his ability to continue the line by begetting his own children, and (symbolic of both those things) the growth of his beard.

Already in the fifth century, the verb *ephēbaō* was one of the vocables in use to articulate those larger social concerns. "Argos was bereft of men to such an extent that their slaves ruled and managed all affairs, until the children [*paides*] of the slain men reached manhood [*ephēbēsan*]" (Herodotos 6.83.1). Eteokles, speaking of Polyneikes, opines, "Justice has never watched over him or deemed him worthy, not when he first fled the darkness of his mother's womb nor in his nurtured years [*en trophaisin*] nor when he reached his prime [*ephēbēsanta*] nor in the dense collection of his chin's hair" (Aiskhylos, *Seven against Thebes* 664–67). But the issues or themes underlying that vocable long antedate its appearance. They are as old as Telemakhos, the first "ephebe" *avant la lettre* in Greek literature, whose just-appearing beard not only precipitates his own tentatively bold moves to confront the despoilers of his father's stores but also consolidates his mother's readiness to consider taking a new husband: as Odysseus had advised her years before, "When you see our son's beard growing, then marry whom you will."[18]

Greek culture generally displays a strong sense of age-classes[19] and a particular fascination with the downy advent of manhood on the cheek.[20] But

who are married) and are commanded by twelve leaders since the citizen body is divided into twelve tribes. The Persian ephebate begins at the age of sixteen or seventeen and lasts ten years. During that time, the ephebes often serve as the King's guard when he goes hunting, "which they consider the truest practice of skills needed for warfare" (1.2.10), and they also man the guard posts (*phrourēsai*), pursue wrongdoers, and intercept bandits. Sommerstein 2010: 50–51 confirms that the word *ephebe* is not in use in the fifth century; he argues that it does not seem to designate a particular status in the case of young men before the formal institutionalization of the ephebate in the mid- to late fourth century.

18. *Od.* 18.269–70; additionally: "now that he is big and has reached the measure of *hēbē*" (19.532, also 18.217); "for now your son has reached that age: you always prayed the gods to see him grow his beard" (18.175–76); "for he is already a man" (*ēdē gar anēr* [19.160]).

19. Roussel 1942 (a book very difficult to obtain); Mette 1982.

20. "Like to a princely youth with his first under-beard, whose *hēbē* is the most gratifying" (*Iliad* 4.347–48); Solon, fr. 27 (West), on the ten heptads of a man's life (the child up to

these perennial preoccupations, the social concerns underlying them, and the undeniable need for some measure of hoplite training for young men do not establish the existence of the ephebate as a formal institution (according to the terms laid out in [Aristotle]'s *Constitution of the Athenians* [hereafter *Ath. Pol.*]) before the 330s, nor does my interpretation presuppose such a thing. The argument I will develop about the *tragōidoi* (or "tragic choristers," the performers who manned the choruses of Attic tragedy) depends only on there having been some recognizable training of some young warriors in Athens in the sixth and fifth centuries: that training need not have been (and I do not believe it was) citywide or compulsory. It is most likely to have been voluntary, especially early on, and a highly sought opportunity for those with sufficient wealth, leisure, and ambition to display their excellence and to win honor while doing their patriotic duty and serving the needs of the *polis*. As Xenophon says, pointedly I think, of cities without the Persian system of public training, "Most *poleis* leave it to individual fathers to educate their children as they wish" (*Kyr.* 1.2.2).[21] Xenophon, as Philippe Gauthier has discerned (see below), had specific recommendations to make about the state-organization and financing of the practices that were equivalent to the Aristotelian (or Lykourgan) ephebate.

Those practices, known as early as Eupolis and Thoukydides, segregated the youngest soldiers into a distinct group (the *neōtatoi*) and assigned them to guard duty on the frontier fortresses, in which capacity they were known as *peripoloi*.[22] Aiskhines twice mentions his service in that corps at that age and refers to himself and his fellow-*peripoloi* as *synephēboi* (co-ephebes): "When I left the ranks of childhood I became a *peripolos* of this territory for two years, and as witnesses of this I shall offer you my *synephēboi* and our commanders" (2.167); "Misgolas in fact is my age-mate [*hēlikiōtēs*] and *synephēbos* and this is our forty-fifth year" (1.49). From the latter passage it is clear that Aiskhines (born 390) served as *peripolos* in 372.[23] Even if his use of the term *synephēbos* were anachronistic (and it does not seem so), it still antedates Epikrates' legislation by some ten years (the speech against Timarkhos was delivered in

---

seven without *hēbē*, the boy up to fourteen who starts to show the signs of *hēbē*, the growing youth whose chin gets downy, and so on), seconded by Aristotle, *Politics* 7.17.1336b37; Plato, *Protagoras* 309A–B; Xenophon, *Symposion* 4.23 and *Anabasis* 2.6.28; virtually *passim* in Greek culture. I do not know why in a representation of the Dioskouroi reported by Pausanias (5.19.2, the chest of Kypselos in the Heraion at Olympia) one is bearded, the other not. Are they two sides of the same ephebic figure, one a boy, the other a man?

21. In the discussion of training for warfare in Plato's *Lakhes* (179A–180A and *passim*), it is up to the individual fathers to ensure their sons' skill and readiness by sending them to specialist instructors.

22. Pélékidis 1962: 35–41.

23. Ober 1985: 93 comes to the same conclusion regarding the date of Aiskhines' service.

346/5) and presents us with a picture of a two-year service on the frontier organized in 372 under commanders and manned by those who have just "left the boys."[24]

Further, Demosthenes specifically refers to Aiskhines' taking of the ephebic oath (*ton en tōi tēs Aglaurou tōn ephēbōn horkon*, 19.303, delivered in 343). The oath itself, an apparently ancient formula, applies to the duties of hoplite warriors in their phalanx:

> I will not disgrace these sacred weapons [*hopla*] and I will not desert the comrade beside me [*parastatēn*] wherever I shall be stationed in a battle line. I shall defend the sacred and holy places. I shall hand over the fatherland undiminished—and greater and better according to my own efforts and with the help of all the other citizens. And I shall obey those in power who give intelligent directions [?] and the established laws and whatever laws shall have been subsequently established intelligently. If someone removes one of the laws, I shall not allow him to do so both by my own efforts and with the help of all the other citizens. And I shall honor the ancestral customs as holy. The witnessing gods are Aglauros, Hestia, Enyo, Enyalios, Ares and Athena Areia, Zeus, Thallo, Auxo, Hegemone, Herakles, the borders of the fatherland, wheat crops, barley crops, vines, olive trees, fig trees.[25]

The language of the ephebic oath not only has the patina of antiquity in its vocabulary but also seems to resonate, at least faintly, in fifth-century literature. Moreau found a reference to the oath in Aristophanes' *The Seasons* (*Hōrai*, produced about 420): "You have corrupted our oath."[26] Pélékidis detects it twice more in Aristophanes.[27] "But I will never ever disgrace the

24. There has been some confusion over the birthdate of Aiskhines. If Aiskhines' birth were placed as early as 399/8 (a possibility set out by Lewis 1958), his "ephebate" would have been in 381. Harris has argued convincingly, however, that Aiskhines was born, as he himself indicates, in 391/90 or 390/89, which would mean that his years in the ephebate were 373–371 or 372–370. See Harris 1988: 213. For a useful discussion of the Athenian system of age-classes, and the system by which young men were moved into the various categories of adulthood, see Davidson 2007: 84–92.

25. The text of this oath is preserved on a fourth-century BCE inscription found at Akharnai; it is easily available (with a literal translation) in Rhodes and Osborne 2004: 440–42. Pélékidis 1962: 113; Daux 1971; Merkelbach 1972. The reliance of a hoplite on his comrades is emphasized at Euripides, *Herakles* 190–94: "A hoplite is the slave of his weaponry; when he breaks his spear he has no way to defend his body from death, it is his one defense; and if those stationed in line with him are not good men he dies through the cowardice of his neighbors."

26. Fr. 579 *PCG* (=fr. 568 Kock); Moreau 1954: 341.

27. Pélékidis 1962: 76, n. 2. He rightly remarks (72) that later authors, such as Plutarch (*Alkib.* 15.4), cannot be taken as decisive when they assume the existence of the oath in the fifth century, though the fact that they can do so is of some weight. Similar references to the ephebate occur in the *Letters of Themistokles* 8 (Hercher 1873: 747) and the Athenian

fatherland," says the First Creditor at *Clouds* 1220, meaning "but I must do my duty." Since it intrudes oddly into his speech, it could well be intended to be recognized as a fixed phrase known to the audience. Pélékidis's second instance is slightly less compelling: "I will not disgrace my clan," says the Sykophant at *Birds* 1451. "My grandpa was a sykophant and so am I." This again could be a reference to a known phrase, given a twisted application.[28] Siewert and Loraux find further echoes of the oath in fifth-century texts.[29]

The text that comes nearest to being decisive on the issue of the existence of pre-Lykourgan ephebic training is Xenophon's *Ways and Means* (*Poroi*), which contains his specific recommendation concerning the corps to which Aiskhines belonged: "If my advice concerning revenues is enacted, I claim not only that the city will be wealthier but also more obedient, more disciplined, and better for battle, for those who are assigned to exercise would do so much more attentively if they received an allowance in the gymnasiums greater than those being trained for the torch-races; similarly, those assigned to guard-duty in the guard-posts and those assigned to light-armed duty and to patrolling [*peripolein*] the countryside—they would do all these duties better if an allowance is granted to each of these jobs" (4.52). Though the passage had been briefly noticed by others,[30] it was Gauthier who first drew the conclusion that Xenophon is essentially recommending (in 355/4) that the several forms of young men's military training should be funded by the state.[31]

This implies both that the state-funded ephebate did not yet exist and also that several "ephebic" duties—training in the gymnasiums, frontier duty, and country patrol—were at least informally recognized, just waiting (as it were) to be organized. Gauthier makes the further interesting suggestion that Xenophon's rather clumsy circumlocutions ("those who are assigned to") are due to his sense that "ephebe" is still too ambiguous a term, mainly referring to an age-class but not to everyone in that class.[32] It is the functions performed by

decree honoring Hippokrates (Hercher 1873: 311; Hippokrates, *Opera Omnia*, vol. IX, p. 402, ed. Littré; Pélékidis 1962: 187).

28. The skeptical side of us, however, might wonder whether what was later called the ephebic oath was in the fifth century taken by ephebes. The answer must be that it is a hoplite soldier's oath and would certainly be taken by all citizen-soldiers from the first time they served, ordinarily in their youthful prime. The open question is whether training for phalanx warfare was conducted as a corporate two-year exercise for all eligible eighteen-year-olds in the fifth century.

29. Siewert 1977 (citing Aiskhylos, *Persians* 956–62; Sophokles, *Antigone* 663–71; and Thoukydides 1.144.4, 2.37.3); Loraux 1986: 305 (citing Aristophanes, *Peace* 596–98; cf. *Akharnians* 995–99).

30. Lofberg 1925; Reinmuth 1952: 37.

31. Gauthier 1976: 190–95.

32. Sommerstein 2010: 50–51 makes the same observation.

certain of those young men, the ones engaged in military exercises, that need to be organized and paid for from the public purse.[33]

This range of evidence supports the moderate or centrist position among the three possibilities for the history of the ephebate in Athens: that the ephebate formally established in late fourth-century Athens was a codification of existing practices. Already before 335/4 BCE, young men underwent military training in a form similar if not necessarily identical to that described in *Ath. Pol.* 42. We do not know whether these young men displayed their close-order drill to the citizen body, or to the *Boulē*, and if so where the performance took place. If it was in the orchestra of the Theater of Dionysos, the analogy between tragic choral dancing and phalanx movement would have been visibly confirmed each year, as it certainly was after 335/4. It is also possible that the ephebic display in the theater was an innovation, but if so, it was one that seemed appropriate to its devisers, because it mirrored the rectangular formation of masked young *tragōidoi* and expressed a roughly equivalent meaning.

In what follows, I will continue to use the term "ephebe" loosely and informally to signify young citizen-warriors in their years of military training, older than boys but not yet men, and well off rather than poor.[34] Readers who cannot dissociate the term "ephebe" from the title formally conferred on Athenian youths by the fourth-century institution of the ephebate or from the historical controversy over the description of that institution in *Ath. Pol.* 42 might simply substitute the phrase "young warrior" for "ephebe" (as I sometimes do). For my hypothesis about tragic performance to work, the *minimum* requirement is only that some visible segment of the young male population of Athens underwent hoplite training of some sort on some days of the year during the fifth and fourth centuries BCE—no more. (It is even possible that the *tragōidoi* were actually recent graduates of such training, rather than eighteen- to twenty-year-olds proper.)

If pre-Lykourgan ephebic training was not publicly financed, then it was, like other forms of education in Athens,[35] privately undertaken—not a universal requirement for *polis* membership but an ambition of those families who could afford it. This corresponds to the picture of the Persian *ephēboi*

33. Plato also experiments with an organizational plan for the military training of young men (ages twenty-five to thirty) as border guards: *Laws* 6.760B–763C; Pélékidis 1962: 25–31.

34. On the cost of hoplite armor, see Connor 1988: 10, n. 30.

35. K. J. Dover, in his edition of Aristophanes, *Clouds* lx–lxi, cites [Lysias] 20.11; Dem. 18.265; Xen., *Mem.* 2.2.6; and Plato, *Prot.* 326C on education as a private endeavor, heavily dependent on wealth. Cf. also Plato, *Prot.* 327D on the competitive pressure to strive for excellence. Loraux 1986: 150–53 has signally clarified the ideological slant that shapes the self-image of Athenian "non-professionalism"; it casts a filtered and flattering light on citizen-soldiers so that they look like aristocratic warriors, whose nature alone (and not any training) is a sufficient explanation of their valor.

described (or invented?) by Xenophon in his *Kyroupaideia*. They do not comprise all Persian youth of the right age (though all are eligible), but only those whose fathers can afford to support them. Sons who must work are not enrolled (*Kyr.* 1.2.15). In Athens, class and wealth seem similarly to have interfered with the universality of military conscription and service. It certainly does not offend our common sense about ancient life to imagine that corporate and individual exercises may have been more pursued by the wealthier and more ambitious families than by those in straitened circumstances. Oarsmen presumably did not need hoplite training; unarmored fighters (*psiloi*) were the poor.[36] "The hoplites" is sometimes virtually a synonym for those citizens who are noble, rich, and good ([Xen.], *Ath. Pol.* 1.2: *gennaioi, plousioi, chrēstoi*). Of course, in all these matters we should not underestimate the messiness of actual arrangements—one citizen volunteers to put up the mess-money for two fellow-demesmen who find themselves short of cash (Lys. 16.14); sailors are conscripted from the deme catalogues for service on a trireme, but "only a few showed up and those were feeble, so I sent them all away" and hired the best available sailors (Dem. 50.6–7).

Not only was ephebic and hoplite status the prerogative of Athens' better citizens before Lykourgos: even the apparent universality of ephebic training in *Ath. Pol.* 42 has been seriously doubted.[37] This is a treatise, after all, whose editorial opinion is that Athens was best organized when citizenship rights were invested exclusively in a hoplite property-class of five thousand (33.2; cf. 23.2). That view was shared by others who put their opinions on record, such as Thoukydides (8.97.2), and corresponds to a general tendency in the period to see the Best Men as the truest representatives of the community: "the hoplites and cavalry, who are evidently preeminent among the citizens in fine human qualities [*kalokagathia*]" (Xen., *Mem.* 3.5.19). Did every Athenian eighteen-year-old male really participate in the late fourth-century ephebate? Does a formal institution necessarily mean a universal one, or did the fourth-century ephebate fall short of universality and continue to favor the elite? How curious it would be if ephebic training passed from being the informal province of relatively well-to-do citizens before about 335/4 to universal conscription in the brief period from about 335/4 to 323/2 and thereafter to an elite school under the aristocratic constitutions of Antipatros and subsequent leaders.[38]

The issue of class ranking in military organization also suggests important issues (which cannot be entered into here) about the class structure of

36. Thoukydides 4.94.1; Plutarch, *Phokion* 12.3; Arrian, *Tactics* 2.1; Gomme, Andrewes, and Dover 1945–81 *ad* 1.15.

37. Rhodes 1981: 503; see also Rhodes 1980, arguing on population figures against Ruschenbusch 1979, who replied in 1981.

38. Pélékidis 1962: 155 ff.; Mitchel 1964 shows that in the oligarchy of Phokion (322–319/8) the ephebate was either seriously diminished or abolished altogether.

Athenian drama, whose early history, more clearly for comedy than for tragedy, seems to have been one of privately sponsored performances incorporated into the system of publicly financed festivals. The Dionysian dances were socially and economically structured as a gift from the wealthy few to the self-sustaining many—a gift that expressed and mediated the privileged position of nobler families, putative descendants of tragedy's old heroes, within the democratic city.[39]

Dionysos and the Apatouria

Now back to the so-called black hunter.[40] In developing this theme, we must allow for (and watch out for) not only a certain play between the looser and stricter senses of "ephebe" and between the older phratry (clan) organization and the newer deme-and-tribe organization of the *polis*, but also the even more important ambiguity inherent in the social meaning of the ephebate itself. Ephebic training is not only a practical induction into the techniques of infantry fighting; it is also a passage between two distinct social identities.[41] "The Spartiates call ephebes '*sideuneis*'; they separate them at *hēbē*, that is when they are about fifteen or sixteen years old, from the younger boys and in isolation they practice becoming men [*kath' heautous ēskoun androusthai*]" (Photios, s.v. *synephēbos*). The ephebate therefore contains not only training in military discipline and in civic responsibility but also rites and fictions that dramatize the difference between what the ephebes were (boys) and what they will be (men). The myth of Melanthos told at the Apatouria expresses the character and status of the new soldiers as in-betweeners, mixing the categories,

39. Wilson 2011: 32–35 argues that the *khorēgia* (private financial sponsorship of the costs of training and preparing a chorus for performance at a dramatic festival) represented a unique form of aristocratic competition within the democratic city: it "gave to the elite a uniquely privileged opportunity for display of cultural and economic prowess and excellence. Yet that display, with all its potential to slip over into tyrannical excess, was tempered by mechanisms of legal control" (34). Wilson 2000 is the standard study of the function of the *khorēgia* in Athens.

40. Vidal-Naquet 1981, 1986a: 106–28. In 1986b, Vidal-Naquet raises some objections to my argument about tragedy: see note 80 below.

41. Thus Artemidoros (*Oneirokritika* 1.54) sees a dream of being an ephebe as symbolic of transitions—for the unmarried, marriage; for an old man, death. Ma 1994 and especially 2008, in a reevaluation of the structuralist paradigm of the "Black Hunter," inveighs against drawing too strict a boundary in ancient Greek society between the categories of "youths" and "adults" in terms of age, social role, status, and military function; he argues for a more prolonged, more gradual, and less sharply demarcated transition between age-classes—for "the existence of a broad band of youthful status, rather than a polarity between marginal youth and incorporated adult: incorporation and socialization take place over time" (2008: 190). "Ephebes" constitute on this view a specific, transitional category within the larger, diffuse transitional zone of "young men" and should not be identified with the whole of that zone.

specifically by an implied contrast between that disciplined and honorable phalanx-fighting on the plains, which was the duty of every citizen-soldier, and Melanthos' tricky, deceitful, solo fighting in the mountains.[42]

To appreciate how shocking was Melanthos' trick one must read chapters 7–9 of W. K. Pritchett's *The Greek State at War: Part II*. Warfare between Greek *poleis* was governed by rules of honor comparable to those for dueling.[43] Enemy armies might camp quite close to each other without fear of surprise attack; battles took place in response to a formal challenge, which might be declined for several days in succession; ambuscades and night attacks were serious violations of honor, at least between Greeks.[44]

There is some indication that the exercises of the Athenian ephebate contained a literal acting out of Melanthos' role, though it may have been rather more symbolic and conventional than the literal program described by Vidal-Naquet. Like all things military and most things archaic, the discipline of the young is best attested for Sparta. There, the sons of citizens were segregated in "herds" (*agelai*), according to a carefully regulated system of age-classes. The training of Spartan youth is known to have included distinctly non-hoplitic exercises: unarmed forays in the hills, feeding off the wild land instead of in a company mess, stealthy night-fighting. Such exercises in wiliness, survival, and what we might call lone wolf tactics do contain a component of the practical, insofar as they promote ruggedness and self-reliance, but on the whole they are quite useless for Greek intercity fighting, since they do not develop that corporate discipline and well-drilled obedience that were the essence of infantry maneuvers.[45]

42. For a perceptive reading of Euripides' *Hippolytos* as reflecting these distinctions, see Mitchell-Boyask 1999: 43–49. Sommerstein 2010 argues that tragedies in the latter half of the fifth century show an increased anxiety over this moment of social transition, suggesting that the previous military training was proving inadequate to educate young men as citizens of the fifth-century *polis* (52–54).

43. "No one who is a man and courageous [*anēr eupsykhos*] thinks it right to kill his enemy secretly, but advances to meet him face to face" ([Eur.], *Rhesos* 510–11). Recent scholarship has challenged the view of Greek warfare as highly ritualized and governed by rules of honor. See especially Dayton 2006, who argues that the view of Greek warfare as "agonistic" is a nostalgic response to the "spiritual strain caused by the potential of modern war" (11). For a careful consideration of the ancient sources on the rules of hoplite warfare, see pp. 52–87. Dayton builds on the important work of Krentz 2000 and 2002; Krentz 2000 provides an overwhelming list of battles from the Archaic through the Classical periods in which trickery and deception played a role. He argues that the rhetoric against deception in battle should be recognized as just that—rhetoric: "While a man might declare his disdain for deception, that does not mean he would hesitate to use it against his enemies" (174). For a contrasting approach that attempts to rehabilitate aspects of the older view, see Schwartz 2009.

44. Zeus exiled Herakles for killing Iphitos *dolōi*, by a trick, when Iphitos' eye was one way and his mind another, looking for his strayed mares: Sophokles, *Tr.* 270–80.

45. Jeanmaire 1913. One must be more reserved, however, than Jeanmaire and Vidal-Naquet about the simple identification of the Spartan *krypteia* as an *ephēbeia*.

The Attic evidence is much sparser but contains some significant parallels. Specifically, the ephebes in Aristotle's account of military training were sundered from all citizen duties or claims at law and were taken out of the city to the series of forts on the perimeter of Attika.[46] It is not necessarily the case that the youngest Athenian soldiers in this period were much exercised in mountain foraging and ambuscades, as Vidal-Naquet concludes from the Spartan parallel.[47] The discussion of border patrol (*phulakē*) at Xen., *Mem.* 3.6.9–11 is quite straightforward and practical, implying that the point of the young soldiers' duty there (Glaukon is not yet twenty, 3.6.1) is mainly to prevent raiding parties of Boiotians from stealing Attic sheep and such.[48] Insofar as the goal of the ephebate was to produce hoplites who would not break ranks, lone wolf training must have formed only a very limited and subordinate part of the program; the purpose that such training served was more symbolic than practical.

We should rather say that in the timespan of the ephebes' novitiate, when they were segregated from the regular community and awaiting entry into the ranks of full citizen-soldiers, the Melanthos tale becomes theirs for its border setting, its patriotism, its unproven hero, and above all because Melanthos is one who has not yet learned the honorable conventions of phalanx battle. Because the ephebate is both a period of practical military training and contains rituals of passage by segregation and inversion, a tale of a fighting trick set on the border captures the very character of the ephebic ideal (or anti-ideal).[49] This is strikingly confirmed when we observe that the mysterious

46. [Arist.], *Ath. Pol.* 42.3–4; *peripolousi tēn khōran*, "they patrol the countryside." Such guard-duty was typical service for young warriors in other cities too: "[For watching prisoners] use should be made, where the system of ephebes or guards exists, of the young men" (Arist., *Pol.* 6.8.1322a27–8). A specific instance was Sikyon, where a fourth-century historian (perhaps Ephoros) described the career of the seventh-century tyrant Orthagoras as follows: "When he moved out of the age-class of boys and became one of the *peripoloi* guarding the countryside" (*Oxyrhynchus Papyri* 1365.22–8 = *FGrHist* 105.2).

47. A more cautious formulation is found in his "Recipes for Greek Adolescence": "What was true of the Athenian ephebe *at the level of myth* is true of the Spartan *kryptos* in practice; the *kryptos* appears in every respect to be an anti-hoplite" (Vidal-Naquet 1986a: 147).

48. The passes are steep and narrow and therefore do not require, indeed hardly allow, full hoplite armor and tactics to defend them: Xen., *Mem.* 3.5.25–28. Munn 2010 and 1996 questions, in any case, the use of border fortifications to control routes into Attika; Munn proposes that their intended use is to protect Athenian agricultural interests in the immediate area of the garrison. On modern sheep-stealing, see Herzfeld 1986.

49. Ma 2008: 190, speaking of the *peripoloi*, argues that "the patrollers appear integrated in the *polis*, whose values and behaviour patterns they reflect"; such integration is not at odds with the paradoxical character of the ephebic ideal but rather constitutes one element of its complexity.

apparition is both beardless (the iconographic sign for ephebes) and black-caped, for Athenian ephebes wore a distinctive black cape.[50]

But, granting all that, there remains a problem. The black-caped apparition is Dionysos, explicitly named in some versions of the story, and well known elsewhere by that title (Melanaigis, "of the black goatskin").[51] Dionysos, as far as we know, has no particular connection with the Apatouria;[52] in fact, the association is distinctly odd.[53] All the same, the place-names Oinoē and Eleutherai fall within his sphere of influence, the former suggesting *oinos*/wine, the latter the title Eleuthereus under which he was worshipped at the City Dionysia, the five-day dramatic festival each spring. The title Melanaigis is explained in the *Souda* by the story that the daughters of Eleuther (the eponymous hero of Eleutherai) saw an apparition of Dionysos wearing a black goatskin and, because they mocked it, went mad; to cure their insanity, their father followed the advice of an oracle to institute the cult of Dionysos Melanaigis. The tale-type is fairly common. Its most significant instance for our investigation is the foundation myth of the City Dionysia: a certain Pegasos of Eleutherai brought the statue of Dionysos to Attika, but the Athenians did not receive it with honor; the angry god then sent an incurable affliction on the

50. Pollux 10.164: "The ephebes' uniform is a *petasos* [broad-brimmed felt hat] and a *khlamys* [cloak]," citing Philemon's *Door-Keeper* (fr. 34 Kock). Artemidoros, writing in the later second century CE, knows three colors of ephebic cloak—white, black, and crimson (*Oneirokritika* 1.54). The substitution of white for black cloaks at the Eleusinian procession was a beneficence of Herodes Attikos about 176 CE, known both from Philostratos, *Lives of the Sophists* 2.550 and a contemporary inscription (*IG* II^2 3606): Roussel 1941; Maxwell-Stuart 1970. The inscription relates the change from black to white with Theseus' failure to change his black sails to white when he returned from Krete. It is just possible, therefore, that Simonides' reference to the fatal sails not as black but as crimson has some bearing on the color of ephebic cloaks (*PMG* 550). Mitchell-Boyask 1999: 47–48 makes the connection between the ephebes' cloaks and Theseus' sails in the context of Euripides' *Hippolytos*. Aristotle, *Rhet.* 3.2.9, speaking of appropriateness, says that the *phoinikis* (a bright red or purplish military cloak) is right for a young man but not for an old man. The cloaks worn by pyrrhic dancers on a black-figure vase in Australia have been painted red, but the significance of this is perhaps diminished by the fact that the artist has also painted each figure's hair, the borders of other cloaks, and alternate palmette leaves red: Australian National University, Canberra, Classics Department Museum Collection 76.08; illustration in Green and Rawson 1981: 31 and in Trendall n.d.: 3 fig. 2.

51. For instance at Hermion, where there were annual contests in music, swimming, and boat racing in his honor (Paus. 2.35.1).

52. None, that is, except for this story, whence the rare report that the Apatouria was celebrated in honor of Dionysos: *Etymologicum Magnum* 118.55.

53. Dionysos does not figure in the list of gods in the ephebic oath; neither does Apollo Lykeios, a principal patron of the accomplished initiation of the ephebes: Jameson 1980. In addition to the gods mentioned above, Hephaistos was honored at the Apatouria by men dressed in fine robes who lit torches from the hearth and sang a hymn to him: Harpokration, s.v. *Lampas*.

genitals of the men that could only be cured (said an oracle) by paying every honor to the god, which the men proceeded to do by fashioning *phalloi* for use in his worship as a memorial of their suffering.[54]

Most telling for our present purposes is the fact that the entry of Dionysos into Athens was reenacted each year by the ephebes (that is, in the years when there were "official" ephebes, post-335; before that we cannot say). They inaugurated the festival by bringing the cult statue in procession from the Academy (just outside the city boundaries on the road to Eleutherai) back to its temple and theater precinct on the southeast slope of the Akropolis. This reenactment for the city of the origin of Dionysos Melanaigis by the ephebes seems to mirror (with the normal cloudiness and unevenness of ancient metal mirrors rather than with the sharpness of our silvered glass ones) those ceremonies of induction and that myth of apprenticeship located at the opposite end of the year.

One might, of course, try either to expunge Dionysos from the tale of the warrior's trick or to sever the tale from the Apatouria.[55] An older style of analysis, well exemplified by W. R. Halliday, excelled in the use of text-editorial methods to detect inconsistencies and to delete intrusive elements in the myth.[56] Like restorers of old paintings, such scholars aimed to uncover the authentic original from centuries of grime and inexpert retouching. The current understanding of such myths, however, recognizes that logical gaps and overlay are sometimes not the unfortunate accretions of time but signs of a social process, of an ongoing negotiation among various groups or points of view. The story of Melanthos' trick of the black goatskin seems caught in some sort of force-field between the Apatouria and the City Dionysia: I propose that a specific feature of these two festivals made it seem to belong to both and that the city's youngest warriors are the link.

54. Scholiast on Ar., *Akh.* 243. Athenian colonies were evidently required to send a *phallos* to the mother city for the Dionysia; we have a record of one such from Brea: *IG* I^3 47, line 12. On the practice of sending offerings from colony to mother city, see Thouk. 1.25.4 and Graham 1964: ch. 8. See also *IG* II^2 673, and the proliferation of phallic *veneranda* associated with Dionysos on Delos: Buschor 1928; Sifakis 1967. A fragment of a Megarian bowl found in a Dionysian context on Delos shows a *phallos* with goat legs: *BCH* 31 (1907): 500–501.

55. At least one ancient scholar understood that *Apatouria* was not derived from *apatē*, "trick," but referred rather to the old community of clans: scholiast on Ar., *Akh.* 146. Szemerényi 1971 derives the word from *ha-patro-woroi*, "watchers, worshippers of the same father."

56. "The proximity to Eleutherai, the name Oinoe, and the name Melanthos may all have played a part in bringing Dionysos Melanaigis into the story" (Halliday 1926: 179). Halliday argues against the theory that the combat of Melanthos/Xanthos, understood as Black Man/Fair Man and Winter/Spring, served as a ritual background for the development of Classical tragedy. Pickard-Cambridge 1962: 120–21.

Paideia/Andreia

Crucial to the establishment of a proper and honorable male identity in the world of Kleisthenes, the fabled tyrant of Sikyon, was military skill—by which I mean a combination of physical strength, endurance of hardships, knowledge of weapons, courage in facing danger, and good judgment. One of the widespread and seriously understudied practices by which such skills were inculcated in youth was dancing, which we must understand as if it consisted not in the casual frolicking of effete neoclassical nymphs but rather (as dancers know) in an exhausting and painful workout, taking the body to its limits.

The athletic abilities required for fighting—strength, nimbleness, speed, and balance—made the analogy to dancing sometimes obvious, as we can see from Hektor's reply to a taunt from Aias in the *Iliad* (7.235–41): "Do not be testing me as if I were some ineffectual boy, or a woman, who knows nothing of the works of warfare. . . . I know how to turn to the right, how to turn to the left the ox-hide shield, . . . I know how to tread my measures on the grim floor of the war god" (Lattimore's translation). "Tread my measures" is *melpesthai*, a word for singing and dancing. The same analogy is implied, later in the epic, by Aineias' taunt to Meriones: "Meriones, if I had hit you, my spear would have stopped you entirely, though you are a dancer [*orkhēstēs*]" (*Iliad* 16.617–18). Meriones had avoided Aineias' spear by ducking down forward (16.611). The agility to dodge a hurtling weapon is no mean athletic skill, and it is naturally harder to do it while wearing full body armor and carrying a three-foot metal shield.

What might in the *Iliad* have been merely a bold metaphor for a warrior's strength and agility certainly became a reality in later times. By way of a very summary account, we can say that dancing with armor and weapons was a regular part of every Greek man's local culture (though presumably not everyone was equally good at it). Styles were traditional and differed by region and *polis*. We know this best from Xenophon's description of a banquet in Paphlagonia (a region in northern Anatolia) where the foreign guests were amazed at the Greek soldiers' dancing skills. Each local contingent had its own form of dancing, featuring leaps or somersaults or mock battles—all in armor and all strictly in time to the playing of an *aulos* (a pipe or wind-instrument):

> After the libations and the singing of the paian, two Thrakians rose up first and began a dance in full armor [*hopla*] to the music of an *aulos*, leaping high and lightly and using their sabers; finally, one struck the other, as everybody thought, and the second man fell, in a rather skillful way. The Paphlagonians cried out in alarm. Then the first man despoiled the other of his arms [*hopla*] and marched out singing the Sitalkas, while other Thrakians carried off the fallen dancer, as though he were dead; in fact, he had not been hurt at all.

> After this some Ainianians and Magnesians arose and danced under arms [*hopla*] the so-called Karpaia. The manner of the dance was this: a man is sowing and driving a yoke of oxen, his arms [*hopla*] laid at one side, and he turns about frequently as if in fear; a bandit approaches; as soon as the sower sees him coming, he snatches up his arms, goes to meet him, and fights with him to save his oxen. The two men do all this in rhythm to the music of the *aulos*. Finally, the bandit binds the man and drives off the oxen; or sometimes the master of the oxen binds the bandit, and then he yokes him alongside the oxen, his hands tied behind him, and drives off.
>
> After this a Mysian came in carrying a small shield [*peltē*] in each hand, and at one moment in his dance he would go through a pantomime as though two men were arrayed against him, again he would use his shields as though against a single antagonist, and again he would whirl and jump somersaults while holding the shields in his hands—ah!, the spectacle was a fine one. Lastly, he danced the Persikon, clashing his shields together and crouching down and then rising up again. And all this he did keeping time to the music of the *aulos*.
>
> After him the Mantineans and some of the other Arkadians arose, arrayed in the finest arms and accoutrements they could command, and marched in time to the accompaniment of an *aulos* playing the martial rhythm [*enhoplion*] and sang the paian and danced, just as the Arkadians do in their festal processions in honor of the gods.
>
> And the Paphlagonians, as they looked on, thought it most strange that all the dances were under arms. Thereupon the Mysian, seeing how astounded they were, persuaded one of the Arkadians who had a dancing woman to let him bring her in, after dressing her up in the finest way he could and giving her a light-weight shield [*aspis*]. And she danced the Pyrrhic with grace. Then there was great applause, and the Paphlagonians asked whether women also fought by their side. And the Greeks replied yes, these women in fact were the very ones who had put the Persian King to flight from his camp. (*Anabasis* 6.1.5–13)

Xenophon's account shows that military dancing in armor was common to many Greek cities; he hints that it was distinctively Greek.[57] The Paphlagonians at least are surprised that one should dance in *hopla*. Xenophon also indicates that its forms were both functional and culturally elaborated.[58] They are obviously functional, insofar as the moves were useful in real-life situations, such as raiding; but they are also culturally elaborated: the mistress of one of the Arkadians is an *orkhēstris*, a professional dancer,

57. On this passage, see further Lonsdale 1993: 141–42.

58. Similarly, Plato thinks of the choral pyrrhic at the Panathenaia as both "useful for battle and a festival event" (*polemou t'en khreiai kai heortōn heneka*, *Laws* 7.796C).

and she can perform the *pyrrhikē* as a showpiece in the same costume used by boys, though her *aspis* is lighter than regulation.[59] We will bring her back for an encore shortly. But first we must look more closely at the pyrrhic—and at the protomilitary dance training specifically of young men.

Several forms of such training are known. They resemble Asian martial arts in their combination of graceful, rhythmic movement with the physical and spiritual training of a warrior-to-be. Athenaios, writing in the early third century CE, praises the ancients for their conscientious focus on the athletic body. Recommending an aesthetics of restraint, Athenaios praises Classical, specifically pre-Hellenistic, culture as a period when the postures of statues and the styles of dancing were equally dignified (14.629B–C). "They transferred the poses [of sculpted figures] to the choruses"—images of effete pseudoclassical dancing may spring to the mind's eye here, but no, for he goes on—"and from the choruses to the wrestling mats" (629B). The governing idea behind this language of dignity in posture and movement is the athletic body, disciplined to a state of tough grace. "In their music and in the care of their bodies they aimed at manliness [*andreia*, down-translated as "courage"], and to be able to move in heavy armor they prepared themselves with song: that is the origin of the so-called pyrrhics and all such styles of dancing" (629C).

The two most prominent versions of this martial dancing for male adolescents were *gymnopaidikē* and *pyrrhikē*.[60] The gymnopaidic dance was a gentler exercise that imitated wrestling and the *pankration*: as Athenaios describes it, "[B]oys dance [the *gymnopaidikē*] naked, performing various rhythmic movements and various figures with their arms in a gentle manner, and thus depict scenes from the wrestling school and the *pankration*, moving their feet in rhythm."[61] The gymnopaidic dance was a preparatory stage for

59. For representations of dancing women in pyrrhic armor, see Poursat 1968; Delavaud-Roux 1993; Goulaki-Voutira 1996. The protodramatic character of some of the dances—enacting a soldier's death in one case and a countryside encounter between brigand and farmer in another—has, in my view, no special relationship to the development of drama in Athens.

60. See Shüler 2017: 7–9 on the *pyrrhikē* as a form of military training; Shüler expands on ideas first put forward in an earlier version of this chapter. Lonsdale 1993: 137–68 provides an excellent discussion of the *pyrrhikē*, its visual representation, and probable ties to religious ritual. Lonsdale sees the dance both as a form of military training and as a rite of transition to manhood. Ceccarelli 1998 undertakes an extended study of the *pyrrhikē*, which she identifies specifically with ephebic training and with rites of passage from boyhood to manhood.

61. Ath. 14.631B–C (translation by Barker 1984: 290–91). Note also "the *gymnopaidikē* is comparable to the tragic dance called *emmeleia*: weightiness and solemnity may be observed in each" (Ath. 14.630E [trans. Barker 1984: 289]). Plato's scheme in the *Laws* for the training of youth to be ambidextrous when they handle weapons (*kai dē ta ge malista pros tēn tōn hoplōn khreian*, 7.794D; cf. 7.795B) categorizes both dancing and wrestling as gymnastic exercises (7.795D–E).

the less gentle, partly weaponed *pyrrhikē*, a fast, warlike dance performed by *enhoploi paides*, older boys in partial armor,[62] about which we know considerably more.

Aristotle derived the name of this second dance from the funeral *pyre* of Patroklos, before which Achilles supposedly first danced the pyrrhic.[63] But another etymology, evidently known to Euripides, traced the term back to Pyrrhos, aka Neoptolemos, the son of Achilles. Both leaping and wielding of the shield are distinctive features of the pyrrhic, and they are described by the messenger in Euripides' *Andromakhe* as Neoptolemos' moves in defending himself against the Delphian ambush.

> He heaved with rigid arm his covering shield
> Here, there, and everywhere, to intercept them.
> No use. For many weapons came at once:
> Arrows and javelins and unfastened spits,
> Meat-cleavers to kill bulls clanged at his feet.
> Then you'd have seen a ghastly pyrrhic, as the boy
> Tried to outtwist them. Men were edging around him,
> Pinning him there, not giving him time to breathe,
> When he suddenly rushed from the sacrificial stone,
> Leaping the leap that Troy knew to its cost.
>
> (1129–36, TRANSLATED BY J. F. NIMS)

When the ambushers first fell on him, Pyrrhos had been unarmed, but he managed to grab some armor hanging on a nearby peg and take his stand on the altar, "looking like a hoplite" (1123). Presumably, he did not have time to tie on a cuirass and greaves, but just took hold of a spear and shield and perhaps a helmet. Thus, he would look very much like the partly armed young men when they did the dance named for him, pretending to dodge missiles and thrusts from all sides, as they would need to do in real combat not many years hence.

The fullest description of a (perhaps idealized) pyrrhic occurs in Plato's *Laws* 7.815A: "The pyrrhic portrays the movements to avoid every kind of blow or missile—by dodging to one side, yielding ground, jumping into the

62. "The pyrrhic is like the satyric, since both are speedy; it seems to be war-like, since boys in armor dance it; speed is necessary in battle both for pursuit and for the losers to flee" (Ath. 14.630D). Downes 1904; Poursat 1968; Scarpi 1979. That the pyrrhicists were somewhat older than the gymnopaidicists is indicated not only by the fact that they needed greater strength to carry the metal equipment but also by such phrases as "beardless pyrrhicists" (Lysias 21.4), indicating that the dancers were man-sized boys.

63. Arist., *Kret. Pol.* frag. 519 = scholiast on Pindar, *Pythian* 2.127: "Aristotle says that Achilles was the first to employ the pyrrhic at the pyre of Patroklos, the dance which, as he says, the Kretans call the *prylis*, so that the name of the pyrrhic comes from 'pyre.'"

air, hunching low down—and also the opposite kinds of movement, aggressive stances adopted for shooting arrows and hurling javelins and striking blows." This seems to be a fair description of the actual pyrrhic, a clearly protomilitary exercise designed to produce, as Plato puts it, "a tough body and a manly soul" (*Laws* 7.814E).

Muscle-building is crucial for young warriors, and the pyrrhic is, among other things, a form of pumping iron. The sheer strength required to dance while carrying a heavy shield may be inferred from the contemptuous reference made by the Older Educational Philosophy (alias Stronger Speech) in Aristophanes' *Clouds* to the namby-pamby modern youth dancing the pyrrhic poorly: "That's the way my training raised real men to fight at Marathon. But you [Weaker Speech] teach today's youth wrapped merely in their cloaks, which made me gnash my teeth when I saw them dance at the Panathenaia and one had his shield at his haunches—no respect for the goddess!" (985–89).[64] Borthwick calls attention to a form of the pyrrhic in which the dancer wraps his cloak around his left arm in place of a shield.[65] What Aristophanes' representative of a more military and disciplined education objects to is the weak arms of contemporary sixteen-year-olds, manifest when one of them could not hold his shield up in a public performance, due to a lack of strength resulting from the habit of practicing with a cloak in place of a real shield.

Both *gymnopaidikē* and *pyrrikē* are simply the Athenian versions of what must have been a universal practice in all Greek cities (Wheeler 1982). In other cities, besides the dances favored variously by the Thrakians, Thessalians (Ainianians, Magnesians), Mysians, and Arkadians that Xenophon describes (*Anabasis* 6.1.5–13), we hear of dances in armor that go by other names: *telesias*, *orsitēs*, and *epikrēdios*.[66] Ephoros, writing in the fourth century BCE, discusses the training of Kretan boys, who from an early age were taught to use army gear (*hopla*), to harden themselves to blows in the gymnasium and in battle formation, and specifically to dance in armor. "In order that courage [*andreia*—i.e., manliness], not cowardice, might prevail, the lawgiver commanded that from boyhood they should be raised with armor

64. The interpretation adopted here was suggested by Borthwick 1968: 65. Others take the lines to mean that boys now practice the pyrrhic while heavily muffled by the cloaks against the cold—an absurd conception of an athletic scene, not to mention the fact that the Panathenaia took place in the hot Mediterranean midsummer (the month of *Hekatombaiōn*).

65. Borthwick 1970: 21 n. 128. The gesture is described in Pacuvius' *Hermione* (186 Ribbeck), probably derived from Sophokles' play of the same name.

66. "That is the origin of the so-called pyrrhics and all such styles of [protomilitary] dancing: numerous in fact are their names, e.g. the Kretans' *orsitēs* and *epikrēdios*" (Ath. 14.629C); "there is also the dance called the *telesias*—a military dance taking its name from a certain man Telesias who first danced it in full armor [*meth' hoplōn*]" (Ath. 14.630A = Hippagoras, *FGrHist* 743 F 1).

FIGURE 1.1. Tondo of a red-figure cup, showing a nude dancer and an *aulos*-player. Attributed to Epiktetos, c. 520 BCE. Vatican Museums, Vatican City, inv. 16575. Photo copyright © Governatorate of the Vatican City State—Directorate of the Vatican Museums.

[*hopla*] and hard labor, so as to scorn heat, cold, rugged and steep roads, and blows received in gymnasiums or phalanx [*kata syntagma*] battles; and that they should practice both archery and armored dancing [*enhopliōi orkhēsei*], which was first displayed by the Kouretes and later by him who organized [*syntaxanta*] the pyrrhic, named after himself, so that not even their boyish play should be without something useful for warfare, . . . and that armor [*hopla*] should be the most valued gift given to them" (Strabo 10.4.16). It is Ephoros, too, who describes a musical and rhythmic chorus of boys at Sparta: "On certain set days, herd [age-class] clashes with herd in rhythmic battle, accompanied by *aulos* and lyre, just as they are accustomed to do in battle situations" (*FGrHist* 70 F 149 = Strabo 10.4.20).

Both of the younger boys' dances (that is, both *gymnopaidikē* and *pyrrikē*) were evidently meant to develop their poise, strength, and stamina as future citizen-soldiers. The dancing of the *tragōidoi* was a still harder exercise displaying the same qualities: just think of the sheer physical endurance required

FIGURE 1.2. Tondo of a red-figure cup, showing an armed dancer and an *aulos*-player. Eukharides Painter, c. 490 BCE. Louvre Museum, Paris, inv. G136. © RMN-Grand Palais / Art Resource, NY. Photo credit: Hervé Lewandowski.

to perform all the singing and dancing of three tragedies and one satyr-play consecutively in a single day. Performing in a tragic chorus must have been an athletic feat as exacting and grueling as any of the Olympic competitions, and one that required youthful strength. Certainly, the older the man, the less all-round vigor he usually has, especially for sustained, energetic dancing—as Teiresias and Kadmos agree in Euripides' *Bakkhai* 175–209.

The look of the pyrrhic is well known from vases showing both solo dancers and pairs. Poursat, who studied the vases in 1968, listed twenty, running from about 520 to 450 BCE. The earliest is a cup in the Vatican by Epiktetos (fig. 1.1): shield, spear, and helmet are the naked dancer's only equipment, and he moves to the music of the *aulos*-player.[67] A similar portrayal of the pyrrhic can be found on a cup in the Louvre by the Eukharides Painter from about 490 (fig. 1.2).[68] Other examples include a pair of adolescent dancers on a hydria in the Metropolitan Museum of Art in New York (inv. 21.88.2), similarly equipped and facing each other on either side of an *aulos*-player: the

67. Vatican City, Vatican Museums, inv. 16575; *ARV*² 73.27; Poursat 1968, fig. 14.
68. Paris, Musée du Louvre, inv. G136; *ARV*² 231.78; Poursat 1968, fig. 15.

FIGURE 1.3. Atarbos statue base, showing Pyrrhic dancers, late Classical to early Hellenistic period. Acropolis Museum, Athens, inv. 1338. © Acropolis Museum, 2018. Photo credit: Yiannis Koulelis.

two youths might look at first glance like they're fighting each other, but they are simply working out in unison. More commonly, pairs of dancers face the same direction, as on a lekythos by the Athena Painter from 490–480, also in the Met (inv. 06.1021.75).

The pyrrhic dancer at the Panathenaia who couldn't keep his shield up gave offense not only because he displayed weakness of arm but also because he spoiled the unity of the ensemble's movement, for pyrrhicists competed at the Panathenaia not as soloists but in squads. A team of eight is represented on a relief in the Acropolis Museum from a statue base set up in 366/5 by Atarbos son of Lys- of the deme Thorikos (fig. 1.3).[69] The relief shows the young men in two lines of four, their bodies in exact alignment.[70] A vase fragment in the Metropolitan Museum of Art, dated to about 500, whose meaning is contested, shows five warriors in an identical pose.[71] The pose is similar to that for an ambush, which would imply that they are "real" warriors, not cadets dancing, but a pillar in the scene seems to indicate a gymnasium.

The division into two groups of four on the Panathenaic relief may indicate that the pyrrhicists were precision dancers performing not in a single line

69. Athens, Acropolis Museum, inv. 1338; *IG* II² 3025. Davies 1971: no. 2679. Poursat 1967 publishes a fragment of a vase (Athens, National Museum, inv. 3854), dated 400–350 BCE, recording a choral victory of pyrrhic dancers.

70. Plato (*Laws* 7.796B) treats the pyrrhic as a choral dance, like the armed choruses of the Kouretes on Krete or the Spartan choruses for the Dioskoroi.

71. New York, Metropolitan Museum of Art, inv. 14.105.9; *ARV*² 354.23; Poursat 1968, fig. 33.

but in two lines of four, a rectangular quasi-military formation. There was at Athens another important occasion for dancing in a rectangle. The choruses for tragedy, consisting of twelve (or later, fifteen) members, were arranged in a rectangle (we'll look at the evidence for this shortly). Dancing, or any kind of concerted motion, in rectangular formation above all requires that the participants move with precision, since they are ordered along two sight lines. Any deviation from the common pattern, to right or left, up or down, is quickly noticed. Circular dancing, by comparison, especially in masses of fifty, as in the case of the men's and boys' dithyramb, can be impressive while admitting a certain degree of looseness.

One ancient scholar almost connects the precision pyrrhic with the choruses of tragedy. Aristoxenos, a prominent fourth-century BCE music historian, himself the author of *On Choruses* and *On Tragic Dancing*, describes a kind of cursus: "The ancients [*hoi palaioi*] first practiced *gymnopaidikē*, then progressed to *pyrrhikē* before they entered into the theater" (Ath. 14.631C). From this we know that Dionysos' theater was and had been since archaic times (in Aristoxenos' view) the final stage where boys well-trained in promilitary dancing would perform. To what might this refer? The boys' dithyramb is a possibility, though nothing suggests that it had quasi-military features. Did the rectangular pyrrhic choruses perform in the theater? We don't know the answer to that question, but we do know that another and extremely important chorus of dancers known as the *tragōidoi* (or "billy goat singers": see appendix I) regularly performed in the theater of Dionysos in rectangular formation, and we further know that those dancers were young men just on the cusp between boyhood and manhood, at the age when their duties as citizen-soldiers were imminent.

Performances/Formations

There are many vase paintings based on tragic plays from which we can cautiously deduce information about plots, scenery, and costumes,[72] but there is only one unbroken representation of the complete (or nearly complete) cast for a tragic competition. It is the so-called Pronomos Vase, a late fifth- or early fourth-century Attic volute-krater, now in the Naples Museum.[73] Its obverse depicts the three actors, each of them dressed for one of the parts of a play and holding the mask that goes with that role (plate 1; details in figs.1.4a–e). On the left, behind Dionysos' couch, stands one actor playing the part of a Trojan king, probably Laomedon (fig. 1.4a);[74] on the right, at the foot of the couch, are the other two actors, dressed for the parts of Herakles and Papposeilenos, the old satyr whose sons form the chorus (fig. 1.4b). Eleven chorus members are shown in costume; ten are holding their masks, but one has donned his mask and is practicing a kick step, under the watchful eye of the poet-trainer Demetrios (fig. 1.4c). Also depicted are the *aulos*-player Pronomos (from whose prominence in the composition the krater gets its nickname, the Pronomos Vase), in full costume and playing his double *aulos*, and an auxiliary lyre-player (fig. 1.4d) as well as the god Dionysos and his consort (perhaps Ariadne), and another figure seated on the divine couch whose sex, identity, and function are debated (fig. 1.4e).

From the fact that the personal names of most of the chorus members and musicians are inscribed, but not the names of the three actors (though the role played by one is labeled Herakles),[75] it appears that this is the victory dedication of a successful ensemble, who have chosen to be portrayed

72. Listed in Webster 1962. There is a fine collection of photos in *IGD*, mainly on play-subjects rather than on theatrical equipment; see also *DFA* ch. 4. See as well Coppola, Barone, and Salvadori 2016. Giuliani 1996 and 2010 argues that the evidence of pottery cannot be tied to individual performances or plays; rather, the potters draw freely on elements of the myth depicted from sources outside of any known drama. On the difficulty of interpreting costumes on vases, see Wyles 2010: 232–48.

73. Naples, Museo Archeologico Nazionale di Napoli, inv. 81673, H3240; *ARV*² 1336.1. Arias 1962: 377–80, with bibliography and plates 218–19; Brommer 1964; Simon 1971. The names, invisible on most photographs, are included in the drawing of the vase in Bieber 1961, fig. 32, and much more visibly in the huge reproductions of Adolf Furtwängler and Karl Reichhold 1904–32. They are also included, conveniently, in the drawing of the full vase in Taplin and Wyles 2010.

74. But see Wyles 2010, who warns about the danger of reading certain costume elements in theatrical representations on vases—e.g., apparently "foreign" dress—on the basis of unsupported assumptions about the roles that the actors are playing.

75. On the omission of actors, *IGD* 29 aptly cites Plato, *Symp.* 173A: the symposion took place on the day after Agathon *and his chorus members* celebrated their victory sacrifice—no mention of actors. Similarly, an inscription published by Mitsos 1965: 163 lists Sokrates as producer (*khorēgos*)—probably Sokrates [II] of Anagyrous, the ancient deme located at Varikasa, where the stone was found (Davies 1971: 131–33); Euripides as

FIGURE 1.4 A–E. Details from the Pronomos Vase (plate 1). 1.4a: An adult actor dressed as Laomedon. 1.4b: Two adult actors, dressed as Herakles and Papposeilenos. 1.4c: A chorus member practicing his kick-step. 1.4d: *Aulos*-player Pronomos and a lyre player. 1.4e: Dionysos, his consort, and a third figure. Red-figure Attic volute-krater, c. 425–375 BCE. From Ruvo di Puglia. National Archaeological Museum, Naples, inv. 81673, H3240. Digital manipulation of a drawing, originally published in Adolf Furtwängler and Karl Reichhold, *Griechische Vasenmalerei: Auswahl hervorragender Vasenbilder*. Images courtesy of T. Mannack, Beazley Archive, Oxford.

in the equipment of their final and more hilarious satyr-play rather than in that of one of their three tragedies.[76] (I am assuming here what has never

poet-trainer (*didaskalos*); and fourteen *tragōidoi*—no actors: see Ghiron-Bistagne 1976: 119–21, and her note 72 on the number of performers.

76. The scholarly consensus now is that the Pronomos Vase does not in fact depict a specific theatrical production but is rather meant to invoke the institution of the Dionysian festival: see Griffith 2010: 48, 52; Csapo 2010: 108; Junker 2010: 136. Csapo 2010 in

FIGURE 1.4 A–E. (continued)

been doubted, that the musical personnel is identical for all four plays by the same playwright-composer. In the later fifth century, the actors were distributed among the three competitors on a rotating basis, but that was after the

particular argues that it is unlikely that the vase is itself a victory dedication, in part because of the prominence of the piper Pronomos on the vase: there was no competition for *aulos*-players. Nonetheless, as even Csapo admits, the vase does seem to draw on the iconography of monumental choregic dedications, albeit in "an abstract and selective fashion" (Csapo 2010: 123). These evolving interpretations of the Pronomos Vase do not in any case affect the central point of this interpretation about the significance of the Vase's portrayal of an age difference between actors and chorus members.

FIGURE 1.4 A–E. (continued)

actors had been separated off from the ensemble-work by a separate prize.) The names are all attested as those of Athenian citizens, many of them found in the wealthiest families (as recorded in J. K. Davies' *Athenian Propertied Families*).[77] Several details on this vase are of uncertain interpretation,[78] but

77. See Osborne 2010 for a thorough investigation into the names on the vase; as he points out, all but three of the names on the vase are either very common or moderately common; those three names, however, are extremely rare, and also suspicious in that they seem to be "speaking names" (e.g., *Eunikos*, "good victory"). Osborne ultimately argues that the names seem to be chosen to represent the idea of Athenian drama, perhaps for the non-Athenian audience of the vase.

78. The feminine-looking couch-sitter seems to be holding the mask and wearing the costume of a fourth role in the play. Since one of the three actors already pictured in other roles would have acted this part, he is not drawn a second time. Some have tried to identify the figure—as Paideia (Bulle) or Tragedy (Curtius) or Paidia (Froning 1971). Hall 2010 suggests that she is the figure of Tragedy herself.

Why eleven choreuts? The poet-trainer Demetrios himself could have performed as the twelfth person in the chorus, presumably the chorus leader, a practice attested for the earliest days of tragedy; but all other evidence points to fifteen as the expected number

FIGURE 1.4 A–E. (continued)

---

of chorus members at this point in time (see note 75 above for an example). Since even inscriptional lists of *Boulē* members sometimes record only forty-nine names, we should not be too surprised at a vase painter's inexactitude. It is also possible that the vase could be taken as evidence for a reduction of the chorus during the Peloponnesian War from fifteen members to twelve, by analogy with the reduction of comedies in that period from five to three (*DFA* 83). The wartime reduction of comedies, however, has been challenged by Luppe 1972. One might speculate that satyr-plays retained the older convention of a twelve-man chorus, even when the chorus of tragedy increased to include fifteen—which would imply that only twelve of the fifteen performed in all four plays. But that would raise other questions: If the vase is a victory dedication for the entire chorus, would the three who performed only in the tragedies be omitted? And why are only nine personal names inscribed? Another possibility is that the tragic choruses were reduced *after* the Peloponnesian War as a small retribution against the pro-oligarchic elite.

The variation in costume is of some interest. Could the chorus member in fancy dress already have changed his clothes for the victory celebration? Why does one chorus member alone wear star-embroidered pants (found on other vases showing satyr-chorusmen or female athletes) rather than the shaggy drawers of the rest? Did they serve as the under-costume for the hairy pelt?

FIGURE 1.4 A–E. (continued)

the matters of controversy do not touch on, let alone affect, one highly significant feature: the division of the performers into two distinct groups—fully mature, bearded men (actors) and young men who have yet to grow a beard (chorus members).[79]

I take it to be significant that the three actors are represented on this vase as full-grown men with beards, while the chorus members have full-grown bodies and just the first sideburn curl that will become a beard: that is, they are, iconographically speaking, ephebes—no longer boys, but not yet men. Although sufficient ingenuity could of course devise other explanations for this visible rule distinguishing actors from chorus members on the Pronomos

79. Even on Ernst Buschor's hypothesis that the roles are taken not by human actors but by the heroes themselves, the contrast is still evident: see Buschor in Furtwängler and Reichhold 1904–32: 3.132–50. Pickard-Cambridge (*DFA* 187) sees a certain "melting" between the faces of the actors and their masks; I should say rather that the actors look very like each other and not particularly like their masks.

At some point, Pronomos' own beard or beardlessness became an issue. "Agyrrhios was an effeminate general who held a command in Lesbos; he reduced the payment of the poets. . . . Pronomos was an *aulos*-player who had a big beard, Agyrrhios was sexually submissive to men: so he borrowed Pronomos' beard and no one noticed that he was a woman" (scholiast on Ar., *Ekkl.* 102). This sounds like a joke from Old or Middle Comedy: in later life, Pronomos was famous either for having a big beard or for having a false one that could be lent out to other, effeminate men.

Vase, the prima facie interpretation is that, in the late fifth century and for some previous time, there was a division between tragic actors and chorus members in terms of age—and, most important for the purposes of this argument, that Attic tragedy was performed by choruses of young men.[80]

The other monuments known to me are consistent with this distinction between actors and chorus members according to age. Among them, I would single out the lovely polychrome fragment in Würzburg, showing an actor with a commoner's face holding the mask of a noble-visaged king; the man has salt-and-pepper hair, which is thinning and receding, and a three-day's growth of stubble on his cheeks and chin (plate 2).[81] Contrast that image with pictures of chorus members. Several vases show two or three chorus members in different stages of dress: a "maenad" (fig. 1.5) holds the costume for a young man who is hurriedly pulling on his *kothurnoi* (buskins);[82] another "maenad" (plate 3), whose face is clearly a mask, does a dance-step, while a beardless youth wearing the same loose-sleeved dress and holding a woman's (?) mask looks on;[83] two ephebes in furry drawers on a bell-krater in Sydney hold satyr masks while a third has donned his mask and is practicing a hip-thrust (plate 4).[84]

The sharp rule formulated above may have to be qualified in one respect. A famous dedicatory relief, found in Peiraieus, shows Dionysos on a couch approached by three persons in costume, two of whom are holding their

80. Unfortunately, the Taranto krater fragments now in Würzburg, Martin von Wagner Museum, inv. 217516, which evidently showed a complete tragic cast with a chorus in female dress, very close in style and date to the Pronomos Vase, are severely broken. Not a single face of an actor or chorister survives (*DFA* 187–88 with plates 50a, b, c; *ARV*² 1338, 1690). Vidal-Naquet 1986b: 137 opines that the Pronomos Vase is too exceptional to support the weight of my argument, but aside from the fact that the Taranto fragments show it not to have been unique, surely its scale and detail do not compromise its information. On the contrary, the inscribed names of its chorus members anchor it more firmly in social reality than any other partial representation of a chorus or of actors that has come down to us. Shüler 2017: 11 cites the evidence of the Pronomos Vase to link the status of young citizen chorus-members to that of ephebes and hoplites.

81. Würzburg, Martin von Wagner Museum, inv. 832, H4600, from Taranto, around 340 BCE; color reproduction in Ghiron-Bistagne 1976, frontispiece; and Mingazzini 1969, fig. 57; see also Bieber 1961, fig. 306 a–b; and *DFA*, fig. 54a. Simon 1968 interprets the role as Tereus.

82. On a red-figure Attic pelike by the Phiale Painter (Boston, Museum of Fine Arts, inv. 98.883); see *ARV*² 1017; Webster 1970, plate 8; *DFA*, fig. 34; Bieber 1961, fig. 90; Taplin and Wyles 2010, fig. 8.5.

83. Red-figure bell-krater, about 460–450 BCE (Ferrara, Museo Archeologico Nazionale di Ferrara, inv. 2299, T. 173C VT); *DFA*, fig. 33, where the mask is said to be certainly that of a young man: it seems to me too poorly drawn to be certain.

84. Apulian bell-krater by the Tarporley Painter, 410–380 BCE (Sydney, Nicholson Collection, Chau Chak Wing Museum, The University of Sydney, inv. NM47.5); *IGD* II.2; Brommer 1959, fig. 7.

FIGURE 1.5. Red-figure two-handled pelike, showing actors preparing for a performance. Phiale Painter, c. 430 BCE. MFA, Boston, inv. 98.883. Caskey-Beazley, *Attic Vase Paintings* (MFA), no. 063. Height: 24.1 cm (9 1/2 in.); diameter: 18 cm (7 1/16 in.). Museum of Fine Arts, Boston; Henry Lillie Pierce Fund. Photograph © 2022 Museum of Fine Arts, Boston.

masks (fig. 1.6).[85] They are often taken to be the three actors of a successful production. The similarity of their costumes, however, might suggest that they are chorus members. The differentiation of the masks would be decisive, if we could gauge it, but unfortunately, of the two masks still somewhat visible, the one held by the right-hand figure is very worn. The left-hand figure

85. Athens, National Archaeological Museum, inv. 1500.

FIGURE 1.6. Relief sculpture from Peiraieus, showing actors and Dionysos, c. 410 BCE. National Archaeological Museum, Athens, inv. 1500. Photo credit: Album / Art Resource, NY.

was evidently wearing his mask, but his head has been completely obliterated. Though the entire surface is in poor condition, there is no real doubt that the two surviving faces of the three standing figures are those of young men.

Though the Peiraieus relief *may* show chorus members, consistent with the strong age distinction between actors and chorus members on the Pronomos Vase, they may also be actors, and this leads to an important qualification. On the Pronomos Vase, not only the chorus but also the poet, the lyre-player, and the *aulos*-player (as well as the god) are young. Though some poets, such as Aiskhylos, Sophokles, and Euripides, lived to be senior citizens and were portrayed by tradition with the dignity of their mature look, dramatic performances were clearly an arena where young men could excel. Tradition puts Aiskhylos and Sophokles somewhere in their mid-twenties when they first exhibited their own plays, Euripides closer to thirty.[86] Aristophanes claims to have been a shy young man at the time of his first production; Menander was only twenty, and Ameinias was officially an ephebe when his comedy *The Fainting Woman* (*Apoleipousa*) took third prize in 312/1 (*IG* II[2] 2323a 46–47). *Mousikē* (poetry, dance, music) is not learned overnight, so we must assume that all these dramatists were active in stagecraft for some years before they took responsibility for mounting a full production of their own. It should not be surprising, therefore, that Demetrios the poet on the Pronomos Vase is a young

86. The *khorēgoi* (producers) could be very young: Perikles was about twenty when he sponsored Aiskhylos' tetralogy containing the *Persians* in 472 (*IG* II[2] 2318); the speaker of Lysias 21 gives an impressive list of choruses he produced, beginning when he was eighteen.

man and that his company of musical personnel are so youthful. Nor would it be surprising if younger men sometimes fulfilled the less musical and less athletic function of *hupokritēs* (actor), which may be the sense of the Peiraieus relief. What would be more startling, however, and what does not seem to exist, is evidence of mature, bearded men as chorus members of tragedy.

The Pronomos Vase is the principal *positive* piece of evidence for the hypothesis that tragic-satyric choruses were composed of young men who were just reaching their *hēbē*. Other literary evidence is consistent with that hypothesis. Direct testimony about the constitution of choruses is extremely meager. Aristotle (*Politics* 3.3.1276b4–6) remarks that the same persons (*anthrōpoi*, not *andres* ["men"]) may perform in a comic and in a tragic chorus, and one vase painting seems to confirm that the comic chorus was composed of youths.[87] A scholiast on Aristophanes says that noncitizens could not perform in the choruses of the City Dionysia, though they could perform (and metics could produce) at the Lenaia, a Dionysian festival held two months before the City Dionysia.[88] Which choruses did that law apply to? [Andokides] 4.20 recounts a fistfight between two *khorēgoi* (producers), Alkibiades and Taureas, over the disputed citizenship of a boy dithyrambist; Plutarch (*Phokion* 30.6) gives an example of a *khorēgos* who allowed some noncitizens to perform in his dithyramb. For tragedy and comedy, we cannot claim to be so sure, though the entire tendency of my argument would suggest that it was properly an affair of citizens.

One occasionally encounters a statement in modern writers to the effect that chorus members had a special exemption from military service, which would imply that they were men rather than ephebes. But this half-truth merely serves to reveal our own collective (I do not exempt myself) insensitivity to age-classes and festivals. There was a military exemption during their year of office for members of the *Boulē* (Lykourgos, *Leokrates* 37) and for customs officers ([Demosthenes] 59.27). Twice Demosthenes mentions such an exemption for choral performers, but then we must ask, performers in what kind of chorus—comedy, tragedy, men's dithyramb (boys' dithyramb is obviously out of the question)—and at what festival? One of Demosthenes' allusions certainly refers to a men's dithyrambic chorus at the City Dionysia (21.15 and scholion); the other also invokes, apparently, the City Dionysia, but what chorus is not clear (39.16).[89]

87. See the bell-krater in Heidelberg (Heidelberg, Antikenmuseum, Universität Heidelberg, inv. B 134, 4648, 390–370 BCE) showing two comic chorus members impersonating women, one with his mask thrown back to reveal a beardless young face: Webster 1956, plate 15a; Bieber 1961, fig. 208.

88. The rule is stated by the scholiast on Ar., *Ploutos* 953: "[I]t was not allowed for a noncitizen [*xenos*] to dance in a City chorus . . . but in the Lenaia it was allowed, since metics too sponsored choruses." A recently discovered example is found in Edmondson 1982.

89. At 21.58–61, Demosthenes refers to two persons who had been convicted of *astrateia* (failure to undertake or evasion of military service) and yet had later directed or

On the surface, this meager evidence about military exemption does not tell against the hypothesis that tragic-satryric choruses were performed by ephebes, youths on the border of manhood; on a deeper level, it speaks for it. The first question to ask is a different one: why should there have been an exemption from marching and fighting for the five hundred men each year who danced the dithyramb in honor of Dionysos? Part of the answer may be sheerly practical—a feeling that in the winter and early spring a busy citizen could be expected to spend about the same amount of time either practicing drill with his (tribal) company and getting in shape for the coming summer's battles or rehearsing the (tribal) dance, but not both. Was there, in addition, any deeper, symbolic equivalence between these two civic duties, which made sense of the exemption? In what framework does a dance for Dionysos equal a season of campaigning?[90] The relation is one of contrast and of similarity. Aristophanes, on the one hand, shows us the opposition in a diptych contrasting the general Lamakhos, called up to military service against midwinter bandits in Boiotia, with Dikaiopolis, the man who refuses to fight, celebrating the Anthesteria with the priest of Dionysos (*Akharnians* 1071–234).[91] The similarity, on the other hand, can be seen in the military tone of some dithyrambs and other choral performances,[92] and in the fact that they were performed, at least for a time, in the region of the Agora that was also the location of war monuments.[93] But the best examples of such mimeto-militarism

performed in choruses. The point is that they were such exceptionally skilled individuals that no citizen who observed them wanted to take the responsibility of enforcing the legal ban on their participation. Presumably, the year in which they had been convicted of *astrateia* was not a year in which they had been dancing for Dionysos.

90. Note that, in the second case cited from Demosthenes, the speaker contrasts military service not only with choral dancing at the City Dionysia but also with the celebration of the Dionysian Anthesteria a month earlier. (At the back of my mind in this argument is the role of army musicians today—"privates on parade"; behind the ideology of the citizen-soldier must lie the practical recognition that not all men are suited to that role.) It must be admitted that it is unclear whether the exemption covered the entire year or only the period of training for the festival.

91. Conversely, Eupolis' *Taxiarkhoi* portrays Dionysos living the hard life of a soldier and learning about military life from the famous general Phormion (fr. 274 *PCG*).

92. Especially the mysterious piece Bakkhylides 18, which is a fully dramatized encounter between King Aigeus of Athens and a chorus of young citizen-warriors (13–14), whom the King has summoned to deal with the advance of an apparent enemy toward the city: that enemy turns out to be the ephebe (*paida . . . prōthēbon*, 56–57) Theseus, wearing the young warrior's cloak (*khlamyd'*, 54). Merkelbach 1973 goes too far in reconstructing the details of its ephebic ceremonial referents, but the general relevance of the poem both to choral drama and to mythic-military subjects is indubitable. Without arguing that this piece was a dithyramb, much less that it was necessarily performed at the City Dionysia, I would observe that early fifth-century dithyrambs were, like this piece, antistrophic ([Arist.], *Problems* 19.15: 918b19–20). See also Burnett 1985: 117–23.

93. Siewert 1982: 150–53. Hammond 1972 emphasizes that early tragic performances were also in the Agora. See now Csapo 2015: 97–98.

can actually be found not in the dithyrambs but in the oldest component of the City Dionysia, the dances of the *tragōidoi*. It is this component of the performance that will justify my reading of the young men on the Pronomos Vase as ephebes in the stricter sense of the word—young citizen-soldiers in training.[94]

One must recall that the history of performances at the City Dionysia is marked by three stages: *tragōidoi* first perform for city-sponsored prizes under the direction of Thespis in about 534 BCE during the long tyranny of Peisistratos (*Marmor Parium, FGrHist* 239 A 43); prizes for men's (and boys'?) dithyrambs are added at the time of the constitutional reforms of Kleisthenes, 509/8 BCE (or perhaps 502/1);[95] *kōmōidoi* (comic choruses) are introduced as a prize category in 486 BCE.[96] (Of course, dithyrambic and comic choruses, at least, are much older than these particular festival arrangements, which simply give a new financial and competitive structure to old traditions.) There are two contrasts in the structure of this set of performances that are "ephebically" significant. The first is that the dithyrambs are designated as belonging to two age-classes, men and boys. "Men's chorus" and "boys' chorus" are the terms, both official and popular, for these dances at all times for which we have records. This is consistent, at the very least, with the hypothesis that *tragōidoi* specifically designated ephebes. When the dithyrambs officially became a competitive event in the City Dionysia, they comprised and were named for

94. Lech 2009a raises careful and systematic objections to this argument about the military formation of tragic dancers, but his objections, while suggestive, are often speculative and not entirely convincing; for some rebuttals, see notes 98 and 104 below. See also Shüler 2017, who argues cogently that the training required to perform in a tragic chorus would also have been effective training for hoplite-fighting. Wilson 2000: 46–47 makes the same point.

95. Hammond 1972: 62–67. The *Marmor Parium* records the first men's dithyrambic victory at the City Dionysia in 509/8; the winning composer was Hypodikos of Khalkis (*FGrHist* 239 A 46). Capps 1904 and 1943 argues that the new Kleisthenic organization of ten-tribe competitions did not begin until 502/1 BCE. See *DFA* 71–72, 102–3; Rhodes 1981: 263 on [Arist.], *Ath. Pol.* 22.2. Capps assumes, in reconstructing *IG* II² 2318, that the boys' dithyramb was present from the beginning, requiring eight lines for each year-entry (one for the Arkhon, two for the boys' dithyramb, two for the men's dithyramb, three for tragedy). But if the boys' dithyramb was, like comedy, a late addition, there would be room on the stone for more year-entries, perhaps allowing the record to go back as far as the first men's dithyrambic victory reported by the *Marmor Parium* for the year 510/9 or 509/8. Wilson 2011 argues that the dithyrambic competition starts at the same time as the creation of the tribes (19–21) and that the dramatic festivals at Athens "represent an entirely new scale of cultural expenditure in Greece, one that far exceeded the possibilities of traditional aristocratic, or even of tyrannical, patronage" (32). Csapo 2015 has now cast doubt on the narrative of an origin with Thespis in the 530s and suggests that tragedy as such did not exist before 508 BCE. See especially Csapo 2015: 81–82, 91–92. See, further, the discussion in the notes to the following chapter of this book, especially chapter 2, note 65.

96. *Souda*, s.v. *Khionidēs*; Capps 1904; *DFA* 82.

the two non-ephebic age groups—men and boys—that bracketed the ephebic age-class. This might imply that those older and younger groups had been previously omitted from the contests of *tragōidoi*.

The second contrast is that men's and boys' dithyrambic dances were circular dances, whereas *tragōidoi* moved in a rectangular formation. Reasonably detailed information survives about this "square" dancing.[97] The chorus members processed in three files and four or five ranks (depending on whether there were twelve or, from sometime in the second quarter of the fifth century, fifteen persons marching). Since they entered the orchestra three abreast from a lateral entrance ramp and the left-hand file was nearest the spectators, the best performers were stationed in the leftmost file.[98] When that file contained five members, the *koruphaios* (chorus leader) occupied the central position. The orchestra in later times was of course a circular space (on its earlier, trapezoidal shape, see the next chapter), but there is no evidence that tragic choruses ever took up a circular formation;[99] on the contrary, the name *kyklios khoros* (circular chorus), which is used as a general term for all dithyrambs, seems to guarantee that *tragōidoi* characteristically performed in rank and file.[100]

We often and quite casually use the term "marching" when referring to the chorus' entrance song with its anapaestic meter, but we don't really think

97. *DFA* 239–54; Lawler 1964. Timaios speaks of "the so-called Lakōnistai who sang in tetragonal choruses" (Ath. 5.181C = *FGrHist* 566F140), but the context and referent are wholly unknown. The rectangular formation of tragic dancing is ignored by Kitto 1955.

98. This arrangement is spelled out by a scholium on Aristeides' *On Behalf of the Four* 154 (scholium 3.535–36, ed. Dindorf). Lech 2009a goes to some lengths to discredit this scholium, arguing that the comments about where to place "the good choreuts" does not refer to a dramatic chorus, but rather to a circular, unmasked chorus. This, however, makes hash of the entire passage, since a circular chorus does not have a "left" and "right" side. Lech's suggestion that the phrase "the good choreuts" really means "the good-looking choreuts" is possible, but not unequivocal in the Greek (τοὺς οὖν καλοὺς τῶν χορευτῶν). The scholiast suggests that the choreuts should be located "looking at the *dēmos*" (ἵνα εὑρεθῶσι πρὸς τὸν δῆμον ὁρῶντες), not that their faces must be seen by the audience. For further discussion of the passage, see Csapo and Slater 1994: 361.

99. *DFA* 239, n. 2.

100. Lysias 21.3; *DFA* 239. Already in the seventh century BCE, at least according to a nameless ancient commentator on Aratos' *Phainomena*, the Spartan poet "Alkman referred to the maidens dancing in order [*en taxei*] as 'in the same file' [*homostoikhous*]" (*PMG* 33); *zygon* and *stoikhos* are the technical terms for rank and file in tragic dancing: *DFA* 239. See Wilson 2007b: 167–68 for evidence that the term *kyklioi khoroi* was closely associated with the dithyramb in Athens and was never applied to tragic choruses. Csapo 2015: 105–6 argues further that the term "dithyramb" itself was never used of those men's and boys' circular choruses in the Athenian Dionysia that modern scholars customarily refer to as dithyrambs or dithyrambic competitions; he contends that originally the dithyramb "was in official discourse more properly confined to the cultic performances of a processional chorus" (105) and that the word was not used to designate any performances in the theater. See further Kowalzig and Wilson 2013.

about the implications of that term. The usual reconstruction of tragic choral movement imagines that the dancers sometimes occupied the center of the orchestra, sometimes split into two groups, at times facing the actors and at other times the audience. But in fact the performance of such maneuvers would have exercised the same precision skills that were required for hoplite marching,[101] since rectangular formation, as I have already noted (in the previous section of this chapter), involves ordering the dancers along two sight lines—unlike circular dancing, which accordingly can afford to dispense with such strictness and rigor. Rectangular formation, by comparison, is unforgiving of sloppy execution when viewed from a distance and from different angles by a large audience. Though I do not imagine that the *koruphaios* actually barked *sotto voce* commands like "Right face," "Company halt," and so forth to his squadron of ephebes, such commands were implicit in the chorus' well-regulated motion.[102] Members of any chorus must focus their attention very carefully on the leader, as Xenophon implies when describing the similar attention rowers give to their boatswain (*Mem.* 3.5.6).

Not only our phrase "rank and file," employed above, but also a number of traditional Greek choral terms point to a homology between the movement of *tragōidoi* and of hoplites: instances include *parastatēs* ("flanking comrade," "wingman") and other compounds of *statēs*; *psileis* ("unprotected"), used to refer to persons with an exposed side in the formation; and *hēgemōn*, applied to the chorus leader.[103] Sometimes the comparison is explicit, as in this very significant fragment of Khamaileon preserved by Athenaios:

> [The older dances were dignified and manly;] therefore Aristophanes or Plato in his *Gear*, as Khamaileon writes, spoke as follows: "So that when anyone danced well it was a real spectacle, but now they do nothing; they just stand in one place as if paralyzed by a stroke and they howl." For the form of dancing in choruses then was well-ordered

101. "There is an enormous difference between an ordered army and a disordered one" (Xen., *Mem.* 3.1.7). Aristotle too notes that the essence of hoplite fighting is coordination (*syntaxis*). Before men discovered *taxis* and so made heavily armored infantry useful, cavalry was supreme: *Pol.* 4.13.1297b18–22. Perhaps the word *epistrophai*, as it is used by the Chorus in Soph., *OC* 1045 to refer to the shift in direction of the enemy squadron in battle, recalls the "strophe" or coordinated turn-around of the chorus as it dances in the theater; if so, the word can be taken to express a homology between military and choral movement.

102. Command words are listed by Asklepiodotos, *Tactics* ch. 12; chs. 10–11 describe the various troop formations for marching and turning: text and translation in the Loeb Classical Library along with military texts by Aeneas Tacticus, Asclepiodotus, and Onasander (1928). For the sixth and fifth centuries, our positive knowledge of military training is almost zero: Pritchett 1974: chs. 11–12; Anderson 1970: chs. 5–6.

103. *DFA* 241. Kreon describes the good householder and citizen: "When stationed in a storm of spears he thinks it right and good to hold firm as a *parastatēs*" (μένειν δίκαιον κἀγαθὸν παραστάτην: Soph., *Ant.* 670–71). Plato Komikos also uses the term in speaking of testicles (fr. 174.13).

> [*euskhēmon*] and impressive and as it were imitative of movements in full armor [*kinēseis en tois hoplois*]; whence Sokrates says in his poems that the finest choral dancers are best in war; I quote, "Those who most beautifully honor the gods in choruses are best in war." For choral dancing was practically like a troop review (or, maneuver in arms, *exhoplisia*) and a display not only of precision marching [*eutaxia*] in general but more particularly of physical preparedness.[104]

Teachers of each discipline are even found giving the same advice to put the best soldiers or dancers in the front and rear ranks, the less good ones in the middle.[105] At other times, a contrast between the two activities reveals that they are assumed to be comparable in ways that would not spring readily to our minds. "The best in the chorus are stationed on the left . . . since in choruses the left side is more honorable, in battles the right."[106] Mention *eutaxia* and the conversation will turn as readily to precision movement in a dancing corps as to gymnastics or the timed stroke of oars (Xen., *Mem.* 3.5.18), even implying that dancing is more disciplined than generalship since war maneuvers are often improvised (Xen., *Mem.* 3.5.21). The grandest such analogy is surely the elaborate comparison of polyphonic choral singing, where all the various voices await the leader's signal, to the coordinated responses of soldiers to a general's command ([Arist.], *De mundo* 399a15–b10).

104. Khamaileon, fr. 42 (ed. Fritz Wehrli) = Ath. 14.628E–F. (This may be two quotations, one from Khamaileon, one from Sokrates.) It is important to note that Khamaileon gets his information, and his authority, principally from Old Comedy, which he cites not only in this instance but also to back up many of his surviving opinions about early tragedy (frs. 40–42 Wehrli). This relocation of their authority at once makes such pronouncements both earlier and more oblique: they remain important evidence even if they were originally the grouchy exaggerations of a curmudgeon about the comic stage. Lech 2009a: 354 argues against the proposition that choral dancing was like precision hoplite maneuvers: "The educational value of tragic dancing would not have helped at the critical point of the clashing of the armies, for the phalanxes ran the last metres before the clash to enhance the power of the impact. No dancing and singing in the theatre of Dionysus could prepare the young men for this." But the rush to meet the enemy line is precisely the moment when a phalanx needed to be able to move swiftly and in a coordinated motion in order to stay in close formation—exactly the sort of movement that synchronized dancing would prepare hoplites for.

105. "In battle the best soldiers should be placed first and last, the worst in the middle, so that they may be led by the ones in front and pushed by the ones in back" (Xen., *Mem.* 3.1.8); cf. *Kyr.* 7.5.5. "The three middle files not visible in some passages are called *laurostatai*; the worse performers are stationed in the middle, the principal ones are placed first and last" (Hesykhios, s.v. *Laurostatai*). "The underlap of the chorus: the valueless positions of the choral station" (Hesykhios, s.v. *Hupokolpion tou khorou*, cited at *DFA* 241 n. 1).

106. Scholiast on Aristeides (3.535 ed. Dindorf), cited in *DFA* 241 n. 1. See discussion in note 98 above.

The homology extends to the accompanying music (Dorian in large part) and the accompanying musical instrument (*aulos*).[107] The presence of an *aulos*-player is one clue that serves to identify the earliest representations of phalanx fighters on seventh-century BCE vases.[108] The Spartans took this musical device so seriously that their infantry employed numerous *aulos*-players in unison (*aulētōn pollōn homou*, Thoukydides 5.70, who does not, *pace* Lorimer and others, say that the Spartans *alone* marched to the sound of the pipe; they may have invented the technique or they may have been best known for it, as Aristotle [quoted by Aulus Gellius, *Attic Nights* 1.11.17–19] alleges, but they did not patent it). Thoukydides also makes it clear that the point of the music is not to raise the hoplites' spirits but to insure their "rhythmic stepping" and so to maintain formation (*taxis*). The *aulos*-player who served on Athenian triremes evidently had the same function: the music would have helped to coordinate the oarsmen and to keep the oar strokes in time (*IG* II^2 1951.100).

We may have a depiction of precision choral dancing on a red-figure column-krater in the Mannerist style, dated to about 500–490 BCE (plate 5).[109] Six performers arranged in three pairs move with identical steps and upraised arms toward or past a tomb, behind which a cloaked figure stands. His open mouth indicates that he is not the trainer or the *khorēgos* or the god Dionysos but a performer, most likely a ghost emerging from the tomb. Invisible on the photograph of the pot, letters at the dancers' open mouths indicate their choral song, though no *aulos*-player is shown. At that period in the early fifth century, the tragic chorus consisted of twelve persons, so this group is half a chorus; perhaps we are to imagine the other half approaching the tomb from the other side.[110]

107. On the Dorian mode and the occasional use of other modes for special effect in tragedy, see *DFA* 258–60. On the musical aspects of hoplite training, see Shüler 2017: 12–14.

108. Snodgrass 1980: 106: "It must be conceded, however, that experiments in the handling of massed infantry had been undertaken before [the mid-seventh century]: an observant critic has recently drawn attention to the presence, in a battle-scene on a Korinthian vase of about 675, of a piper [i.e., *aulētēs*]—an indispensable participant in the later Spartan phalanx where his music kept the men in step, and therefore perhaps a sign of incipient phalanx tactics, although the moral-boosting effect of military pipers, as modern parallels show, is not confined to those operating in close formation." For a general study, see Lorimer 1947.

109. Basel, Antikenmuseum Basel und Sammlung Ludwig, inv. BS 415: Schmidt 1967.

110. Conceivably relevant is an Attic black-figure neck-amphora, dated to c. 520–510 BCE, showing on one side a stately Dionysos with two dancing satyrs and on the other a procession of five or six women—stately but with hair unbound. The first and third pair are clearly drawn, but between them is a single woman, whom Beazley thought had an invisible companion: Shapiro 1981. There is, perhaps one should mention, a Korinthian aryballos with six youths processing in pairs; they are led by an *aulos*-player and a leaping youth: Boegehold 1965.

M. Schmidt, who first published this vase, was inclined to believe that the performers were dancing a dithyramb, but their rectangular formation and their costumes argue for tragedy rather than dithyramb.[111] Dithyrambists could perform in splendid array,[112] but not in masks or character costumes. (The attempt to see a satyr chorus on a red-figure krater by Polion of about 425 BCE as dithyrambic performers in costume misreads that vase entirely.[113] The label *OIDOI PANATHENAIA*, "Singers at the Panathenaia," above three aged Papposeilenoi does not mean that actual dithyrambic choruses at the Panathenaia did or could dress up as satyrs, nor even that there were comic turns at the Panathenaia.[114] The *aulos*-player facing them holds his pipes down at his sides, in consternation not only at the incongruous presence of these singers' lyres[115] but also at the singers' very identity.[116] For these are not regulation contestants but wild men—i.e., satyrs—who, monkey-like, imitate forms of civilized behavior.[117]) It seems likely from their chin line that the six choristers on this red-figure column-krater are actually wearing masks, in which case they would be, on my interpretation, ephebes dressed as a chorus of ephebes, as in Aiskhylos' *Neaniskoi* or Thespis' *Eitheoi*. More important for the correct interpretation of this vase, dithyrambists formed themselves into a circle, not a rectangle. For contrast, consider the dithyrambic men's chorus represented on an Attic red-figure bell-krater in Copenhagen, dated to about 425 BCE (fig. 1.7).[118] Five bearded (not masked) men in single file, the central one facing forward, are dressed in fancy khitons and wrap-around cloaks (not in theatrical costume, as if they were characters), and they are singing to

111. Froning 1971: 23–24; Simon 1982: 8–9.

112. Demosthenes sponsored a men's dithyrambic chorus in 351/0 whose members wore gold crowns (21.16).

113. New York, Metropolitan Museum of Art, inv. 25.78.66; Bieber 1961, fig. 17; Pickard-Cambridge 1962: 20, 34, plate 1.

114. Beazley 1955: 314–15; Bieber 1961: 6, fig. 17 relates the depiction to a comedy, Kratinos' *Satyroi* (424 BCE), without commenting on the label *PANATHENAIA*.

115. "It would be very remarkable for participants in a dithyrambic chorus each to play his own instrumental accompaniment" (Froning 1971: 25).

116. "The *aulos*-player stands there thunderstruck like a tavern-keeper who one day sees three of his best customers, now converted soldiers in the Salvation Army, march into his saloon with bible and hymnbook in hand rather than their usual bottle and drinking-mug" (Roos 1951: 228). Roos sees the scene as a comic take-off on Perikles' reorganization of musical contests at the Panathenaia and suggests a relationship with three lyre-playing satyrs on a black-figure amphora of the late sixth century (pp. 227–30, figs. 32–33). Froning 1971: 25–26 suggests that it represents a satyr-play on the subject of the founding of the Panathenaia, comparable to Aiskhylos' *Isthmiastai*.

117. Elsewhere, satyrs pretend to be honest citizens by wearing cloaks (*ARV*² 175, no. 16; Brommer 1959: 59 n. 40 lists examples from the second half of the fifth century) and by carrying staffs instead of *thyrsoi* (*ARV*² 785, no. 11). See Lissarrague 1990.

118. Copenhagen, The National Museum of Denmark, inv. 13817 (Beazley no. 215175); *ARV*² 1145.35; Pickard-Cambridge 1962, plate 1b; Johansen 1959.

FIGURE 1.7. Red-figure Attic bell-krater, showing a dithyrambic chorus. Attributed to the Kleophon Painter, c. 425 BCE. The National Museum of Denmark, Copenhagen, inv. 13817 (vase no. 215175). Licensed by The National Museum of Denmark, license type CC-BY-SA. Photo credit: John Lee.

the accompaniment of an *aulos*-player. While five unmasked and uncostumed men in a ring may represent fifty dithyrambists, six masked and costumed performers in rectangular formation cannot be dithyrambists but must represent a semichorus of early fifth-century tragedy.[119]

The rectangular movement of ephebes in the orchestra of the Theater of Dionysos thus has two forms: the tragic chorus and the year-end military display. It would seem that the analogy would have been obvious to every citizen-spectator. Yet several features also keep the two performances at a distance from each other. First, the *tragōidoi* are of course masked and costumed, most often in the guise of characters far removed in age or gender or class, as well as in time and space, from the young Athenian males they actually are. Second, the *tragōidoi* are only a small set, no more than a tenth, of their age-class; twelve—or, later, fifteen—chorus performers for each of the three competing tragedians would amount to a total of thirty-six or forty-five, whereas the yearly crop of eighteen-year-olds fluctuates in the neighborhood of five

119. Csapo 2010: 96 argues that the scene on this vase (pictured here as plate 5) is "unambiguously tragic"; the "three ranks and two files of young men in rectangular formation" are "a certain synecdoche for a full tragic chorus which in this period moved in three files and four ranks."

hundred when we can determine their numbers from ephebic inscriptions in the later fourth century.[120]

The third difference is an offshoot of the second—the late appearance of the institutionalized ephebate. I have argued that the fourth-century Lykourgan ephebate is a codification of practices that were formerly the preserve of the wealthy and ambitious. *Tragōidoi*, it would seem, like our balancing friend Hippokleides, must tend to come from the wealthy and well-born youth of Athens, its *jeunesse dorée*: they at least are the ones who would have both the leisure and the ambition to spend time learning complicated songs and precision dances lasting much of the day—a very taxing physical performance. With the Lykourgan reforms, the ephebate now extended to all young citizens (or at least to the top three property classes). We can actually trace the growth, in fourth-century writings, of the idea that military training should be centrally organized and financed, rather than left up to the initiative and resources of private individuals.

The novelty of this idea and its institutionalization stand out with particular starkness against the ideological background of an earlier, distinctive social ethic that regarded manhood as a personal achievement, to be won by one's own efforts, rather than something that could be granted by the state or tribe. Indeed, the fifth-century evidence suggests that hoplite or cavalry service was seen not as a duty so much as an arena for voluntary excellence—an opportunity to acquire and display honor (*timē*), motivated by personal ambition (*philotimia*), within a controlling matrix of patriotic necessity. Where there is no public ceremony to grant and guarantee that a youngster is now a man, the individual youth must seek out suitable occasions for winning that status and be watchful of chances to exhibit—and thus, in the community's estimation, to achieve—his *andragathiē*.

In my first publication on this topic, I maintained that there was a connection between the performance of tragedy and the city's training of ephebes (Winkler 1985). Now I would make that connection more precise by arguing that the character of, and the social need for, tragedy and comedy—along with performances of other social scenarios of risk, such as jury trials—were shaped precisely by the *absence* in pre-Lykourgan Athens of an organized, citywide ephebate or indeed of any rite guaranteeing the transition of boys to adult male status. It is not the existence of the ephebate that gave rise to Athenian drama. Rather, it is the lack of a recognized rite of passage from youth to manhood at Athens that led to the multiplication of more spontaneous occasions

120. As Wilson 2011: 26 points out, by the fifth century, "an entirely unparalleled percentage of the citizenry was directly involved in choral performance: 1,145 men and boys each year." Most of those choral performances, however, were in the men's and boys' "circular choruses."

on which the issues of manhood and its acquisition could be acted out (for examples, see chapter 3).[121] The late fourth-century Athenian ephebate was a short-lived attempt to regularize and formalize that status transition for the entire male citizenry.

The whole city, of course, sees itself as a military corporation of citizen-householders ready to face danger in defense of their territory, and a body of new work on Attic drama emphasizes that the City Dionysia is not merely five days of musical festivity, or a seasonal rite, but an occasion for the display of the civic ideology—that is, the self-understanding of the *polis* in all its moral and emotional complexity. I would emphasize, as Loraux has done in *The Invention of Athens*, not only that the *dēmos* at large saw itself in the light of a hoplite ideal but also that it was quite ready to acquiesce in an essentially aristocratic interpretation of that ideal. The *tragōidoi* are just that: both quasi-hoplites and representatives of the best and noblest manliness, *andragathiē*, that the city contains.[122]

Perhaps I have said enough to indicate why it might have entered Hippokleides' head that he could win honor in the eyes of his fellow-banqueters and his prospective father-in-law by an exhibition of solo dancing in several regional styles. He was not wearing armor, to be sure, which might have contributed to the deep (and ultimately disastrous) ambiguity of his performance, but at least we can see why, in very general terms, it would have been an intelligible move in the game of asserting his superior manhood, specifically his athletic-aesthetic skills, to engage in that demonstrative display. But to achieve a proper roundedness and complexity in our social reconstruction, we must also try to identify the local framework within which Kleisthenes, so far from admiring Hippokleides' performance of manliness, could be shocked at his shamelessness.

Playing with Manhood: Women in Armor, Men in Drag

At the beginning of this chapter, I referred to Kleisthenes' banquet hall as a "theater of excellence." The small-scale symposion too could be a kind of theater, in which performers took on some accoutrements and exhibited

121. Sommerstein 2010: 54, remarking on the depiction of *ephebe*-like young men in a number of tragedies of the later fifth century, makes a similar argument: "I wish to suggest that, rather than reflecting the pattern of an existing Athenian ephebic transition-scheme, what they reflect is contemporary anxieties arising precisely from the fact that such a scheme did *not* exist."

122. See Griffith 1995 and 2011 for arguments about the representation and advancement of aristocratic ideals within the somewhat democratized world of the Greek tragedies.

some movements that pertained to social roles different from their own. On fifth-century vases representing symposia, we find two forms of quasi-dramatic entertainment relevant to our larger theme. Both involve dancing in costume.

The first appears on a series of Attic vases, mainly red-figure, produced between 510 and 460 BCE. Known as the "Anakreontic vases," they portray fully-grown men, usually sporting long and rather bushy beards, but wearing gauzy, ankle-length khitons, with a woman's turban or hair-net on their heads, and either waving a parasol or strumming a barbiton, an elongated lyre.[123] The costume is not an instance of female impersonation or drag, though the apparel is certainly associated with women and more generally with the softer, refined lifestyle of Greeks in Ionian colonies on the Asian coast of the Aegean. Rather, these men of Athens simultaneously display their most masculine feature, the extended beard, while they also appropriate certain signs of the feminine, of the poetic, and of the luxurious. Indeed, the prominence of the beards leads Frontisi-Ducroux and Lissarrague, who have studied these scenes, to describe them not only as fundamentally male but also as "radically barbocentric."[124] Women are occasionally present in these scenes, but when they are there, "their role is entirely accessory and their function purely instrumental," which is of course consonant with the setting of a symposion.[125] In some representations, the artists seem to delight in establishing significant contrasts, for instance on the tondo of a black-figure plate in Basel between a straight-backed female *aulos*-player, hired for the occasion, and the sinuously turning gentleman, loose-limbed (because well-lubricated). While she works, he plays (fig. 1.8).[126] Or on a red-figure cup in Munich, which could be seen as a before-and-after picture: there are two symposiasts of essentially the same physique and status, but one is in a state of noble nudity while the other is swishing his way through a stanza of Anakreon.[127] What these contrasts seem to indicate is that the complexity of manhood permits, or even encourages, a certain deliberate playing at the borders of a man's normal regimen.[128] At some symposia, some men

123. For an extensive discussion of these vases, see Price 1990 (with exhaustive bibliography), who interprets the paintings on "Anakreontic vases" as burlesque portrayals of Ionian lyric poets, possibly mediated by representations on the Athenian comic stage. See also Miller 1999.

124. Frontisi-Ducroux and Lissarrague 1990: 228.

125. Frontisi-Ducroux and Lissarrague 1990: 228.

126. Basel, Antikenmuseum Basel und Sammlung Ludwig, inv. Kä 421.

127. Munich, Staatliche Antikensammlungen, inv. 2647; *ARV*^{2} 438.132, 1653.

128. Plato is thus close to actual practice when he proposes, as a theory of the symposion in *Laws* I, that men should expose themselves to the enticements of pleasure, just as they are tested by exposure to the pain of battle (633D ff.). The only question is, do the Anakreontics go too far?

FIGURE 1.8. Tondo of a black-figure plate, showing an *aulos*-player and a male lyre player, 550–500 BCE. Antikenmuseum Basel and Sammlung Ludwig, Basel, inv. Kä 421. © Antikenmuseum Basel and Sammlung Ludwig.

could costume and disport themselves in a way that verged on the unmanly, but always with (as it were) their fingers crossed.

The second form of flamboyant display can be found on a series of vases, running from about 470 through the end of the fifth century, which portray *orkhēstrides*, dancing women, performing specialty numbers for the entertainment of men. The dancers of concern to us here are dressed like boys doing the pyrrhic in partial armor. There are twenty-four figures in the series, ranging from solitary dancers—as on a mid-fifth-century lekythos in the manner of the Carlsruhe Painter, now in Cape Town (fig. 1.9),[129] and a pyxis in Naples dated

129. Cape Town, Iziko Social History Collections, South Africa Cultural History Museum, inv. 1345; *ARV*[2] 677.11.

FIGURE 1.9. Red-figure lekythos from Athens, showing an armed dancer, middle of the fifth century BCE. © Iziko Museums of South Africa, Cape Town, Social History Collections, inv. 1345.

to about 480–470 (figs. 1.10a and 1.10b)[130]—to more complex groups, in which the dancer is accompanied by an *aulos*-player.

A single male spectator is quite common—as on an oinokhoe in Vienna (about 440, fig. 1.11)[131] and on two bell-kraters, one by the Munich Painter

130. Naples, Museo Archeologico Nazionale di Napoli, inv. 81908, H3010.

131. Painter of Louvre Centauromachy: Vienna, Kunsthistoriches Museum, inv. ANSA IV 1043; *ARV*[2] 1094.103; Poursat 1968: 590–91; Van Hoorn 1951, fig. 184.

FIGURE 1.10 A–B. Red-figure pyxis, showing a solitary armed dancer, c. 480–470 BCE. National Archaeological Museum, Naples, inv. 81908, H3010. Printed with the permission of the Ministry of Culture, National Archaeological Museum of Naples. Photo credit: Giorgio Albano.

(about 430, fig. 1.12)[132] and one by the Dinos Painter (about 420, fig. 1.13).[133] Some have taken this standard male onlooker to be a dancing instructor (Poursat 1968: 607), but I think he is meant to be a customer. The point is that the woman is not dancing on her own initiative or for her own pleasure: depictions of armed females are not a glimpse into the women's quarters of Athenian homes; they show working women, hired for a men's banquet.[134] We have three representations of such symposia where the men lie on couches

132. Munich Painter 2335: Rome, Museo Nazionale Etrusco di Villa Giulia, inv. 50479; *ARV*² 1164.57; Poursat 1968: 592–93.

133. Ferrara, Museo Archeologico Nazionale di Ferrara, inv. 2685, T. 695 VT; *ARV*² 1154.34.

134. See Goulaki-Voutira 1996: 5–8, who offers additional support for this interpretation.

FIGURE 1.10 A–B. (continued)

while a woman dances the pyrrhic for them. The clearest is on a bell-krater in Naples by the Lykaon Painter from about 440 (plate 6).[135]

Side by side these two series become even more interesting, since each shows a partial crossover in costume and movement. On the one hand, dignified men may take on some female or soft trappings and sway to exotic rhythms, but without obscuring their status as men and as masters; on the other hand, *hetairai* (courtesans) could entertain their clients by imitating the military dancing of citizen boys, moving athletically to the accompaniment of martial music, and again not obscuring their real status as female and as paid workers in what is nowadays called the sex industry. In the same social

135. Naples, Museo Archeologico Nazionale di Napoli, inv. Stg. 281; *ARV*[2] 1045.9. A puzzling Korinthian bowl by the Q Painter (*ARV*[2] 1519.13; *JdAI* 97, fig. 25; Luce 1930: 339, fig. 4) should perhaps be placed here: if the choruses of a tragedy and satyr play are composed of young male citizen-soldiers, then this might represent a dancing-girl who, like her pyrrhic sisters, has taken on some of the trappings associated with her social opposite, the citizen male in training.

FIGURE 1.11. Red-figure Attic oinokhoe, showing an armed dancer and one spectator. Painter of Louvre Centauromachy, c. 440 BCE. Kunsthistoriches Museum, Vienna, inv. ANSA IV 1043. Photo © KHM-Museumsverband.

context, then—the setting of an Attic symposion—we find these two mirroring modes of protodramatic performance, two styles of costuming and dancing that partially reverse the polarities of gender and class that define male citizens and female workers. Yet they both refer, even in the breach, to matters of manhood: at least, I would maintain that these carefully contained and highly stylized transgressions of gender decorum tell us that the aesthetics of dance and costume are fundamentally perceived in terms of masculine comportment and its deviations.

FIGURE 1.12. Red-figure bell-krater, showing an *aulos*-player, an armed dancer, and a single spectator. Munich Painter, c. 430 BCE. National Etruscan Museum of the Villa Giulia, Rome, inv. 50479. © Museo Nazionale Etrusco di Villa Giulia. Photographic Archive. Photo credit: Mauro Benedetti.

Let us here recall from the wings, where she has been waiting for the encore we promised her, Xenophon's dancing girl doing the pyrrhic for the Paphlagonians. It appears now that her act was neither original nor even uncommon. In fact, she would have learned it in class with other women in this service profession.[136] A hydria by Polygnotos in Naples from about 430 shows such a school in which the *hetairai* are learning and practicing various specialty numbers for men's parties: one of them is actually doing the pyrrhic.[137] On the far right in that group scene, a naked *hetaira* is practicing another party

136. Isok., *Antid.* 287 refers to the schools for flute-girls as places where young men hang out: *polloi d'en tois tōn aulētridōn didaskaleiois diatribousi* ("Many waste time in the schools of the [female] flute-players").

137. Naples, Museo Archeologico Nazionale di Napoli, inv. 3232.

FIGURE 1.13. Red-figure bell-krater, showing an armed dancer, a male spectator, and a female *aulos*-player. Possibly Dinos painter, c. 420 BCE. National Archaeological Museum, Ferrara, inv. 2685, T. 695 VT. By permission of the Ministry of Culture—Photographic Archive, Regional Directorate of the Museums of Emilia-Romagna (further reproduction or duplication by any means is prohibited).

trick—handstanding on a table and using her feet to lift a drinking cup to her mouth. And on another portion of the same vase, we see a *hetaira* about to dance in the midst of knives planted in the earth. On an Apulian squat lekythos from about 340, another acrobatic *hetaira* not only does the knife dance but flips up onto her hands.[138] Xenophon describes a hired dancer, performing at a symposion, who somersaults through a hoop lined with swords: a man in the audience suggests that her master should put her on official display to the city so that Athenians could learn to be bold in facing spears.[139]

138. Naples, Museo Archeologico Nazionale di Napoli, inv. 2854. On the sword dance: Schneider-Hermann 1982, plates 140–41.

139. Xen., *Symp.* 2.13. At 7.3 Sokrates calls that performance a "model display of danger [or risk-taking]" (*kindunou epideigma*).

The wondrous abilities of acrobatic dancers were also featured on the comic stage in South Italy. On a kalyx-krater (plate 7), generally attributed to the painter of Louvre K 420, the respectable women can be seen in the upper-story windows of the house, while outside Dionysos and a comic actor watch a naked female gymnast perform.[140] On a Paestan kotyle in the Ashmolean Museum (plate 8), another comic actor turns the ropes on a revolving wheel while the acrobat doing a handstand keeps her balance.[141] Xenophon mentions such an act in his *Symposion* (7.2–3), where the woman not only balances on a spinning potter's wheel but also reads and writes while doing so. Xenophon does not describe how she does this, but it may have involved using her feet to hold the scroll or stylus. To illustrate the extremes of pedal dexterity, of using one's feet as hands, I offer you this Berlin pelike (fig. 1.14), on which a female performer shoots a bow and arrow—for all we know through twelve axeheads.[142]

And now finally we can return to Hippokleides. In striving to outdo his competitors with an untoppable performance in Kleisthenes' theater of excellence, Hippokleides boldly and deliberately played with the boundaries of his own dignity, as the Anakreontic singers do. His initial dancing, for all that it did not suit Kleisthenes' idea of decorum, might have been well within the range of competitive display tolerable at a drinking party, but in upending himself and using his feet as hands he certainly went one step too far. I think of it as an unwitting act, invented on the spur of the moment and in the heat of *eris* (competition), but an act that in Kleisthenes' eyes violated the syntax of proper manhood.[143] One can take the measure of its lack of social gravity by noting that, at least in later times, such a performance is attested only for acrobatic call-girls, performing for hire and for the pleasure of men.

A sketch of manhood's poetics, which stressed only the athletic and military ideal and did not include the playful and teasing experiments in recombining elements of the sign-system, would be seriously inadequate. As the symposion was an occasion for both serious singing of patriotic *skolia* (drinking songs) and not-so-serious fooling around, so the City Dionysia contained both serious and comic performances, both of which expressed aspects of the city's self-understanding.

Hippokleides, if I may confess what should be obvious, is not of much concern to me—*ou phrontis moi*—though he has provided me with an occasion for setting out some information and ideas about dramatic and paradramatic performance, mainly in Athens. It seems to me that we can open up

140. Lipari, Museo Archeologico Regionale Eoliano Luigi Bernabò Brea, inv. 927, T367.

141. Oxford, Ashmolean Museum, inv. AN1945.43; Beazley no. 425002.

142. Berlin, Antikensammlung, Staatliche Museen, inv. F3444 (525); Richter 1942.

143. See in this connection a red-figure stamnos by the Peleus Painter, dating to 450–440 BCE, depicting the dancing Hippokleides as a dwarf: Erlangen, Kunstsammlung, inv. 707; *ARV*² 1039.6; Lippold 1937, fig. 14.

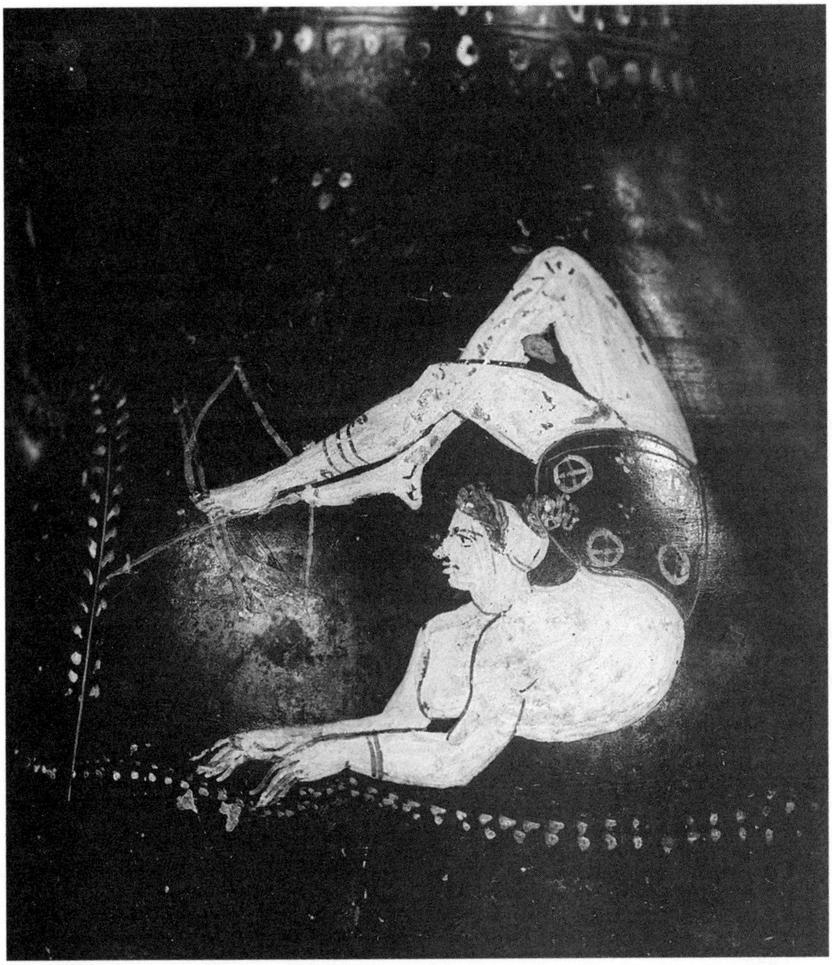

FIGURE 1.14. Red-figure pelike from Naples, showing a female acrobat shooting a bow with her feet, fourth century BCE. Antikensammlung, Staatliche Museen, Berlin, inv. F3444 (525). Photo credit: bpk Bildagentur / Antikensammlung, Staatliche Museen, Berlin / Art Resource, NY.

our understanding of Attic drama by cutting athwart the received categories—specifically by looking at the *codification of masculine identity through performance*, and generally by exploring the *stylization of public life in terms of performers acquiring and displaying a social identity before audiences*. Being literally performative, masculine identity in particular is a sometimes precarious achievement, in which the performer's fortunes and reputation may hang in the balance between honor and shame, between hero and clown, between butch and femme.

Hippokleides the social actor—wealthy, handsome, aristocratic, vigorously competitive, and in the flower of his youth—is significant insofar as he and his type were central to some frameworks of value that organized Greek society, both in its oligarchic and in its democratic forms. In the next chapter I will look at some of the ways in which the Athenian democracy harnessed and incorporated the performing talents of its own elite, using both serious (tragic) and playful (comic) formats as ways of representing the body politic.

CHAPTER TWO

Phallic Theatrics

STAGING THE BODY POLITIC

IN THE DEBATE (*agōn*) at the culmination of Aristophanes' revised *Clouds*, the personification of Stronger Speech (*Kreittōn Logos*) tries to win the allegiance of young Pheidippides to the principles of old-fashioned education by presenting a comparative chart of the two body-types that result from his training and from that of his opponent, Mr. Weaker Speech (*Hēttōn Logos*). "If you do what I say and pay careful attention, you will always have a rippling chest, glowing skin, broad shoulders, a tiny tongue, a solid rump, and a teeny pee-pee; but if you follow the modern practices, . . . you will acquire a sickly complexion, narrow shoulders, a nothing chest, an enormous tongue, spindly thighs, and an immense subpoena" (Ar., *Clouds* 1009–18).[1]

What Stronger Speech outlines for us here is a system—or rather a humorous parody of a system—for evaluating the best and worst in male bodies. It falls short of being an adequate code or rule-set for assessing the male body, in two respects: it is not complete, since it leaves out facial features and hair and other pertinent points, such as the waist-line; and it is one-sided, too rigorous in its perspective, not a sophisticated, complex, and nuanced statement of what ideal manhood means for the *polis*. For *andragathiē* involves much more than physique and body-building; it includes all the mental abilities and practical skills and refinements of character valued in a worthy citizen.[2] But, however crude or unaccommodating, the basic point is a valid one: in the face-to-face maneuvering of a highly competitive society, the very look of a man may in itself provide an opening for praise or blame, for admiration or

1. The translation of *psēphisma*, legislative proposal, as "subpoena" is inspired by Douglass Parker's translation of *The Congresswomen* (*Ekklēsiazousai*), line 980. I follow K. J. Dover's text of the *Clouds*.

2. Isok., *Ad Demon.* 6.

disapproval, for defense or attack.[3] If a young man is in poor physical condition, he is subject to abuse for being a bad warrior—that is, a bad citizen.

Sokrates berates the young Epigenes in just these terms:

> Many, thanks to their bad condition, lose their lives in the perils of war or save themselves disgracefully. Many, for this same reason, are taken prisoners, and then either pass the rest of their days, perhaps in slavery of the hardest kind, or, after meeting with cruel sufferings and paying sometimes more than they have, live on, destitute and in misery. Many again, by their bodily weakness, earn infamy, being thought cowards. (Xen., *Mem.* 3.12.2)

We can bring out the political (which, in this context, means the social) implications of Stronger Speech's cartoon bodies by comparing two similar arguments, one in Aristophanes' *Wealth* (*Ploutos*), another in Xenophon's handbook on hunting (*Kynēgetikos*).

The ideal male body was, to some extent, traditionally that of the young aristocrats, habitués of the gymnasia, who are figured on so many Attic vases. But in his play *Wealth*, Aristophanes stages a debate between Wealth and Poverty in which Poverty claims to turn out better men in mind and body than Wealth. Aristophanes remarks on one feature of the male body in particular—a feature that is crucial in all discussions of the ideal citizen-soldier, that serves as a fulcrum for representations of youth, maturity, and middle age, and that plays a decisive role in articulating (or, we might say, shaping) the dramatic genres: the waist-line. "From [Wealth]," claims Poverty, "we get the gouty men with paunches and waddling calves, the shamelessly fat, whereas from me come the sleek and wasp-waisted who are terrors to our enemies" (558–61). The irony is underlined by Khremylos, who immediately remarks that Poverty slims his ideal warriors' waists by simply starving them (562).

As we shall see in this chapter, the waist-line was arguably more important than the phallos for the political symbolism of the male body in Athens. From a survey of the early and later history of that body's symbolic representations, it appears that the absence of a pot-belly hanging out over one's belt was the central *definiens* for military, civic, and personal manhood—particularly as manhood was encoded on the stage. Modern medical science, always on the march, has recently laid down a distinction between gynoid fat and android fat: android fat is upper-body frontal fat, gynoid fat is that which collects on the lower body, and it appears that android fat is a considerably greater health risk than gynoid fat. Both men and women can have either kind of fat, but the

3. Thus, the speaker of Lysias 10.29 alludes to the defendant's impressive height and manly good looks, and claims that this is all the more reason he should be held accountable for his cowardly behavior.

typical configuration, giving the two fats their names, is that men collect their spare tonnage on the stomach, women on hips and thighs.[4]

This modern insight, like so many, is based on ancient wisdom: men and women have somewhat different worries about flab. Sokrates, in Xenophon's *Symposion* (2.19), is concerned that his stomach is disproportionately large, so he has taken to dancing in private. By this, we are not to imagine an occasional foxtrot with Xanthippe across their living room floor, but rather a strenuous workout in one of the dance-like martial arts described in chapter 1.

Even so, it is not the case that men were always evaluated in a straightforward, Procrustean fashion on the basis of their waist-lines. There are many complexities involved in the application of this standard by social actors, occasions on which it is invoked with fingers crossed, as it were: those who apply that standard also know how to exempt themselves from it. One such ambiguity pertains to age, since the naturally slim-waisted are the young, while men sliding into middle age find themselves increasingly paunchy. Though men of greater age and avoirdupois may idealize the "sleek and wasp-waisted who are terrors to our enemies," they are not about to devalue the other qualities of experience that come, like a flabby belly, with age.

The debate in the *Clouds* is a familiar text. Xenophon's *Kynēgetikos* is a less familiar one, but it is based on the same pattern of thought. In that text, the author constructs a one-sided comparison between the manly discipline of hunting and the greedy self-indulgence taught by sophists. Among the contrasts is an invidious distinction between bodies: the pupils of sophists "have the worst, the most shameful bodies for warfare, incapable of hard work, but hunters have splendid bodies and possessions to support the common good of their fellow-citizens" (13.11). Xenophon has less to say about the details of body proportion than Stronger Speech does (it takes a comic character to dwell on the obvious) and more to say about the social meanings invested in a taut rather than a slack masculine physique. The goal and standard of a proper education, including a superb physique, is to be good at the practices of war, and this can be touted as a service to the city. The argument of Xenophon's pamphlet begins with the general statement: "I advise young men not to scorn hunting or the other forms of education, for from these pursuits they become good at all the practices needed for warfare, and good at all things which are the necessary foundation of thinking well, speaking well, and acting well" (1.18). The rewards of hunting are rather extravagantly summarized toward the end of the work. "Those who pursue hunting will derive many benefits: it makes their bodies healthy so that they see and hear better, they age less quickly, and most of all it educates them in the works of war" (12.1).[5]

4. For a recent study correlating the android/gynoid fat ratio in boys with LDL + VLDL, i.e., "bad" cholesterol, see Samsell, Regier, Walton, and Cottrell 2014.

5. On the function of hunting in Athenian education, particularly as a preparation

Xenophon, of course, writes for the wealthy ephebe, the supposed embodiment of natural ability and effortless *aretē* (virtue, skill, performance). But that ideal standard is a mirage. It is easy to represent youth as effortlessly beautiful, since not too many of the young are naturally paunchy, but in middle age all men tend to look like Poverty's anti-ideal. Therefore youth and aristocracy are given a representative value, symbolizing the best there is for the body politic, even though the audience knows that both youth and the aristocracy are potentially dangerous, in different ways, to the democratic city. In Xenophon's text, the young and well-born are allowed to be a screen onto which are projected the values held—and held in check—by the male community as a whole. This is a community whose collective goal is warfare and general *aretē*, and whose members seek to be admired by others, to resolve disputes, and to win battles. Hunting is one way in which young men bask in the glow of male admiration, both from the older audience and from their teenage *erōmenoi* (boyfriends): they can see themselves being seen. This constant inspection and evaluation are effectively extended in the practice of drama, which can be considered a venue for watching masculinity's ups and downs.

Putting the *Clouds* and Xenophon's *Kynēgetikos* side by side, we can see a common underlying schema or habit of representation. Value is discussed in terms of polarized opposites, in this case educational programs. The competition between the two is motivated by similar goals—particularly, by a desire to win the vote or the allegiance of an audience. And although the discussion is presumably addressed to the entire audience in the theater or to the entire readership in the case of the written texts, the fictional audience is characterized as young and wealthy: Pheidippides and Xenophon's generalized young men.[6]

Let's now extend this look at the social meanings attached to the male body, young and old, rich and poor. First we can consider its representations on the stage, noticing the three axes of value—age, class, and (of course) gender—along which those representations may slide. Then we can juxtapose to those theatrical images a different politics of the body, represented in the herm.

---

for warfare, see Barringer 2001, esp. 10–70. Barringer argues that scenes of hunting on Athenian pottery "provide evidence for the critical place that the hunt occupied in the construction of male gender in Athenian aristocratic culture" (10).

6. The difference between Aristophanes and Xenophon may be due to the different social contexts for which they were composing: the relative dignity of Xenophon's description conforms to the decorous tone assumed by elite writers addressing members of the propertied classes, whereas the Dionysia (the religious festival at which Aristophanes' *Clouds* was performed) is characterized by wilder images of unrestrained manhood—such as satyrs, phallic processions, and ithyphallic comic choruses.

The Politics of Costume

The body contrast described by Aristophanes is found in the Attic theater in the opposition between the general look of tragedy and comedy. From the evidence of ancient vases, reliefs, and terracottas, we know that tragic characters were costumed and proportioned in a way that heroized or ennobled them, while comic characters were contrived to look squat, fat, and grotesque. A generous selection of pictures is available in A. D. Trendall and T. B. L. Webster's *Illustrations of Greek Drama* (abbreviated here as *IGD*).[7] In studying comic and tragic costume, I will try to show how the very look of characters on the stage, their costumes and masks, set up two parallel languages or dialects in which the issues of proper civic masculinity could be represented, debated, and played with.[8] The core concern that generates those images (and is variously supported or challenged by them) is the military fitness of each male citizen—the physical and psychic qualities enabling him to face ultimate risks for the common good, and sometimes the very survival, of the entire *polis*.

Our exploration of comic and tragic costume will begin in Athens during the fifth century BCE, but soon it will take us far away—to Korinth in the late seventh century and to Sparta in the sixth, for it is there that the elements of dramatic costuming (body-suits and masks) are first found, and it is in the Spartan material that we can first begin to recover a tentative sense of the larger social issues involved. Then we will return to Athens and to the sixth-century performances that have hitherto been called "animal choruses," but that need to be renamed. Finally, we will consider the archaeology of the orchestra and the auditorium of the Attic theaters, for there too the basic system of shapes and seating-arrangements bespeaks a concern for the proper display and articulation of the body politic—that is, both the bodies of individual citizens and the corporate body formed by their serried ranks in the theater.

The look of Attic comedy and tragedy can be reconstructed from several sources: vases, terracotta figurines, relief sculpture.[9] For both tragedy and comedy there is also a very large number of fourth-century vases manufactured

7. As Giuliani 1996 and 2010 has shown, the title of this book is misleading: often the fourth-century "Apulian" pots do not seem to be illustrating a particular production of a drama, but rather the elements from the myth that the painter considers important. See Giuliani 1996 for a convincing demonstration that one such krater illustrating the myth of Rhesos draws both from book 10 of the *Iliad* and the pseudo-Euripidean play. On the difficulties of interpreting tragic costumes on vases, see Wyles 2010: 232–48.

8. Foley 2000, extending and qualifying Winkler 1990c (an earlier version of this chapter), argues that "the valence of theatrical costume is not so simply oppositional as Winkler would have it" (284), pointing to the ways that tragic actors are sometimes feminized (284–86), along with the ways that comic actors are often identified, despite their large-bellied, slack appearances, as regular citizens (303–4).

9. *IGD*; *DFA*. On the depiction of drama on vases, see in particular Green 1991b.

in southern Italy, whose relation to Attic drama is in some cases demonstrably close.[10] For any single vase painting or sculpture, we might wonder how accurately the artist portrayed what he saw—that is, how far his intention to represent actors was realized in a drawing or figure that showed what was actually there or what was only imagined to be there.[11] But the aggregate of surviving theatrical depictions builds up a well-defined field whose boundaries, particularly in the differentiation of comedy and tragedy from each other, are unmistakable.[12]

Let us approach this topic from the body shapes contrived in comedy, starting with the evidence from Athens itself. Plate 9 is a khous (wine pitcher) from Meidias' workshop, dating to 410–400 BCE. Now in the Hermitage Museum in Saint Petersburg, it shows five children dressed in theatrical costume, two in the ankle-length embroidered robes worn by *aulos*-players and by some tragic actors, three in the padded body-suit with long phallos worn in comedy.[13] The artist has taken great pains to illustrate the leotard and body-stocking, with lines at ankle and wrist, which stand for stage nudity in comedy. About the same time, 410, the Nikias Painter depicted Herakles in the chariot of Nike (Victory), which is drawn by four centaurs and led by a leering man with two long torches (fig. 2.1).[14]

10. For example, in the case of the *Telephos* parody vase representing Aristophanes' *Thesmophoriazousai*, see Csapo 1986; Taplin 1987: 38–40; Austin and Olson 2004: lxxv–lxxvii. Csapo 1986 makes a strong and specific case for the vase as an illustration of the Aristophanic play, and thus for the *phluax* vases as representing, in some cases, Attic Old Comedy. The similarity of themes and types has been argued by Radermacher 1924 and Webster 1948. As Giuliani 1996: 73 points out, however, we must exercise caution: not a single Apulian vase depicting a tragic myth seems to show the action taking place on a stage.

11. Sometimes vase scenes show what happened in the narrative of a messenger's speech, such as the dragging of Dirke by a wild bull in Euripides' *Antiope* (*IGD* III.3.14–15), Medeia's murder of her children in Euripides' *Medeia* (*IGD* III.3.36), or the thunderstorm that put out the burning pyre under Alkmene in Euripides' *Alkmene* (*IGD* III.3.6–8). Background figures, personifications, and gods may illustrate some aspect of a play's contents, even when they did not figure explicitly as characters in the script. See Giuliani 1996: 85 for the argument that the painters are more concerned with the myth than with illustrating individual dramatic productions.

12. As Giuliani 1996: 74 points out, the vases depicting *comedies* often show clearly that the character is in costume. On vases that have been associated with tragedies (or, perhaps more accurately, the myths of tragic texts), the characters are depicted in clothing appropriate to the character, but not in anything that can be identified as dramatic costume. Green 1991b: 34–40 makes similar observations, and argues that this difference can be attributed to the different conventions of tragedy and comedy: whereas comedy often breaks the fourth wall and calls attention to the conventions of the theater, tragedy more consistently maintains the dramatic illusion. The discussion below focuses on the pots as evidence for comic productions.

13. On khoes in general, see Van Hoorn 1951; studies of khoes after Van Hoorn are listed in Simon 1983: 95. This khous is: Saint Petersburg, The State Hermitage Museum, inv. ΦA1869.47; Van Hoorn 1951: 137, #585; Stone 1981, figs. 5a–d; *IGD* IV.3.

14. Paris, Musée du Louvre, inv. N3408; *ARV*² 1335.34; *IGD* IV.2; Stone 1981, figs. 3a–b; *DFA* fig. 77.

FIGURE 2.1. Red-figure Attic oinokhoe, showing Herakles in a chariot pulled by four centaurs. Nikias Painter, c. 410 BCE. Louvre Museum, Paris, inv. N3408. © RMN-Grand Palais / Art Resource, NY. Photo credit: Hervé Lewandowski.

All the faces are recognizably those of Old Comic masks, but the artist has given us more of what the mind sees—Nike's wings perhaps, certainly the centaurs' horse bodies. For the leering groom he shows us both a naked torso, which is what the mind's eye saw, and the loose leggings that the actor actually wore. The overstuffed look of the children in plate 9 and the slimmer characters in figure 2.1 define the range of comic corporeality: neither has the noble look of athletic excellence.

Five unglazed, polychrome khoes, four of them found in a well in the Athenian Agora that was abandoned and used as a dump soon after 400 BCE, evidently show comic characters. Of the two vases illustrated here (figs. 2.2, 2.3), one portrays a fat man rowing a fish and the other is a fragment with two figures labeled [Di]onysos and Phor-.[15] It is quite possibly an illustration of Eupolis' comedy *The Squadron-Leaders* (*Taxiarkhoi*), in which the Athenian general Phormion took the raw recruit Dionysos and whipped him into shape with proper military discipline. The unglazed surface is very worn, but one can certainly make out the dumpling-shaped bodies and the slack postures of the two characters.

15. London, British Museum, inv. 1898,0227.1, and Athens, Agora Museum, inv. P23985; both images here are watercolors of the objects by Piet de Jong. Crosby 1955, Webster 1960.

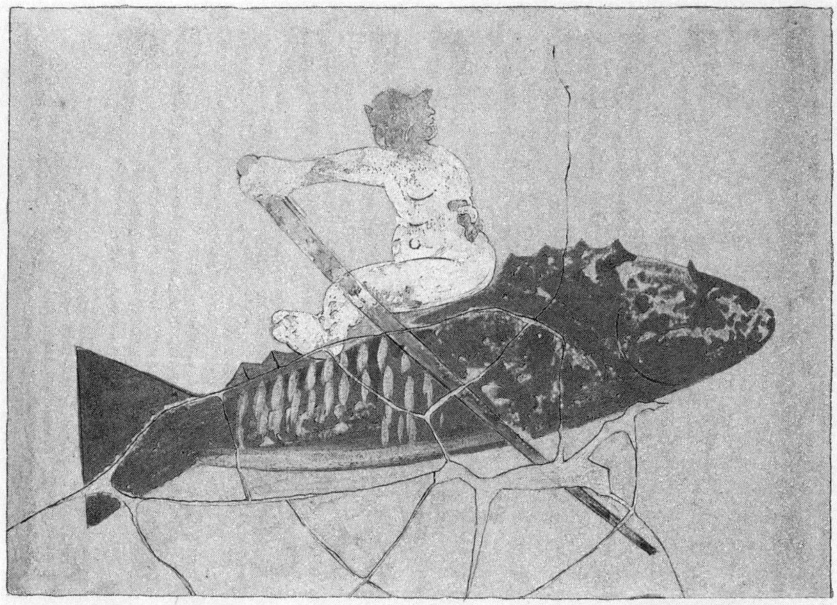

FIGURE 2.2. Watercolor by Piet de Jong of a vase painting in the British Museum, showing a man rowing a fish. Agora Excavations, Athens, drawing DA 13058. Original object in London, British Museum, inv. 1898,0227.1, c. 350 BCE. Credit: American School of Classical Studies at Athens, Agora Excavations.

On the famous Perseus parody from 420 BCE (fig. 2.4),[16] the presence of a stage platform and audience show that a comic performance of some sort is intended (though the audience's chairs suggest that they are not in the theater of Dionysos: perhaps it is a rehearsal, watched by the producer and playwright). In portraying the actor on the stage, the artist has selected several signs of a comic look—a wispy beard, an inelegant pose, squat proportions—but has not (or perhaps the producer has not) endowed the actor with a notable paunch, at least not one that can be seen frontally. The lines at the wrist are the only certain acknowledgment by the artist that this is not a naked man dancing but an actor whose precise *quality* of nakedness has been contrived by a costumer. The artist's omission of the usually obvious leotard and wrinkled sleeves and leggings is very exceptional and has led to this figure being called a dwarf (Van Hoorn 1951: 37). The preponderance of vases, however, will show that, though the point is well taken, it is probably too literal, since the overall effect of comic padding was to give the actor the proportions, especially when seen at a distance, of a dwarf.

The proper way to establish the corporeal code, of course, is to look at contrasting bodies by the same artist. Thus, on the Perseus vase there is a clear

16. Athens, National Archaeological Museum, Vlastos-Serpieri Collection, inv. VS518, red-figure oinokhoe from Anavyssos; *ARV*[2] 1215.1; *DFA* fig. 76; *IGD* IV.1.

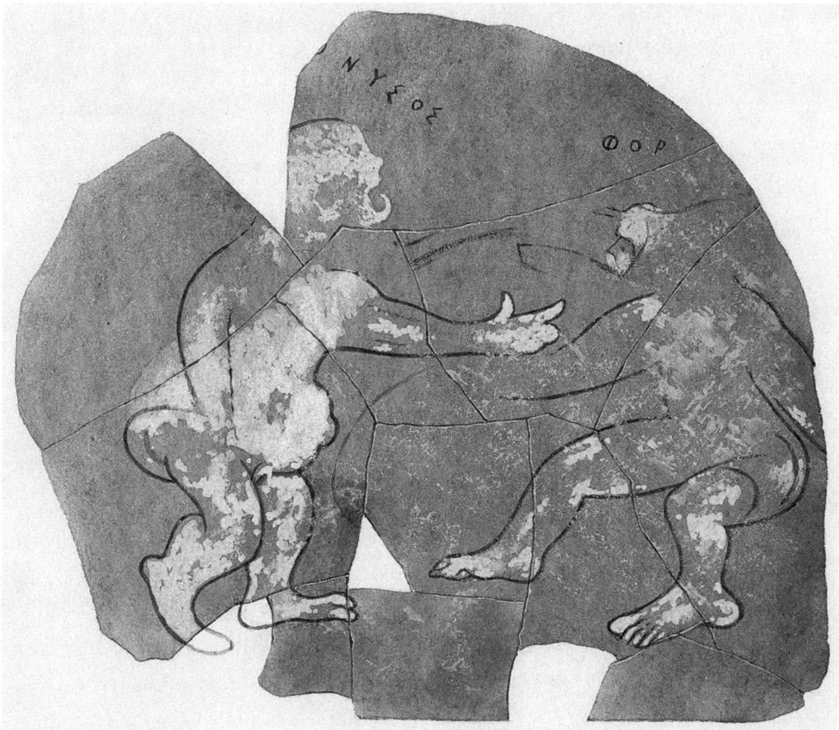

FIGURE 2.3. Watercolor by Piet de Jong of a vase fragment from the Athenian Agora, showing two actors. Agora Excavations, Athens, drawing DA 10672. Original object Agora, inv. P23985, c. late fifth century BCE. Credit: American School of Classical Studies at Athens, Agora Excavations.

contrast between the faces of the gentlemen in the audience and the face (that is, the mask) of the actor on the stage. The Karouzou khous (fig. 2.5) in the National Archaeological Museum in Athens gives a more complete version of the code.[17] One of the figures depicted on it wears a grotesque mask, comic padding, and a big, artificial phallos; another figure, a youth with a Dudley Do-Right profile, is portrayed in what is meant to be a state of noble nakedness. The pair might almost serve as an illustration of Stronger Speech's point, except that the unsteady youth pictured drinking between them is faced not with a choice between two "real" bodies, but with one ideally "real" body, that of the youth, and one man dressed in a funny suit.

17. Athens, National Archaeological Museum, inv. 17752. Fig. 2.5 shows incompletely the paintings on the vase described in the text; fuller images are available in Karouzou 1946, figs. 10a–c. See also Van Hoorn 1951, fig. 148. Karouzou, who found the pot in a shop on the Odos Pandrosou and persuaded the dealer to present it to the National Archaeological Museum, reads the scene quite differently, as an actual children's play about Orestes, with the right-hand figure being interpreted as a Fury (Karouzou 1946). A similarly dressed boy can be found on Van Hoorn 1951, fig. 87, wearing an open coat with sleeves.

FIGURE 2.4. Red-figure oinokhoe from Anavyssos, showing an actor on stage with two seated spectators, c. 420 BCE. National Archaeological Museum, Athens, inv. VS518. © Hellenic Ministry of Culture and Sports/Hellenic Organization of Cultural Resources Development (HOCRED). Photo credit: Konstantinos Kontos.

At this point we might ask why it is that almost all the early Attic evidence for comic costume and performance occurs on khoes (wine pitchers). The middle day of the Anthesteria festival was called "Khoes," and the mass of big and small pouring pitchers seems to have been especially used on that occasion. Drinking contests, both in private groups and under state sponsorship, were held in which the first man to swallow his entire jug of wine won a cake

FIGURE 2.5. Red-figure khous from Athens, showing naked and padded actors, c. 400 BCE. National Archaeological Museum, Athens, inv. 17752. © Hellenic Ministry of Culture and Sports/Hellenic Organization of Cultural Resources Development (HOCRED). Photo credit: National Archaeological Museum, Athens.

as his prize.[18] Though it was a festival of Dionysos (only his temple *en Limnais* was open on those three days), there were no dramatic contests. The Anthesteria was what we might call a festival of individuation: people ate separate

18. And a grander version was held under the supervision of the priest of Dionysos (Ar., *Akh.* end), with a wine-skin as prize.

rather than common meals and drank silently from individual pitchers and cups rather than from a commonly mixed krater.[19]

Such an event can be very disturbing to children, so they were treated specially. Indeed, the miniature khoes were gifts to children, and that day was a kind of communal birthday party for them. During the festival, children were introduced to wine and inebriation on a small scale. Swinging, which is represented on a number of these khoes, may have been intended to produce a feeling akin to drunkenness. Each of the children had a little khous, which held considerably less than the adult's three-quart size. In fact, the age of children can sometimes be determined by the number of khoes they possessed—one for each year of the festival.

Many of these little pitchers are illustrated with homely and undignified subjects that were normally filtered out of the vase-painter's repertoire as unbefitting—such as children playing with toys or hand-standing. Comedy is picked up as a subject partly because it is undignified and partly because the physical proportions of babies and little children tend to be like the proportions of comic characters: short and squat. Probably, though, we should put it the other way around and argue that one of the templates by which the significance of comic costume should be measured is that it makes adult men look like children. Certainly, the behavior of Philokleon and the Sausage-Seller and many other comic characters is rampantly self-indulgent, unpredictable, and energetic—in a word, childish.

Greek artists of the Classical period seldom portrayed fat, phallic, and grotesquely leering men, apart from satyrs (and even those satyrs are often lean-bodied and small-phallosed).[20] When they did so, it was regularly with unmistakable indications that such a physique was not a natural state but an artful contrivance, a costume donned for a special occasion. There seems to have been a sort of practical ban on showing unbecoming bodies, unless it was made perfectly clear that their fatness and slackness were artificial.[21] Even on the numerous Attic terracottas from the late fifth century, the leggings

19. Orestes was said to have been the ancestor of this custom. The reference in the *Akharnians* to a drunken Orestes assaulting Antimakhos, the stingy *khorēgos*, may simply mean that, on the day of Khoes, Orestes prowls the city or that a drunken, unsocial man could be called an Orestes on that day (the fictional setting of the end of the *Akharnians*).

20. Some black-figure artists liked showing athletes in the heavy-weight class, such as the wrestlers by the Painter of Tarquinia, R. C. 3984 (Tronchetti 1983: 74–75) or the pugilists by the Altalena Painter (Tronchetti 1983: 77–79), whom Beazley characterized as a comedian, or the "tubby boxers," as Michael Vickers calls them, of the Michigan Painter's stamnos in the Ashmolean (M. Vickers 1978, no. 30).

21. Foley 2000: 310 suggests accordingly that ugly or shameful bodies, as portrayed on vases or displayed on the comic stage, functioned as an artificial disguise, beneath which viewers could perceive the continued existence of normative, even heroic citizens: "The harmless, laughable costume is worn, like a jester's cap and bells, to license citizen actors to parody and distort normal civic activities with the aim of correcting, educating, and illuminating the audience."

FIGURE 2.6. Red-figure *phluax* vase, showing two actors, c. 375 BCE. National Archaeological Museum, Taranto, inv. 20353. © National Archaeological Museum of Taranto.

are wrinkled and the cuff-line clearly indicated. The heads, too, are distinctly big—large enough to give the impression that this is a person wearing a mask. The popularity of such terracottas, which are found in great numbers in many locations outside Athens, whether they are souvenirs from a visit to Athens or manufactured on the spot to accompany local comedy, tells us more than that audiences liked comic images. What is striking about these popular artifacts is less the grotesqueness of the figures in itself than the insistence on showing the artificiality of the look.

That artificiality is clearest on the numerous South Italian vases showing what have been called *phluax* actors and *phluax* plays.[22] These vases are immensely entertaining as well as important; their closeness in some cases to Athenian comedy has been demonstrated by Oliver Taplin.[23] Two images, both from *phluax* vases in Taranto, are sufficient to give the general idea. The reveler in figure 2.6, holding a torch, wears a khiton that significantly fails to

22. On the meaning of this term, see appendix II.

23. Taplin 1987, with an extended argument in Taplin 1993. Further arguments have been made by Csapo 1986. See, however, the criticisms of Giuliani 2010: 254–55; 1996: 85. While Giuliani does not believe that the painters had particular productions in mind, he does agree that the vases are evidence for comic costumes.

FIGURE 2.7. Fragment of a red-figure *phluax* vase, showing a comic king, fourth century BCE. National Archaeological Museum, Taranto, inv. 121613. © DeA Picture Library / Art Resource, NY.

cover his genitals.[24] That is a defining feature of the costume. The roly-poly creature in figure 2.7 is a king, with crown and scepter, and he too is clothed in a way that reveals his nakedness.[25] Both have a generally dwarfish or child-like look, caused by their body proportions and by their style of clothing: they look like children playing grown-up. The typical *phluax* actor, representing the whole genre, is always a single man, never a single woman (though many scenes show groups, and in those larger groups women are included).

Plate 10 presents an excellent example of stage padding. A slave is about to thrash an old man whose hands are tied above his head; the words coming out of the slave's mouth are metrical but nonsense, while the old man is speaking Attic, saying, "My hands are tied." It looks as if he is about to be punished for killing the old woman's goose. Off to the left stands a rather slim young man

24. Taranto, Museo Archeologico Nazionale di Taranto, inv. 20353.

25. Taranto, Museo Archeologico Nazionale di Taranto, inv. 121613.

FIGURE 2.8A. Red-figure Apulian bell-krater, showing comic actors. Attributed to the Schiller Painter or an associate, c. 380 BCE. Virginia Museum of Fine Arts, Richmond, inv. 78.83. Adolph D. and Wilkins C. Williams Fund. © Virginia Museum of Fine Arts. Photo credit: David Stover.

labeled *tragōidos* (tragic chorister), waiting for his group's turn to perform. The old man's stomach is clearly a pillow tied to the actor's waist, the rump is stuffed cloth, and you can even see the skin suit hanging loosely about the old man's neck.[26]

Our impressions of the comic look are confirmed by comparing the front sides of these vases with their backs, which frequently show a pair of ephebes, as on an Apulian bell-krater in the Virginia Museum of Fine Arts (figs. 2.8a, 2.8b).[27] Obviously, this artist could show a male nude in classic *contrapposto* when he wanted to. The idealized youthful body on the reverse provides a

26. New York, Metropolitan Museum of Art, inv. 24.97.104.

27. Richmond, Virginia Museum of Fine Arts, inv. 78.83.

FIGURE 2.8B. Reverse of vase in 2.8a, showing two youths. Virginia Museum of Fine Arts, Richmond, inv. 78.83. Adolph D. and Wilkins C. Williams Fund. © Virginia Museum of Fine Arts. Photo credit: David Stover.

kind of baseline against which the deliberate deviancies of the comic body are measured.

Similarly with the masterpiece by the painter Asteas, shown in plate 12: the lips of Zeus and Hermes, as they approach Alkmene's second story with a ladder, are bright orangish-red, and the stomach and pectorals are highlighted with a similar color.[28] This might suggest that a second standard against which the comic male body should be measured is the feminine. But, since middle-aged men sometimes have sagging breasts, perhaps we should not insist too strongly on the feminizing effect of this costume. Rather, both

28. Vatican City, Vatican Museums, inv. 17106.

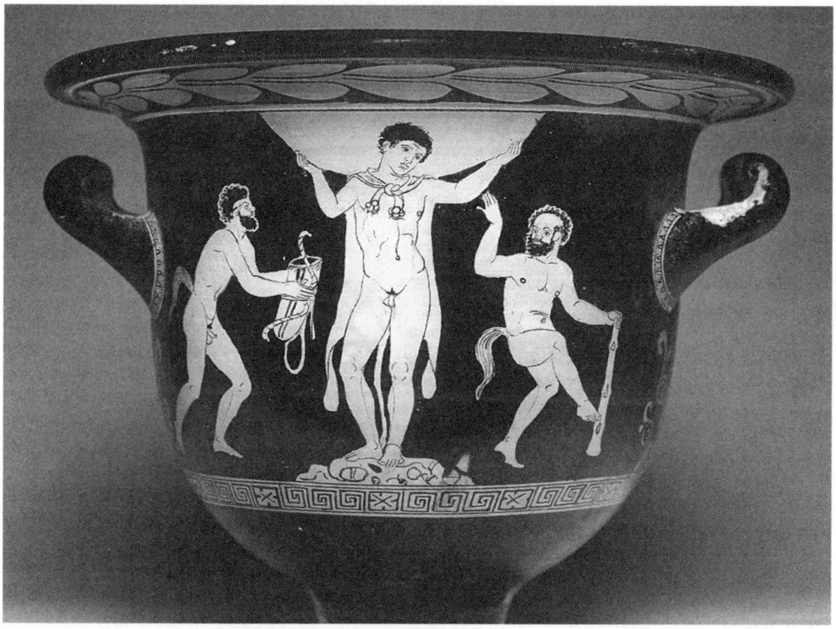

FIGURE 2.9. Red-figure Paestan bell-krater, showing Herakles holding up the world, with two satyrs. Choregos Painter, c. 380–370 BCE. From Ruvo di Puglia. Civic Archaeological Museum, Milan, inv. A 0.9.2841. © Comune di Milano—Civico Museo Archeologico.

baby fat and female fat are perceived as forms of slackness, falling short of the ideal body of a mature young man.[29]

On another vase, a bell-krater by the Choregos Painter, the artist has drawn Alkmene's son Herakles in a scene from a satyr play in which Herakles obtains the golden apples of the Hesperides by relieving Atlas of his burden for a time (fig. 2.9).[30]

We can compare that idealized image of Herakles with a decidedly comic version of the same hero on a khous in Taranto (plate 11).[31] Here Herakles has abandoned his bow and club in favor of a whirling love charm called an *iunx*. The other characters, who need his help, are expostulating with him to get over his love-sickness and get back to his heroic labors—and to saving the world.

29. See Foley 2000: 291–95 for the androgynous aspects of the comic costume as it is depicted on vases.

30. Milan, Civico Museo Archeologico, Athos Moretti Collection, inv. A 0.9.2841.

31. Taranto, Museo Archeologico Nazionale di Taranto, inv. 56048. Green 1991a argues that the Tarentine *phluax* vases are of local manufacture and represent "Greek comedy as seen and understood in Taranto" (56).

FIGURE 2.10. Red-figure hydria, showing a scene from the *Telephos*, fourth century BCE. National Archaeological Museum, Naples, inv. 86064, RC141. By permission of the Ministry of Culture, National Archaeological Museum of Naples. Photo credit: Giorgio Albano.

FIGURE 2.11. Red-figure South Italian bell-krater, showing a scene from the *Thesmophoriazousai*, parodying the *Telephos*, c. 370 BCE. Martin von Wagner Museum, Würzburg, inv. H5697. © Martin von Wagner Museum, The University of Würzburg. Photo credit: C. Kiefer.

Let us continue our principle of establishing systematic contrasts of costume, body, and genre. A hydria in Naples (fig. 2.10) shows one of Euripides' most popular plays, *Telephos*, in which the Mysian king, Telephos—exhibiting a typically heroic physique—whose wound can only be cured by rust from the spear of Achilles who wounded him, has crept into the Greek camp in disguise as a beggar and here holds baby Orestes hostage at the altar, threatening to kill him.[32] There are many vases of this scene, including a splendid parody, a South Italian bell-krater from about 370 (fig. 2.11).[33] As Oliver Taplin (1987: 38–40) has argued, the artist has not merely imitated the serious iconography of Telephos: rather, he has also represented a play that parodies Euripides' *Telephos*, the *Thesmophoriazousai* by Aristophanes.[34] In that play, Euripides'

32. Naples, Museo Archeologico Nazionale di Napoli, inv. 86064, RC141.

33. Würzburg, Martin von Wagner Museum, inv. H5697.

34. See note 10 above. Of particular interest is Csapo 1986.

relative, disguised not as a beggar but as a woman, infiltrates the women's Thesmophoria festival, and when he is discovered he grabs not a baby but something even more precious to the women, a wineskin.

The interpretation of this vase as an illustration of Aristophanes' play is confirmed by several details. The man on the altar is wearing a woman's dress—therefore the phallos is not visible—and there is stubble on his face. In the beginning of the play, you may recall, Euripides' relative is shaved by the women who detect him in disguise. Most important, the wineskin is wearing little booties, which are referred to in the script as *persikai*. Given the immense popularity of Euripides in South Italy during the fourth century BCE, it is not surprising that a play of Aristophanes devoted mainly to him should have been reperformed there. This raises the question, however, of how many other of the so-called *phluax* vases actually represent performances of Attic comedy. The reverse of the bell-krater shows, as so often, two ephebes, whose faces and physical proportions embody the ideal—of age, class, and gender—against which the comic characters are measured . . . and found human.

Although men are central in these representations, as they are in the conventions—or fictions—of Greek social life, women (that is, representations of women) are clearly important, too. For Athens, we have the testimony once again of the terracottas, which represent a variety of types of women. However, to illustrate the contrasting possibilities of female representation, we can compare the lovely drawing of Sappho on an Attic krater produced in about 470 with the not-so-lovely Sappho on a second Attic vase, chewing a stylus as she composes her poetry: a scene in a comedy.[35] There were at least six plays whose titles are recorded that were devoted to the comic Sappho, and the second vase gives us a chance to see what she looked like when viewed through the distorting lens of the comic stage, rather than through an idealizing lens.[36]

Finally, here are two versions of the Antigone story. In figure 2.12, a serious Antigone is being led by the guards to Kreon.[37] Contrast that with plate 13, which shows the *Cage aux folles* version of the same scene: an old man who is an Antigone impersonator, wearing a woman's robe—transparent enough that you can see his phallos through it—and carrying a female mask and a funeral urn, is being led away from his confrontation with Kreon.[38] The play is unknown, but it is clearly a comedy.

35. Bochum, Kunstsammlungen, Ruhr-Universtität, inv. S508. An image of the first Attic vase is available in Yatromanolakis 2001, plate 1. [We have been unable to identify the second Attic vase referred to here.] See, further, Yatromanolakis 2008.

36. Testimonia 25–26 in D. Campbell 1982; Greek fragments collected by Kock. The playwrights in question are Ameipsias, Amphis, Antiphanes, Diphilos, Ephippos, and Timokles.

37. London, British Museum, inv. 1867,0508.1330 (formerly F 175). The interpretation of this vase as showing a scene from the *Antigone* is disputed.

38. The bell-krater referred to is sometimes known as the "Sant' Agata Antigone." It is in a private collection in Italy and is reproduced here by the kind permission of the owner.

FIGURE 2.12. Detail from a red-figure Lucanian nestoris (two-handled jar), possibly showing Antigone attended by two guards. Attributed to the Dolon Painter, 390–380 BCE. British Museum, London, inv. 1867,0508.1330. © The Trustees of the British Museum / Art Resource, NY.

Phallos Politikos

The interpretation of dramatic costume that I have been offering is political and social. There is an alternative view, which focuses not on the taut or slack quality of the entire male body in the context of a military ideology but simply on the presence of the phallos, understood as a survival from primitive fertility rites. The padded characters, on this view, can be described as descendants of vegetation demons in the entourage of the archaic Dionysos. Such a theory has more to do with our own embarrassment at exposed genitality than with the authentic meanings of the male body to the original audience of Athenian drama, to say nothing of the meanings of Greek drama itself. We cover our embarrassment by making an immediate leap over the social to the "primitive"—a code word for that Other which is so distant from us as to be exempt from our taboos. That Other tells us more about what we have repressed than about what the Greeks displayed.

I offer a different strategy of interpretation, one that privileges the social and present meanings of Attic body imagery over putatively natural and timeless ones. When representations of the body are viewed in terms of biology and anatomy, we lose the historical dimension of their meaning. Anatomy, we might even say, is politics: that is, the field we call anatomy was coded for the Greeks with social messages about class and status. To look at the anatomy and not at the society effectively conceals what the Greek artists and symbol-shapers revealed.

Consider for a moment the political fortunes of the phallos in democratic Athens. As David Halperin has shown, Athenians of the Classical period attributed to Solon several sweeping changes in the laws that in effect redefined the conception of the citizen body (Halperin 1990a). A citizen could no longer be made a slave for his unpaid debts: his physical person at least was untouchable. He could not be manhandled as slaves and foreigners could be, and he could not be tortured to produce evidence in a court of law as slaves and in some cases foreigners could be. In principle, the body of the citizen (perhaps because he was one who could be called to put his body on the fighting line for the common safety of the *polis*) was declared to be a free zone, exempt from physical intimidation, and this remained a fundamental rule for the democracy.[39] At the same time, Solon was said to have instituted public brothels with price supports, enabling all male citizens to have equal access to a subsistence level of sexual pleasure.[40] Together, these two regulations served to increase the status of the ordinary man who had no special claim to honor from family or wealth. Simply by being a male member of the civic corporation, he is honored with a minimum physical impunity (the dignity of his masculine person may not be breached) and with an easily available symbol of his equality as a man with all other male citizens—his access to the *polis*' *pornai*, the city's whores.

The pressure toward greater democracy came in waves, not in a single explosion, and it is quite possible that by the fourth century some historically later developments were being read back into Solonian times. What matters for us is not the literal truth of the story about Solon's institution of public brothels; what matters is the symbolic effect of the cumulative strategy, over the course of the sixth and fifth centuries BCE, by which the city-state consistently expressed a distinct political message in terms of the bodies of its eligible participants.

One development, distinctive to Athens, can be dated to the late sixth century. It is the creation of a type of monument that regularly marked the sameness of all male citizens and that was deliberately indifferent to distinctions of class or achievement. I am referring to the herm, a plain rectangular pillar, adorned only with a carved head, shoulder holes, and an erect penis, used to signpost the boundaries of temples and houses.[41] The invention of

39. Winkler 1990a: 48–49.

40. Philemon, fr. 4; Nikander, fr. 9 (*FGrHist* 271–72), cited by Athenaios 13.569D–F. This passage is discussed by Halperin 1990a: 13.

41. A suggestive analysis of the Attic herm, which several times approaches the views

herms and their use to mark the halfway point on roads from Athens to its rural demes are attributed to Hipparkhos, in the last, balmy days of the Peisistratid tyranny before democratic pressures were renewed and culminated in the reforms of Kleisthenes.[42] The absence of herms in earlier Greek culture and their specific invention by an Athenian ruler indicate that this kind of phallos, at least, had more to do with political meanings than with rituals of agricultural fertility.

The democratic ideology that the herm acquired in the post-Kleisthenic period is perhaps clearest in the celebrated Eion monument. When the Athenian generals defeated the Persians at Eion, probably in 476 BCE, they asked to be honored by the city with a public memorial. Their request was granted by the Athenian democracy with a strict proviso: no individual leader was to be named. The honor was to be spread equally over the entire body of citizens. Three herms, inscribed with epigrams glorifying the military *andreia* of Athens, but mentioning no generals' names, were erected in the Agora. This famous monument again suggests that the specific meaning of the herm in Athens was democratic, that it was a symbol of the sameness and equality of all the city's capable fighters.

We can extend this analysis to the herms that stood by the doors of individual houses. In the ancient understanding of democracy, each male citizen represented not just his own interests but also those of a household, a group of dependents and social minors (women, children, slaves).[43] In a political community whose atomic units are representatives of family groups, the herm expresses the notional equality of each household, represented in the person of its patriarch and symbolized by a simplified image of the man—a bearded face and an upright phallos.[44]

The herm is thus a leveling sign.[45] At least, it came to be such when it was widely used under the fuller democracy of Kleisthenes.[46] By contrast, the body

---

expounded here, is to be found in Osborne 1985. Many of Osborne's points were already made by Crome 1935–36. Quinn 2007 expands on Osborne's argument and on the earlier version of this chapter (Winkler 1990b), arguing that the figure of the herm replaced the statuary figure of the *kouros*, and that this shift signals a move from aristocratic ideals to a democratic aesthetic.

42. Such are the chronology and interpretation of [Plato], *Hipparkhos*, the main source for the invention of herms; a different but related account is found in [Arist.], *Ath. Pol.* 18.1.

43. This is not to imply that each male citizen actually possessed a separate domicile—quarters could be rented in tenement blocks—but where the herm was used for private houses, it had such a meaning.

44. As the modern Kabyle proverb for the fundamental equality of all men puts it, "I too have a mustache" (Bourdieu 1977: 13); cf. Herzfeld 1986: 11–15.

45. Quinn 2007 supports and extends this argument for the interpretation of the herm as a symbol and expression of fifth-century Athenian democracy's egalitarian ideology.

46. It is unclear whether Hipparkhos' motive was antidemocratic (to segregate the city's active political life from the rural residents, as Osborne 1985 argues) or a concession

languages of comedy and tragedy carry a different sort of political meaning, since they continually mark the degrees of better and worse in corporeality: they may therefore be called class conscious. This accords well with the flourishing of comedy and tragedy in sixth-century Athens, in what must have been more aristocratic than democratic contexts. Or rather, extending our terms a bit, we might allow that the dialectic and debate between epic notions of heroic excellence and forces promoting the inclusion of a wider population under the aegis of that excellence must have had a centuries-long history, and one of the many venues of this unfolding social process was provided by choral performances involving music, dance, and costume, both in a serious, epic-based mode and in comic distortions.

Such performances were controlled, according to [Xenophon]'s *Constitution of the Athenians* (1.13–14), by the wealthy and well-born, the best men in the city, whose traditional prerogatives were based not on the prestige of land and money (though they had plenty of that), but on their military role as defenders of the people's safety from external aggression. In the seventh and sixth centuries, fighting procedures and citizenship rules underwent a major restructuring—a reformulation of tactics and a redistribution of honors known as the hoplite revolution.[47] I now propose to extend my political interpretation of dramatic costume to the evidence, fragmentary as it is, for late seventh- and sixth-century costumed choruses, associating that evidence with just such issues of military manhood and its deviations.

Archaic Costume

Our earliest representations of costumed dancers from the seventh and sixth centuries are found in Athens, Korinth, Boiotia, and Sparta. On several cups from Attika (figs. 2.13, 2.14, 2.15) dated to about 585–565, the raised feet and gesturing arms indicate dancing; the padding at the stomach and rump is unmistakable and has led to this type being called "padded dancers."[48] The

to democratic feeling, such that the herm could then be taken over and exploited on a large scale by the Kleisthenic democracy. In either case, what for our purposes is significant is that the herm could be taken over, appropriated by the fuller democracy, just as modern political symbols in our world can become sites of disputation and quarrels over who owns them—witness the American flag in the era of the Vietnam war or in the period after 9/11.

47. The "hoplite revolution," as it has come to be known, continues to be a hotly debated topic. For good overviews of the subject, see Raaflaub 1997 and 1993; for a defense of the "hoplite reform" against the arguments of Latacz 1977, see Snodgrass 1993a.

48. Paris, Musée du Louvre, inv. E742; Athens, National Archaeological Museum, inv. 528; Berlin, Antikensammlung, Staatliche Museen, inv. 1966.17. Compare the vase in Taranto, Museo Archeologico Nazionale di Taranto, inv. 50677, also from Athens, attributed to the C Painter; the padding is a matter of interpretation. For detailed discussion of these vases, especially their depiction of clothing/padding and dance/gestures, see T. Smith

FIGURE 2.13. Black-figure Attic cup, showing padded dancers. Attributed to the KY Painter, 575–565 BCE. Louvre Museum, Paris, inv. E742. © RMN-Grand Palais / Art Resource, NY. Photo credit: Maurice and Pierre Chuzeville.

FIGURE 2.14. Black-figure Attic cup, showing padded dancers, c. 575 BCE. National Archaeological Museum, Athens, inv. 528. © Hellenic Ministry of Culture and Sports/Hellenic Organization of Cultural Resources Development (HOCRED). Photo credit: National Archaeological Museum, Athens.

dancers are wearing body suits, but evidently not masks.[49] Unfortunately, we have virtually no literary tradition to help us interpret these vases. I suggest that the fatness of the dancers, conveyed by their padding, makes sense as

2010: 35–40, 52–56, 63–66; Rothwell 2007: ch. 1. See also the useful discussions in Csapo and Miller 2007.

49. T. Smith 2010: 35 observes that there are a very few vases on which "male dancers at times appear with frontal faces, resembling satyrs; however these are the only examples in which the wearing of a mask seems feasible."

FIGURE 2.15. Detail from a black-figure Attic colonette-krater, showing padded dancers around a wine cauldron. Attributed to the KY Painter, c. 575 BCE. Antikensammlung, Staatliche Museen, Berlin, inv. 1966.17. Photo credit: bpk Bildagentur / Antikensammlung, Staatliche Museen, Berlin / Johannes Laurentius / Art Resource, NY.

a portrayal of the anti-athletic and the unmilitary—in short, the deliberate negation of the civic ideal.[50] Note that the phallos, so prominent in the agricultural and primitivist interpretations of Greek drama, is absent.[51]

Consider also a magnificent Spartan cup, attributed to the Rider Painter, organized in three horizontal bands: noble characters at the top, a cockfight in the middle, and padded dancers below (fig. 2.16).[52]

Padded dancers may happen to crop up in greater numbers on Archaic vases from Korinth, which has led to them often being referred to as "Korinthian padded dancers," but in fact the type is proportionately just as frequent in Sparta and is found in many other places. Phalloi sometimes occur on these vases, but the distinctly drawn padding is the essential trait. Again, there is no literary tradition of any kind to guide us in interpreting these figures.[53]

50. Isler-Kerényi 2007: 84; Carpenter 2007: 41 confirm this point.

51. Also observed by Foley 2000: 276–77.

52. Taranto, Museo Archeologico Nazionale di Taranto, inv. 20909. Pelagatti 1957: 36–39.

53. Green 2007; T. Smith 2007: 66; Carpenter 2007; and Rothwell 2007 all provide useful discussions of the uncertainties here.

FIGURE 2.16. Black-figure cup from Sparta, showing padded dancers in the lower register and a cockfight in the middle register. Attributed to the Rider Painter, c. 550 BCE. National Archaeological Museum, Taranto, inv. 20909. © National Archaeological Museum of Taranto.

A second body of material that might plausibly be linked with pre- or proto-dramatic representations of the human form is found from about the same time at the temple of Artemis Wortheia in Sparta.[54] It consists of clay masks—some are small, but others are almost life-size, and some have the apertures for eyes and mouth opened as if for actual use. The fact that not all the eyes, mouths, and noses are pierced, however, shows that at least some of these masks are votive copies, presumably of masks that were actually worn. They fall into two broad types: first, the idealized faces of warriors and youths—the warriors with full beard and helmet, the youths having neither beard nor helmet (figs. 2.17,

54. Worthasia appears to be the oldest spelling found on inscriptions, gradually succeeded by Worthaia, Wortheia, Bortheia, and finally (in Roman days) Ortheia: Woodward 1919–21: 117; Jucker and Risch 1979: 27. For a discussion of the extent of the cult of Artemis Ortheia, see Wide 1898: 113; Dawkins 1929. The masks are found partly below (300+ fragments) and partly above (3,000+ fragments) a layer of sand deposited to level the ground for a major rebuilding: that sand layer was dated by the British excavators to about 600 BCE, by Boardman to about 570/560, and by Catling to about 600/590. Boardman 1963; Catling 1977: 42.

FIGURE 2.17. Mask from Sparta, showing a young male warrior, date uncertain. Sparta Archaeological Museum, Sparta, no inventory number. Ephorate of Antiquities of Lakonia—Regional Office. © Hellenic Ministry of Culture and Sports/Archaeological Resources Fund. Photo credit: Sarah Brucia Breitenfeld.

2.18);[55] second, various sorts of nonideal faces—some grotesques, partly animal, many of them wrinkled seniors, probably old women (fig. 2.19).[56]

55. Sparta, Sparta Archaeological Museum, no inventory number (Dawkins 1929, plate 53, no. 2); Sparta, Sparta Archaeological Museum, inv. 12.

56. Sparta, Sparta Archaeological Museum, inv. 1 (Dawkins 1929, plate 47, no. 1). Guy Dickins, in his chapter in Dawkins 1929 on the masks from the sanctuary, divided them into seven types. J.-P. Vernant, however, noted that "a sharp dividing line separates two kinds of masks and clearly opposes them. On one side, the figures of men, adolescent or

FIGURE 2.18. Mask from Sparta, showing the lower half of a young man's face, date uncertain. Sparta Archaeological Museum, Sparta, inv. 12. Ephorate of Antiquities of Lakonia—Regional Office. © Hellenic Ministry of Culture and Sports/Archaeological Resources Fund. Photo credit: Sarah Brucia Breitenfeld.

For the purposes of our investigation, it is interesting not only that this group of masks as a whole reveals the same broad contrast of ideal and non-ideal facial types as is later found in tragedy and comedy, but also that the serious faces are all male and military. Jane Carter has tried to interpret them in the light of Near Eastern parallels and to see them as reenacting a fight between a hero and a monster, but the division into men and ephebes for the

mature, bearded or unbearded, representing warriors in their 'normal' aspect as *kouroi* and *andres* . . . ; on the other, figures which, contrasting with the regular models of the young man and the adult, present a varied range of departures or deviations expressing ugliness, old age, monstrosity, horror, the grotesque" (Vernant 1991: 226).

FIGURE 2.19. Mask from Sparta, showing a grotesque, possibly an old woman, 600–570 BCE. Sparta Archaeological Museum, Sparta, inv. 1. Ephorate of Antiquities of Lakonia—Regional Office. © Hellenic Ministry of Culture and Sports/Archaeological Resources Fund. Photo credit: Sarah Brucia Breitenfeld.

serious masks suggests to me that we should think rather of a ceremony in which that distinction was prominent.[57] As it happens, we have a secure liter-

57. J. Carter 1987. The masks described by Carter as grotesquely furrowed demons may equally well be seen as very wrinkled old women. That some of the "old women" have a bit of beard and whiskers is not untrue to life (J. Carter 1987: 356). Pollux 4.104

ary tradition about the Artemis Wortheia shrine, testifying to the existence there of rites of passage for boys, who had to endure whipping to prove their manhood while the priestess held the statue up to watch them.[58] That does not automatically tell us, to be sure, what kind of scripts were followed by the persons who wore these masks, but it does set up an environment in which an interpretation of these protodramatic masks in terms of the poetics of manhood is eminently reasonable.[59]

For a third body of early dramatic representations, we return to Athens and the years 560 to 480 BCE. This series was first discussed as relevant to the animal choruses of Aristophanes' comedies by Smith in 1881 and Poppelreuter in 1893. It is often referred to as a series of "animal chorus" vases.[60] Smith and Poppelreuter were basing their description on just three instances: a red-figure khous showing bird-men in full feather; an oinokhoe with wattled, bird-faced men wrapped in cloaks; and an amphora with boys riding on men dressed as horses. But now that the series has expanded to include some seventeen vases, all showing strangely dressed choruses, mostly led by an *aulos*-player, it appears that what ties them together is something more specific than the idea of animal choruses.[61] The birds are not just any birds but specifically fighting cocks; the horse-riders are cavalrymen. The formula for the series seems rather to be the combination of something military with something preposterous or playful, such as warriors riding on dolphins or ostriches. A stronger connection between Aristophanic comedy and an item in this series is furnished by

---

mentions a Lakonian dance to Artemis and Apollo called *baryllika*, performed by women, and Hesykhios cites a similar word, *bryllikhistai*, as designating "men who put on ugly women's masks and sing hymns." Another entry in Hesykhios, whose text is corrupt, seems to identify *brydalikha* as a Spartan word for ugly and funny female masks worn by men in women's clothing. As usual, we must cross our fingers and hope that textual and mental inconcinnities are not leading us into a quagmire of confusion, but it appears that the Spartan celebration of Artemis (and Apollo?) was on record as featuring choral performances by men masquerading as comic old ladies. There may also have been a real women's dance called *baryllika*, which the masked and costumed men who were called *bryllikhistai* parodied.

58. Xen., *Lak.* 2.9; Plut., *Thes.* 31, *Inst. Lac.* 40, *Lyk.* 18; Paus. 3.16.7–17.1, 8.23.11; Them., *Or.* 21.

59. Lonsdale 1993: 159 notes, "The discovery of grotesque masks at the sanctuary of Artemis Orthia as well as at Tiryns has led scholars to postulate a ritual struggle between young males and a masked dancer."

60. C. Smith 1881; Poppelreuter 1893: 6–22. For a recent, and different, interpretation, see Rothwell 2007, esp. ch. 2, who provides a thorough discussion of these vases and who argues that they are not clearly associated with any particular ritual context; rather, he sees them as congruent with the development of symposia. Green 2007: 101–4 is also skeptical of any link to tragedy or comedy. Even so, the element of military parody in the images remains relevant to the argument advanced here about the social meanings of the contrast between the civic male ideal and its opposite.

61. Csapo 2015: 87 notes that the term is insufficient; he proposes to call them "komos vases."

FIGURE 2.20. Black-figure Attic oinokhoe, showing men with apparently large erect phalloi under their cloaks, c. 510 BCE. Martin von Wagner Museum, Würzburg, inv. L344. © Martin von Wagner Museum, The University of Würzburg. Photo credit: P. Neckermann.

a black-figure oinokhoe from about 510 (fig. 2.20), showing warriors whose cloaks cover something long and extended in front of them.[62] Toward the end of *Lysistrata*, Spartan and Athenian emissaries come on stage looking like this, in the ultimate throes of suffering from their wives' sex strike. A jolly skyphos

62. Würzburg, Martin von Wagner Museum, inv. L344.

FIGURE 2.21. Black-figure skyphos from Tanagra (Thebes), showing old men marching with torches, c. 480 BCE. Archaeological Museum of Thebes, Thebes, inv. 64.342. © Hellenic Ministry of Culture and Sports—Ephorate of Antiquities of Boeotia—Hellenic Organization of Cultural Resources Development (HOCRED).

from about 480, one of the latest in the series, has white-haired old men running with torches on one side and hand-standing on the other (fig. 2.21; only one side of the vase is shown here).[63] There is nothing animal about them: we might think of them as spry or rejuvenated veterans.

The only framework we have for understanding what kind of Athenian performances were represented by these fantasy military vases is provided by two facts: at one end of the historical sequence, the *Marmor Parium* records that a prize for comedy was awarded in Athens from some time before Peisistratos' reign—some time, that is, in the 560s—which is the period of the earliest of these vases; at the other end, Edward Capps has reconstructed an inscription (*IG* II^2 2323) that shows that comedy began to be financed by the democratic state in 486, which is the decade of the last of these vases.[64] It appears that both tragedy and comedy in the sixth century were essentially aristocratic

63. Thebes, Archaeological Museum of Thebes, inv. 64.342, which dates this cup to the end of the sixth century BCE.

64. *Marmor Parium* (*FGrHist* 239A39): "[x years] from the date at which a [kho]r[os of] kōmō[idoi] was established in Athens, the men of Ikaria being the [fir]st to perf[orm], Sousariōn being the inventor, and the prize at first established was a wicker basket of dried figs and a measure of wine" (Capps 1904). This text has recently been discussed by Csapo 2015: 90–91. Csapo points out that the text is uncertain in many places; the restoration of Athens as the place where the comic choruses were instituted may well be wrong, and the text as we have reconstructed it seems at odds with the later entry on the *Marmor Parium* concerning Thespis (*Marmor Parium* 58–59, *IG* XII 5, 444).

entertainments that, in the fifth century, were taken over by the democracy in stages—first tragedy, then comedy as well—and that both the serious and playful modes of representing the body politic antedate the full democracy and were ultimately incorporated into its series of self-representations.[65]

The Shape of the Theater

We might see a trace of this shift toward democracy in the design of the orchestra, which in the earliest surviving Attic theater, that at Thorikos from the late sixth or early fifth century, is not circular but rectangular or trapezoidal. The area contains not only a long, straight grandstand rounded at one end and angled at the other but also a temple of Dionysos located in a position analogous to that in the City theater in Athens.[66] The earliest excavators of the City theater were guided in their reconstructions by the Roman architect Vitruvius' description of the typical Greek theater (in his day) as having a circular orchestra. The famous theaters at Epidauros and elsewhere lent support to the inherently powerful idea of a perfectly rounded dancing area. But the stone remains now in Athens are mainly from the Lykourgan rebuilding of the theater in the late fourth century.[67] Earlier building on the site can only be reconstructed when it was done in stone, and it appears that the previous structures there were mainly wooden and gave way quite gradually to stone replacements, in phases lasting over two centuries. Csapo's analysis of the leasing of theater operations in the fifth century makes it clear that the fifth-century theater in Athens (as elsewhere) contained a relatively small seating area, on which wooden benches were constructed for the dramatic festivals.[68]

At the City theater, in any case, the few traces of an archaic sublevel that are plausibly related to the oldest dancing area are not evenly rounded in a continuous arc: one segment forms a straight line, the other an unevenly

65. Csapo 2015 has challenged the common belief in a sixth-century origin for Attic drama. He argues that although the Dionysiac procession seems to have flourished in the sixth century, and may well have featured brief dithyrambic songs at various stops on the procession, nothing like the extended narrative directed at a focused audience can be seen before the end of the sixth century, after the reforms of Kleisthenes. See especially Csapo 2015: 82, 93, 97–98, 106–7. Csapo's contentions are intriguing and may, if accepted, alter some of the arguments advanced in this chapter; they also, however, oppose what is for now the prevailing understanding of the early evolution of Attic drama.

66. From the Attic regional theaters at Ikaria and Rhamnous, dating to the fifth century, only front-row seats survive, but these are placed in a straight line, evidently defining the front side of a rectangular orchestra (Gebhardt 1974: 434–36).

67. Wurster 1979 provides an excellent summary of the state of the questions concerning the theater.

68. Csapo 2007: 96–100. [Winkler was early in realizing that the fifth-century theater had a rectangular (or trapezoidal) orchestra; his conclusions here have been repeatedly confirmed by the work of Csapo, Wilson, and others.]

rounded line.[69] Either or both of those foundation lines could be interpreted as part of an orchestra that had the form of an irregular rectilinear figure, like the old orchestra at Thorikos.[70] In the late fifth century, the Athenians constructed new chambers for the Council. The Old Bouleuterion had rectangular seating; the seating in the New one was semicircular (Rhodes 1972). The date when the orchestra and seating of the City theater went circular is harder to determine, but it had certainly happened by the late fourth century, when the massive Lykourgan building program petrified the entire complex and made it permanent for us to see today.[71] At any rate, so far from being the almost mystically primitive shape of a Greek dance floor, the circular orchestra now appears to be a later contrivance, obscuring for us the earlier nature and function of quasi-military dancing on four-cornered fields of action.[72]

If we were to speculate on the attraction of a circular orchestra, we might say that one of its features is that it gives an equally good view of the dancing to all in the audience—right, left, and center. A semicircular seating area surrounding it also enables the members of the audience to view one another. These are democratic principles, and the Athenians organized their seating in a way that showed the structure of the Kleisthenic democracy, divided into ten tribes, as well as the fundamental equality of all its qualified participants. The layout of the auditorium formed (at least ideally) a kind of map of the civic corporation, with its various tensions and balances.[73]

69. The two segments are of different material and may not have been part of the same structure. See the confirming arguments of Csapo 2007: 99; and Goette 2007: 116–21. Goette 2007 provides a detailed reconstruction of the fifth-century theater from the existing archaeological evidence, which is admittedly scant.

70. Perikles installed at least some stone seating for dignitaries. Pöhlmann 1981 (esp. 140–45) argues from the shape of these stones that they must have been arranged in a straight line, marking the edge of a more or less right-angled orchestra. Dinsmoor 1951 tried to save the possibility of a circular orchestra by reconstructing the blocks in a polygon enclosing the circle. See also Dilke 1948, 1950; Ashby 1988. As Csapo 2007: 99 puts it, "Thus, the Classical auditorium was constrained by a straight face on the south and a straight back on the north. When this evidence is combined with comparative evidence from other fifth- and early fourth-century theatres, all of which are trapezoidal or rectilinear, the case for a trapezoidal *theatron* for the fifth-century theatre of Dionysos seems conclusive." See Csapo 2007: 99 n. 20 for relevant bibliography. Lech 2009b: 223 adduces scant but intriguing literary evidence for the existence at Athens of a "rectangular/trapezoidal *theatron* [grandstand] constructed of wooden benches (*ikria*)" as late as 424 BCE.

71. As Csapo 2007: 106 points out, "We know of no circular theatres until the stone theatres of Lykurgos at Athens, Epidaurus, and Megalopolis."

72. Not that there was no circular dancing in early times: Tölle 1964.

73. Ober 2008 demonstrates that the Athenian democracy spent considerable resources, beginning early in the fifth century, building civic buildings that were "inward looking." He suggests that the function of this architectural preference may have been to promote civic interaction resulting in "substantial net gains in common knowledge" (203–6; quotation on 205).

The fundamental contrast was that between the internal competition of tribe against tribe, which is mirrored on other levels of Athenian society by the always vigorous competition of individuals and households, and the equally strong, insistent ethic of honoring and obeying legitimate authority, so that the *polis* as a whole would display a united front against its enemies. These two vectors of civic manliness cross at a balance-point that is a locus of no little anxiety, particularly since the unit of intra-Athenian competition, the tribe, is also the unit of military organization.[74] In describing the concerns that were written into the physical organization of the audience, we will at the same time be characterizing the expectations of that audience, its readiness to perceive certain messages eliciting its sympathy and anxiety—in the language of Aristotle's *Poetics*, *eleos* (pity) and *phobos* (fear). Ultimately, this will explain why the city's youngest warriors were placed precisely at the cross-hairs of the powerful contrasting forces of competitiveness and solidarity, tribal rivalry and civic unity.

Consider first the seating of the ten tribes. Three statue bases found at the feet of three of the thirteen seating sections (*kerkides*, or "wedges") correspond to the traditional order of the ten tribes, assuming that the central wedge was that of the *Boulē* (Council) and the two outermost wedges were assigned to noncitizens, perhaps to citizen wives.[75] The statue bases are of Hadrianic date in the early second century CE and are located at the feet of the first, sixth, and eighth wedges (as one looks from the orchestra to the audience). Of course, the number of tribes did not remain constant over the years, and the different revisions to them may also be interpreted in the light of theater and assembly seating. Changes to the tribes were made in 307, 224, 201 BCE and in 126 CE. An interesting feature of these rearrangements is that the added tribes are placed sometimes at the beginning of the list (Antigonas

74. Ridley 1979.

75. Seating: *DFA* 270. Tribal seating in the theater was first suggested by Pickard-Cambridge in his revision of Haigh (see Haigh 1907: 337 and n. 5). Of the two theaters at Peiraieus, the one still visible, at Zea, also has thirteen wedges (Arias 1934). It is only in the lower auditorium that the seating sections numbered a full thirteen, hence only in that portion was the political structure of the city mapped.

On citizen-wives in general, see Patterson 1987. The perennial question of whether women attended the theatrical performances is hard to answer. I believe that they did, on the basis of Aristophanes' *Skēnas katalambanousai*—if it means *Women Occupying the Stage*, a thoroughly Aristophanic conception—because a fragment of that play represents a woman speaking of her *syntheatria*, fellow-spectatrix. The audience is always addressed, by Aristophanes and Menander, as composed of men in various age-classes, which means that the notional or proper audience is one of men. But women, aside from the priestesses in the front row of thrones, may have sat in the outer two wedges and even more likely in the higher regions, where there were fewer than thirteen seating wedges. At all events, their presence was no doubt socially marginal and physically restricted. On this question, see Goldhill 1994 and Henderson 1991, both of whom survey the ancient evidence with a critical eye. D. Carter 2011a: 50 makes a strong case for women being in the audience; see his n. 15 for bibliographic references.

and Demetrias), sometimes at the end (Attalis), and twice in the very center (Ptolemais, Hadrianis).[76]

One can understand the conservativism that consists in making additions at the beginning or at the end of the traditional list, which keeps the previous order internally untouched. But why, on two occasions, did the Athenian body politic rearrange itself with a new unit in the center? On both occasions, it was an increase from twelve tribes to thirteen, and the additional tribe is located as number seven on the new list, dividing the previous twelve tribes into two groups of six. I propose that the rationale for placing the new tribe in this position is that, even though it may have caused a greater disturbance of the *polis* operations governed by tribal order, it produced a minimal disturbance to the seating plan in a thirteen-wedge theater—if we assume that the central wedge in the ten- or twelve-tribe system had been occupied by the members of the *Boulē*.[77] Much earlier evidence pertinent to seating exists in the form of lead theater tickets, whose spelling conventions and letter forms put them at least as early as the early part of the fourth century BCE, if not earlier. These tickets are marked with tribal names.[78]

If the citizens are seated—at least *grosso modo*—by tribal affiliation,[79] the original ten tribal blocks would inevitably have taken on the character of cheering sections during the dithyrambic competition, which unlike comedy and tragedy was a competition among the tribes. Each of the ten tribes entered a chorus of fifty men in the men's dithyrambic contest and another chorus of fifty boys in the boys' contest. The two contests therefore represented a perfect homology with the *Boulē*, the Council that administered the daily political business of the city, since it was composed of five hundred men, fifty from each tribe. That Council had a special block of seats in the theater[80] (as in later times the ephebes did too), and, to make the analogy complete, a prize

76. For corroborating evidence from elsewhere in the Greek world, see Chaniotis 2007: 60, who describes theaters from Makedonia and Kaunos that had tribal names inscribed onto lower blocks of seats, and who paraphrases an inscription from Samos: "A Samian decree (IG XII 6, 172 A ll.3–8) instructs the *prytaneis* to invite the members of the assembly, which convened in the theatre, to take their seats there according to the subdivisions of the citizen-body (*chilyastyes*); signs were to be set up in order to determine the place reserved for each *chilyastys*. . . . When citizens, ephebes, or young men attended processions, they did so divided into *phylai*."

77. One inscribed stone from the late-fifth century theater "subsequently built upside down into the outer western wall of the auditorium (where it may now be seen) bears the inscription *bolēs ypēreton* ['servants of the Council']" (Pickard-Cambridge 1946: 20, where the stone is illustrated).

78. On the tickets, see *DFA* 270–72; Jentoft-Nilsen 1982.

79. I do not want to insist that everyone always sat where they were supposed to sit, only that provisions existed for each tribe to have its own wedge.

80. Ar., *Birds* 794 and scholion (=*Souda*, s.v. *Bouleutikos*); Pollux 4.122; Hesykhios, s.v. *Bouleutikon*; Trugaios at Ar., *Peace* 887 addresses the *Boulē* and *prutaneis* directly as audience members; the scholiast on *Peace* 882 confirms the seating arrangement.

was awarded at the end of the year to that tribe of Councilors who had best conducted the city's business.

The panel of ten judges for all events was selected on the basis of tribal membership, one judge from each tribe, and as a matter of course they were carefully sworn not to show favoritism. Of the ten ballots cast, five were selected randomly to count as votes, while five were discarded. The recorded instances of bribery and cheating show that the oath and other such safeguards were necessary.[81] Isokrates claims that a man named Pythodoros had tampered with the ballots naming judges for the dramatic competition. More directly, Demosthenes maintains in his *Against Meidias* that, when Demosthenes was sponsoring a dithyrambic chorus, Meidias corrupted his chorus trainer, bribed the Arkhon, turned the chorus-members against him, disrupted the judges while they took the oath of impartiality, blocked the normal entranceways for the chorus, and ultimately bribed the judges—before physically assaulting Demosthenes himself.[82] In addition, as Wilson points out, the texts of comedy contain frequent denunciations of bribery and corruption, but on occasion comic characters themselves offer bribes (*Ekkl.* 1140–43; *Birds* 1102–7; *Clouds* 1115–20). While these "bribes" cannot be taken at face value (the chorus of the *Clouds* offers to keep the judges' fields well-watered in times of drought), they suggest that the Athenian *dēmos* understood that bribery and corruption were possible risks of intense tribal competition.[83]

In short, the lateral spread of the auditorium formed an axis of competition among the ten citizen groups, with the *Boulē* as its representatives and mediators at the center. But here, too, considerations of democratic equality were balanced by interests of wealth and position. The vertical axes up and down the blocks displayed relative prestige. *Prohedria*, front-row seating, was one of the highest honors that could be bestowed on benefactors and special friends of the city: it is attested in numerous decrees—and in one funny story about Demosthenes.[84] If the democratic *polis* is organized on principles of internal balance and competition, it does not entirely ignore the preeminence

81. See *DFA* 96–101 for a general discussion of the judging, along with evidence of bribery and corruption. A more cautious treatment of the evidence is provided by Wilson 2000, 98–102.

82. Isok. 17.33–34; Dem. 21.17–18.

83. Wilson 2000: 102: "The genre which frequently rages against the operation of bribery, threats and similar abuse in the political realm ludically turns those very modes of action to its own ends, for the virtuous purpose of making its vision of political rectitude triumphant before the city."

84. The inscriptional evidence is surveyed in ch. 4 of Maass 1972. See also Pöhlmann 1981. The Demosthenes anecdote can be found in Aiskhines, *Against Ktesiphon* 76. When the Athenians took over control of Delos in the mid-second century BCE, they transferred the announcement of civic honors from the Apollonia to the Dionysia: Sifakis 1967: 14.

of its own best citizens, whether they hold office by lot or have a traditional family claim to precedence.[85]

The entire audience is thus seated and disposed in a way that demonstrates its corporate manliness as a *polis* to be reckoned with, comprising individuals who are vigilant to assert excellence against their competitors and equals—namely, the other members of the democratic city (tribe versus tribe)—but who are still ranked to show orders of precedence; by accepting their placement in the theater according to acknowledged degrees of excellence, the audience members affirm their due willingness to honor and obey the legitimate authority of their superiors: the laws and the city's rulers. In sum, the city sees itself and shows itself as an entity that maintains all the traditional forms of heroic manhood, even as it now spreads them out over a larger population of male citizens.

This tension between egalitarianism and hierarchy is what we find in the social articulation of the theatrical festivals as a whole. Just as dithyrambic competitions are structured, like the democratic *Boulē*, by the division of tribe, so tragedy and comedy, which date back to an earlier period and constitute older, predemocratic modes of civic play, dispense with the tribal system and feature a hierarchical distinction between better and worse kinds of people—along with their taut or slack bodies—as well as between true manly excellence and its radical subversion or caricature.

Together, then, tragedy and comedy present the sort of social contrast between better and worse, or stronger and weaker, that is also visible in the vertical as opposed to the lateral axes of the theater. The democratic *polis* does not reject its best and brightest: on the contrary, it engages their services—we may even say it features them as the star attraction of the festival, both in seating arrangements and as subjects of the drama—and it uses tragedy and comedy, those older traditions of representing and parodying *andragathiē*, as a device for enhancing its own self-awareness.[86]

It was not only in the City theater that seating was organized according to the division of tribes. A similar seating arrangement into ten wedges for the ten tribes seems to have existed for the Pnyx, in which the full citizen Assembly met four times a month.[87] The homology between the citizens assembled in

85. On the tension between democratic and elitist tendencies in the social and political culture of Classical Athens, see Ober 1989 and, more recently, Morris 1996, Kurke 1999, Kistler 2004, Duplouy 2006, Fouchard 2010. Griffith 1995 and 2011 discusses how the texts of the Athenian tragedies continued to negotiate this conflict.

86. See Griffith 1995 and 2011, Burian 2011, and D. Carter 2011a.

87. McDonald 1943: 71–75; Staveley 1972: 81–82; Kolb 1981: 93; *contra* Hansen 1977 (but citing Aiskhines 2.64–68, where two members of tribes contiguous in the official order are seated adjacent to each other) and 1982. My argument does not require that all citizens always sat in the wedge assigned to their tribe, either in the Pnyx or in the theater, only that the number of wedges in both cases was notionally related to the configuration of the

the theater and in the Pnyx should be pressed. Some Assembly meetings were actually held in the theater. Of the two theaters in Athens' harbor town Peiraieus, the one at Mounikhia, which is now entirely covered by modern buildings, was used for some Assemblies, particularly in times of crisis, according to Thoukydides and Lysias.[88] The other at Zea is still visible, and its auditorium is divided into thirteen wedges. Theater attendance therefore can be seen as a properly political event. At the Great Panathenaia, the money paid out to citizens to attend the festival was distributed by deme and was tied to registration on the deme census lists (Dem. 44.37). The same procedure for distributing attendance monies presumably held good for the Dionysia.[89]

Recent work has confirmed just how embedded was the tragic festival itself in the political and military life of the city. For one thing, as Wilson has argued, the Dionysia required a level of civic expenditure that exceeded the financial resources of even the wealthiest tyrants.[90] The texts of the plays themselves, moreover, allowed for a complex structure of debate and questioning of civic roles that is quite unlike anything exhibited by the choral songs presented at, say, the Theban Daphnephoria, in which "the performance of the Theban chorus was . . . very much a family affair, and during its tenure of this choral honour that family in some sense 'stood for' the wider community."[91] No such appropriation of the chorus by a clan was possible in Athens.

Instead, the dramatic competitions in Athens were organized in such a way as to give a starring role to the *polis* itself. As Simon Goldhill points out, before the performance of the tragedies at the Dionysia, the audience saw a parade of the city's war-orphans, who would be cared for by the state, followed by a display of the year's tribute from Athens' military allies (which is to say, other members of the Delian League).[92] If the tribute and the presence of the city's friends represent her active military alliances, the war orphans who are ready to become soldiers in their fathers' places inevitably bring to mind the city's battles, both past and future.[93]

---

citizen body into ten tribes. The argument for tribal (and trittys) seating has been extended to include Pnyx I and II by Stanton and Bicknell 1987, who notice other tribally seated theaters on pp. 86–87.

88. Thouk. 8.93.1, 3; Lys. 13.32, 55; cf. Xen., *Hell.* 2.4.32. See Chaniotis 2007 for a discussion of ritual and political uses of theaters throughout the Greek world, drawing largely from Hellenistic and Roman-era evidence.

89. Csapo 2007: 100–103 discusses the evidence for a public dole to attend the City Dionysia, which later authors ascribe to Perikles.

90. Wilson 2011: 23–26, 32.

91. Wilson 2011: 24, drawing on the work of Kurke 2007. On Greek tragedy as democratic in its discursive structure, see also Burian 2011.

92. Goldhill 1990: 101–2.

93. The city's military preparedness was also advertised by the ten generals (one per tribe), who offered a ceremonial libation at the beginning of the performances. Plutarch attests to this practice and establishes an early date for it (468 BCE) in a story about a

This description may make Athens' dramatic festival sound like a West Point graduation ceremony, which is not my intention, but it is nonetheless important to underscore the fact that the *toto caelo* difference we experience between the military realm and the theatrical, between marching to war and going to a play, did not apply to the City Dionysia. In the *Frogs*—to cite a caricature whose degree of truth will later become apparent—Aristophanes presents Aiskhylos as claiming that his *Seven against Thebes* made every man in the audience lust for battle (1022). On that account, at least, tragedy is a martial art.

Bodies, Costumes, Auditoria, Politics

What I have tried to do in this chapter is to question the two assumptions that are usually made about phallic imagery in ancient Athens generally and in the dramatic performances staged by the Athenians particularly—namely, that it is "primitive" (which is not the same thing as saying that it is early) and that it is bound up with fertility.[94] Instead, I have tried to distinguish and to specify two different significations, or fields of meaning, of the phallos in ancient Athens: an elitist or hierarchical signification, in which the obtrusiveness or unobtrusiveness of the represented phallos is correlated, respectively, with excess and restraint, grotesque abandon and manly control, unmilitary slackness and heroic discipline, comedy and tragedy; and, by contrast, a democratic or egalitarian signification, visible in the herm, in which the phallos serves as a marker of the notional equality of all the male householders and citizens of Athens. Moreover, I have tried to show how these two different sets of meanings, with their implied tensions between aristocracy and democracy, elitism and egalitarianism, were articulated, elaborated, and enacted in Athens in the staging of dramatic performances, both in the costuming of the players and in the seating of the spectators. My emphasis throughout has fallen on the political signification of the body—on the coding of the male body with social messages about class and status as well as gender. For it is by means of some such semiotic analysis of the politics of masculinity, I believe, that we may achieve a better anthropological understanding of Athenian drama.

---

competition so fierce that the Arkhon refused to select judges by the usual lot and instead persuaded the generals, who were present for their customary libation, to act as the panel: *Kimon* 8.7–9. This passage is discussed by Goldhill 1990: 100. On the generals' *prohedria* in the theater, see Ar., *Knights* 573–77, 702–4; *Thesm.* 832–35; Theophrastos, *Characters* 5.7; *IG* II^2 500.32–35.

94. If the latter were true, as Walter Burkert objects, why did Athenians put the *wrong end*—i.e., the base, not the head—of the phallos into the ground?

CHAPTER THREE

Scenarios of Risk

COCKFIGHTING AND *KINDUNOS*

WHEN THE ATHENIAN audience took its place in the theater for a dramatic festival, its seating arrangement reflected competing and complementary principles of manly excellence, balancing democratic rivalry among equals against an older, elitist order of hierarchical prestige in which heroic virtue contrasted with its comic opposite. Similar tensions played themselves out onstage before the eyes of the assembled citizen-spectators. Contemporary sources from Athens provide us with a uniquely eloquent image of this combative community defining and testing its own manhood at the Dionysia.

The image appears on the central throne in the front row of the theater (fig. 3.1).[1] On either side of that throne, where the priest of Dionysos sat to watch the performances of comedies and tragedies, there are relief carvings of winged youths readying their roosters for a cockfight. The carvings constitute one of only two known sculptures of a cockfight from the Classical period of ancient Greece (though cocks figure frequently in vase paintings, in both agonistic and erotic contexts). Why, then, do we find that sculpture here, in the theater? What, we may ask, do theater, young men, and cockfighting have to do with one another? Further inquiry into this question will reveal the cockfight to be one of the central and underrated topoi in the Athenian poetics of manhood.[2]

1. Line drawing by Kevin Boyer; Risom 1913, figs. 9–11; Bruneau 1965, no. 74, fig. 21; Maass 1972: 60–76, plate IIa.

2. See Csapo 2006–7 for a clear discussion with numerous illustrations, including a photograph of the throne shown in fig. 3.1. In addition to the points made here, Csapo demonstrates that cocks in Athens were particularly associated with ephebes as they made the transition to becoming hoplites; he also shows that defeated cocks could be associated in the Greek imagination with *kinaidoi*, the cultural opposite of a hoplite and the

FIGURE 3.1. Detail of the seat of the priest of Dionysos in the Theater of Dionysos in Athens. Original object late fourth century BCE. Line drawing by Kevin Boyer. © Kevin Boyer.

We can confirm that proposition by consulting another appearance of the same image, a dramatic one this time. The central *agōn* of Aristophanes' revised *Clouds* provides one of the clearest surviving examples from ancient Athens of a clash of philosophies over the proper education of young men. As we saw at the beginning of the previous chapter, the antagonists in this contest are two personified abstractions, "Stronger Speech" and "Weaker Speech": they stage a debate for the benefit of a youth, Pheidippides, each of them trying to convince him to subscribe to a particular pedagogical method. Stronger Speech is a traditionalist, concerned with producing another generation of men who could live up to the values and valor of the glorious Athenians of the past. Weaker Speech is a product of the new-fangled sophistry, guided by an explicitly self-interested ethic and prone to what we would call cultural relativism. Both are concerned with the best method of turning young Athenian men—the same group that I have identified as ephebes in a loose, informal sense—into full adult citizens.

anxiety-producing emblem of manhood gone wrong. In this latter observation, Csapo draws on the work of Winkler 1990c.

Stronger Speech begins with a description of the method of education that he prefers, hearkening back to a time when "temperance" or "self-restraint" (*sōphrosunē*) was the norm:

First, there was no need for the boys to say anything;
they went through the streets together, accompanied by kithara-music
and naked, even if it was snowing like oatmeal.
Then their teacher would teach them to memorize a song, and they
would not rub their thighs together. . . .
When sitting in the gymnasium, the boys had to cover their thighs
so that they would show nothing tormenting to those outside.
And when a boy stood up again, he would sweep the sand, and take
care
not to leave an image of his youthful beauty [*hēbē*] for his lovers.
And no boy would oil himself below the navel, back then, so that
soft dew grew on his privates and downy fuzz, as on peaches.
He would not go to his lover, concocting a pretty voice
nor pimping himself out with his eyes.
He was not allowed at dinner to choose the head of the radish,
nor to snatch dill or celery from his elders,
nor to eat fish nor giggle nor hold his feet crosswise.

(AR., *CLOUDS* 961–83)

Though a stern moralist of the old school, Stronger Speech appears to have something of a lascivious interest in the boys who would be educated under this system, as K. J. Dover noted, and his loving description of their genitals shows his pedagogical program to be motivated by more than philosophical principle.[3] But if his method of education is self-serving, it also is calculated to produce young men who are ideal *erōmenoi*—that is, both objects of adult male desire and future citizens of Athens. In his next brief tirade (985–86), in fact, Stronger Speech suggests that this is the method that gave rise to the men who fought at Marathon in 490 BCE.

Stronger Speech goes on to list the desirable results of his pedagogical principles, and to contrast them with the product of Weaker Speech's methods (here is the entire passage, whose opening lines will be familiar from the previous chapter):

If you do what I say
and pay careful attention,
you will always have

3. See Dover 1968: lxiv–lxvi and *ad* 977: "[I]t is as if a modern preacher, having thundered 'No girl ever wore trousers in those days!' continued, 'And sometimes you glimpsed the satiny flesh on the inside of her thighs.'"

a rippling chest, glowing skin,
broad shoulders, a tiny tongue,
a solid rump, and a teeny pee-pee;
but if you follow the modern practices, . . .
you will acquire
a sickly complexion, narrow shoulders,
a nothing chest, an enormous tongue,
spindly thighs and an immense subpoena,
and he [Weaker Speech] will convince you that everything shameful
is admirable, and that what is admirable is shameful
and on top of that he will fill you
with the anal inclinations [*katapugosunē*] of Antimakhos.

(AR., *CLOUDS* 1009–23)

In other words, Stronger Speech claims, his educational method will produce ideal young men, valorous citizen-soldiers of highly desirable male beauty; that of his opponent, frail weaklings who are also sexually passive.[4]

Weaker Speech responds, not with a set oration, but in the more sophistic form of a series of questions posed to his opponent. His initial arguments are deliberately specious and trivializing. Eventually he comes to his final point, namely that Stronger Speech should not object to those citizens of Athens who are "wide-assed" (*euruprōktos*)—that is, who have been sexually penetrated in their youth (or, possibly, since); indeed, as he causes Stronger Speech to realize, most of the members of the audience belong to this disreputable category. Stronger Speech, recognizing he is outnumbered, abandons his cloak and leaves the stage in a gesture of utter and complete surrender, declaring that he will desert to the side of "those who are screwed" (*kinoumenoi*). Pheidippides' father thereupon turns his son over to the victorious Weaker Speech, entrusting his offspring to the sort of education that, as he thinks, will help him win lawsuits (Ar., *Clouds* 1085–1110).

Such, then, is one of our most explicit, if comic, debates about the proper method of educating young men in Athens. While both participants in the debate prove to be ridiculous in one way or another, their comic bluster reveals the outlines of a duel between the idealized manhood of an unreal, nostalgic past and a form of weak, unattractive masculinity supposedly produced by modern educational methods—a duel disparagingly characterized by one of

4. The word *katapugōn* is of uncertain, and perhaps indeterminate, meaning. Literally it means "down the buttocks," and so may suggest a man who is interested in being anally penetrated. But, as Worman 2015: 212 argues, its use in comedy "covers quite wide-ranging notions of behavioral excess." Hubbard 2003: 84 n. 100 generally translates the word as "anal" and suggests that "[i]t seems to be used of both active and passive participants in anal sex." We know of no clear example of it being used of the penetrating partner.

the combatants as a choice between butch and femme. What is particularly interesting about this *agōn* for our present purposes is not only the words that were spoken in the course of it but also the manner in which it was performed. For when Aristophanes staged this contest, the abstract characters of Stronger Speech and Weaker Speech were costumed to look like fighting cocks.

This information has been transmitted to us by a scholiast writing in the late third or early second century BCE.[5] It has been confirmed by an image on an Attic vase from the late fifth century BCE, a near contemporary of the play.[6] On this vase, carefully analyzed by Oliver Taplin and Eric Csapo, two men dressed as fighting cocks gesticulate, facing each other, while an *aulos*-player stands between them. As Csapo notes, the vase-painter has indulged in some unnecessary anthropomorphism in representing this *agōn*: not only do both men in costume have visibly erect (hyperhuman) phalloi; the cocks' spurs have been represented as erect phalloi as well. This bit of gratuitous visual play was perhaps suggested by the fact that the word used to denote a cock's "spur," *kentron*, is also commonly used in Greek comedy to refer to a man's "prick."[7] In other words, we have both lexical and ceramic evidence to suggest that this famous scene from Aristophanes, a debate between an old moralist and a young sophist about how to produce good Athenian men, was presented to the Athenian audience as a literal cockfight, in both senses of the word.

Equally important in this context, though perhaps less visually arresting, is the image on the other side of the vase. There we see an ephebe receiving his armor, while his parents look on. As Csapo has proposed (developing a suggestion made in an earlier version of this chapter), the scene seems to be a variation on the more common depiction of a hoplite departing for battle in the presence of his parents or wife.[8] Though the decorative elements on different sides of Athenian vases need not be related, the correspondence here is irresistible: on side A, a representation of a theatrical scene about the

5. Scholium on Ar., *Clouds* 889, attributed to Aristophanes of Byzantium. See Csapo 2006–7: 20.

6. Attic red-figure kalyx-krater, c. 420 BCE: Naples, Museo Archeologico Nazionale di Napoli, inv. 205239 (formerly Malibu, J. Paul Getty Museum, inv. 82.AE.83, side A; online photo available at http://www.perseus.tufts.edu/hopper/artifact?name=malibu+82.ae.83&object=vase, accessed August 30, 2021). The vase was first proposed as representing the *Clouds* by Taplin 1987. Taplin retracted much of this argument in Taplin 1993: appendix 1. See the discussion in Revermann 2006: 217–18. Though J. R. Green has suggested that the scene here represents a choral action from the *Birds* (see Green 1985), Csapo argues convincingly that this cannot be a choral scene, and he makes a strong case for the *Clouds*. See Csapo 1993a: 1–7; 2006–7: 20–21 and nn. 2–3.

7. Csapo 1993a: 6 and nn. 21–22; 2006–7: 20–21.

8. See Csapo 1993a: 7–8 and plate 2a, who refers to a passage in Winkler 1990c: 41, which first outlined the argument now fully laid out in this chapter. Csapo 2006–7: 23 argues, further, that the usual "departing warrior" scene has been modified here to emphasize the youth of the ephebe: "The focus on the boy's youth, and the absence of a wife or child, strongly suggest that he is about to go to war for the first time."

education of young men; on side B, the depiction of an ephebe at the moment of his transition to manhood—that is, his graduation to the status of hoplite. The vase presents the perfect trifecta for rehearsals of manhood on the part of young citizen-warriors: cocks, theater, training.

Cocky Ephebes

In order to examine more closely the poetics of manhood outside the theater, not now in costumes and dancing and seating but in forms of behavior, let us consider a remarkable real-life drama that elaborates the image of combat inscribed in the cockfight and highlights its role in the self-definition of Athenian men. The first scene of this drama is set in one of the ephebes' encampments at Panakton, the second in the Agora one evening when a fight broke out, and its climax was reached in court. Our hero is a young Athenian ephebe named Ariston, assigned to guard duty at Panakton along with many others his age.

Panakton is an interesting place. In the Athenian ephebic oath, the young citizen-warriors swear not only by the great gods Zeus and Athena and Hestia and such, but also by the wheat and barley, plus the vines, figs, and olives of the countryside.[9] The identity of the fully socialized adult Greek male as a member of his *polis* rested not only on knowing and being integrated into the *polis* proper but also on knowing and cherishing the *khōra*, the agricultural countryside.[10] It is in the countryside that the young warriors train, particularly at the series of towers and forts dotted along the perimeter of Attika—Panakton, Eleutherai, Melainai, Oinoē. Such outposts for patrol-duty are sometimes called *peripolia* and the young soldiers stationed there *peripoloi*, since they patrol (*peripolein*) the countryside. These are mainly mountainous areas, rough and wild, the usual points of entry for enemy warriors or raiders, overlooking plains that are often disputed territory.[11] (Recall the old tale of the duel on the border, from chapter 1.)

9. The oath is quoted in chapter 1 at note 25. The ephebes at Dreros on Krete similarly swore by the Earth and Sky and fountains and rivers: *IC* I ix 1.31–36 (=Chaniotis 1996, text 7). The Athenian ephebic oath also invokes in its list of witnesses the *horoi tēs patridos*, "the boundaries of the fatherland." That was clearly a resonant theme. At the end of Euripides' *Elektra*, Elektra laments being exiled from "the border of her fatherland" (1314–15).

10. Osborne 1987: 145–49. In Xenophon's *Memorabilia*, Sokrates examines Glaukon (Plato's older brother), who wishes to be a leader of the Athenian state, though he is not yet twenty years old at the time of their conversation. In the course of discussing how Glaukon will benefit Athens, Sokrates presumes that he must know the current condition of the many guard-stations (*phulakai*) and guards (*phrouroi*) that Athens has. Glaukon, embarrassed, must admit that his rather sweeping opinions on the topic are not based on personal observation (Xen., *Mem.* 3.6.9–11).

11. Aiskhines 2.167 makes a strong connection between being an ephebe and being a *peripolos* (border guard): ἐκ παίδων μὲν γὰρ ἀπαλλαγεὶς περίπολος τῆς χώρας ταύτης ἐγενόμην δύ᾽ ἔτη ("for when I grew out of boyhood, I became a *peripolos* of the countryside for two years"). See Pélékidis 1962 for further examples.

Ariston and his mess-mates have pitched their tent and are busy about their exercises when a terrible commotion interrupts their work. Their slaves, who have been fixing a fire for dinner, come running to them, wailing and bloody and with a strange smell emanating from their clothes. It seems that the smoke from their fire drifted toward the neighboring tent, occupied by Konon's sons, wastrels who had been drinking from early in the day. These no-good ephebes, apparently annoyed by the fumes, roughed up Ariston's slaves, kicked over the utensils and chamber-pots, and as the ultimate insult did what men who have drunk a lot are ready and able to do: they urinated on the cowering slaves. When the sons of Konon would not listen to reason, Ariston and his mess-mates complained to the general, who gave the bad ephebes a dressing down. But later that night the offenders, undeterred, broke into Ariston's tent and started beating him up, making so much noise in the process that the general and the division commanders came over and stopped the fracas.

Scene 2 takes place back at Athens, some time afterward. Ariston is taking an evening walk in the Agora with a friend. One of Konon's sons sees them and goes to his father's house, where a drinking party is in progress. Konon, his son, and his cronies arrive in the Agora, accost Ariston, pin the arms of his friend, tear off Ariston's cloak, trip him, and throw him into the mud, kicking and beating him about the head until he has a split lip and can't open his eyes. Then, just as the sons had added insult to injury when they mistreated Ariston's slaves, so now Konon proceeds to crow, like a victorious rooster in a cockfight, and—encouraged by his friends—he actually flaps his bent elbows like wings.

Since the body of a democratic citizen is sacrosanct, Ariston is fully entitled to bring suit, which he does.[12] And so it is that we happen to know about this series of incidents. Our information comes from Demosthenes' fifty-fourth speech, commissioned by Ariston and written to be delivered by him in his role as prosecutor at a trial of Konon for assault. The great value of courtroom speeches is not that they give us the truth about real events. Ariston may have been lying about what happened, for all we know, or he may have suborned the witnesses who supported his version of the story. Rather, courtroom speeches provide us with conventional cultural images, the common clichés about propriety and impropriety in social behavior. Ariston's (or Demosthenes') task is to generate and mobilize a set of representations—in this case, a series of plausible, persuasive, and recognizable portraits of good and bad ephebes—that will command the assent of several hundred average citizens.

12. See Winkler 1990a: 48–49 and chapter 2 of this book at note 39. The trial takes place some two years later (Dem., *Against Konon* 3). The date of the speech is unknown, but Ariston's walking in the Agora might imply that the whole affair predated the building program of Lykourgos and the institution of the formal ephebate. The delay of the trial might suggest that there was at that time a ban, analogous to that reported by [Arist.], *Ath. Pol.* 42.5, on ephebes being involved in legal action, but see the instances cited in note 24, below.

To our dossier of cockiness we may now add the information provided by Lucian, writing some five hundred years later of course, and perhaps about a custom not yet established in the fifth century BCE—though he puts it in the mouth of Solon, the notional sixth-century founder of Athenian democracy. Explaining Athenian and Greek customs to the visiting Skythian sage Anakharsis, Solon says, "We stage competitions between quails and between cocks, and they are very popular. . . . By law all men of military age are required to attend and to watch the birds battling to their last breath" (*Anakharsis* 37). Lucian also tells us the meaning of these performances—namely, that they are designed to promote manly spirit: "[T]he souls of the audience are subtly infiltrated with an enthusiasm for facing dangers [*kindunoi*]." He does not say where in the city the official version of this bloody spectacle took place. Although we know that taverns and gambling shops were the scene of ordinary cockfights (Aiskh. 1.53), the cockfight to which Lucian alludes probably took place in the theater: Aelian, writing in the next generation after Lucian, records that it was an Athenian custom established after the Persian wars to hold a public cockfight in the theater on one day of the year (*Var. Hist.* 2.28). Aelian's account of the custom's civic significance is as follows. Themistokles, he says, was leading the troops against the barbarians when he happened to see two cocks fighting. He made the army stop in its tracks and said, "These birds are enduring great pain—not to defend their fatherland or their paternal gods or their ancestral tombs, not for glory or freedom or for the sake of their children—but simply because each wants not to be shown weaker than the other one and not to give ground to the other."[13]

Now, as I say, the staging of a cockfight for the edification of all citizen-soldiers may or may not have been a fifth-century practice. But whenever it was installed in the calendar of civic events—the carved throne for the priest of Dionysos in the theater might seem to take it back at least to the late fourth century, and the scene from the *Clouds* to 423 BCE—it was seamlessly woven into the texture of public representations of *andragathiē*. Even if it was not as ancient as Solon or Themistokles, the story of compelling citizen-soldiers to witness a cockfight does record the beating pulse of endangered and combative manhood. The comments of Lucian and Aelian on the cultural meaning of the cockfight, as a symbol of fierce determination not to yield in the face of danger (*kindunos*), provide us not only with a precious interpretation of the civic ideology embodied in that spectacle but also with the general program that should be read into all the many cocks and cockfights shown on black- and red-figure vases throughout the sixth and fifth centuries.[14] Cockfighting

13. Both of these examples are discussed briefly by Csapo 2006–7: 25.

14. Fighting-cocks are among the most common "courting gifts" on pots that depict paederastic courtship: see Lear and Cantarella 2008: 238 n. 40. But Parker 2015: 69–80 points out that mentions of courting gifts are almost nonexistent in Greek literature and

was manhood itself in action, its perfect butch apotheosis starkly opposed to its femme (or effeminate) other: as an unidentified comic playwright put this gendered contrast between assertiveness and surrender in a nutshell, "You'll never see a cock that is a *kinaidos*."[15]

With this context in mind, we can now return to Ariston's speech, which tells us several interesting things about cockiness in Athenian social life. His suit was not brought against the bad and too-cocky ephebes, who started the quarrel in the camp, but against their father, Konon—no youth, he, but a man over fifty, who made a spectacle of himself flapping his arms and crowing (Dem. 54.9). By this strategy, young Ariston shows the jury his good sense, his maturity, his tolerance. For cocky behavior is, like everything in the game of manliness, a complex entity. In some situations, such as facing danger in battle, it is a good thing; in others, such as assaulting an innocent fellow-citizen, it is bad.[16] For some social actors—young men spring to mind—it may be regarded as the excusable effervescence of their age. But for a dignified older gentleman, who should be setting a good example for his sons, it is shameful and actionable. Ariston goes quite far in making allowances for the youthful folly of Konon's sons, admitting that youth in itself, though it does not excuse outrageous behavior, may be a mitigating circumstance when it comes to judging such behavior at a trial. Drawing on what he assumes will be the defense's argument about the natural high spirits of youth, Ariston even informs us about bands of young Athenian toughs—youth gangs with terrifying names, who get drunk and fight over their favorite prostitutes. Unlike our urban gangs, however, these are wealthy young men of good family, the sons of *kalokagathoi* (14); families of this sort finance the city's festivals and fleet with their donations, their "liturgies." Hence, their sons are tempted to take liberties that would not be tolerated in more modestly placed youth.[17]

The names of these gangs, by the way, let us glimpse some of the complex underpinnings of Athenian masculinity. The gangs are called such things as *Triballoi* (39), *Ithyphalloi*, and *Autolekythoi* (14, 16, 20). *Triballoi* are a wild Thracian tribe, *Ithyphalloi* are the Erect Phalloses, and *Autolekythoi* may be a colloquialism with a similar meaning, since the lekythos was a rather narrow, upright cylindrical vase, averaging some six to twelve inches in height.

---

that some animals in courting scenes that scholars have taken to be gifts would in fact make very implausible presents. Lear is mistaken when he states that "there is no Greek text which calls cockfighting educative" (74).

15. *Com. Adesp.*, 1213 Kock. But was that claim partly bluster? See Csapo 2006 for some striking counterexamples: Aristophanes, *Birds* 70 and a scholiast on that passage suggest that the cock who loses a cockfight becomes a "slave" to the cock who defeated him and allows himself to be penetrated (28–29 and n. 47).

16. See the brief discussion in Csapo 1993a: 20–21.

17. See now Csapo 2006–7: 31, 36 for a corroborating discussion. Skinner 2013 [2005]: 146–54 also provides a useful discussion of this speech and its participants.

Autolekythoi therefore means something like "those who make themselves lekythoi." These gangs of assertive and reckless young aristocrats take names that challenge conventional models of propriety, intending to signify (presumably) that they are dangerous young bucks, not to be messed with, because they may not follow the local rules of *andragathiē*. In other words, they want everyone to know that they do not adhere to the chaste image of proper young men put forward by Stronger Speech. Theirs is a defiantly aggressive style of manhood, displaying youthful cockiness at its most extreme.

The Theater of Youth

The ambiguity of cockfighting, as both a military, masculine ideal and a potential terror to the less aggressive, picks up the ambiguity of young manhood itself. That ambiguity emerges with particular clarity from John Campbell's portrait of the Sarakatsani, shepherds in modern Greece.[18] Like the information from post-Classical writers such as Lucian and Aelian, descriptions of social life in modern Greece are sometimes very expressive of the meanings latent in the ancient material, provided they are used with reasonable caution. Evoking the ideal youth, endowed with physical and moral excellence, Campbell notes that the appropriate term for him is a double one, *levendēs kai pallēkari*. Campbell continues, "The first of these terms is perhaps the more composite, describing a youth who is handsome, manly, narrow-hipped, and nimble; such a youth will distinguish himself at a wedding by his upright carriage, restrained manner toward his elders, and his agility in the dance. *Pallēkari* is rather the hero warrior with physical strength and assertive courage who is prepared to die, if necessary, for the honour of his family or his country. Caution must always be foreign to his nature."[19]

Drawing partly on Campbell's and Michael Herzfeld's accounts of the poetics of manhood in modern rural Greece, and tentatively aligning their observations with a broad range of ancient evidence, I would like to maintain the following thesis: the ideal ephebe, at once admirable and dangerous, is a kind of *theatrical event* for his elders, indeed for the entire community.

And that for three reasons.

First, each young man is carefully watched to see how and when he will first show his manliness, first assert his independence. That is because he will be, from that point on, a social actor to reckon with, and it is important for all his enemies and allies to know his particular strengths or flaws of character. As Campbell says, "It is during these years of early manhood that the community begins seriously to take stock of a man. . . . [T]he critical moment in the development of the young shepherd's reputation is his first quarrel. Quarrels

18. J. Campbell 1964.

19. J. Campbell 1964: 278–79.

are necessarily public. They may occur in the coffee-shop, the village square, or most frequently on a grazing boundary where a curse or stone aimed at one of his straying sheep by another shepherd is an insult which inevitably requires a violent response." (For village square, read "Agora"; for boundary, read "Panakton.") Campbell goes on: "Some account of the event becomes public property. If the quarrel occurs before unrelated bystanders, the community may obtain a reasonably factual account of the fight. If it is not witnessed by an impartial audience, the contestant with the fewer marks of injury and the greater number of persuasive kinsmen wins the day. It is the critical nature of these first important tests of his manliness that makes the self-regard (*egōismos*) of the young shepherd so extremely sensitive."[20] Or, to put it another way, it is because so many people are watching, discussing, and evaluating a young man's behavior that some of these ephebes have a hair-trigger and go off, as we say, half-cocked.

Second, youth is an idealized time of life when a young man is just entering his physical prime and is not yet encumbered by family responsibilities. He can afford to be cocky, more than can a father and husband whose dependents need him. Young men are thus the freest of all male actors to play the risky and dangerous game of manhood to its limits. Older men, having established their character, need not reassert it on every occasion. They may also claim exemption from certain challenging situations for family reasons.

Given these two considerations, the drama of living up to the community ideals of masculinity may center in a special way on the performances of the young. I take it that this is why so many myths and, indeed, so many tragedies, if we take into account all the lost plays, are concerned with the fortunes of a young man—whether it is Orestes, returning to claim his paternal lands usurped by Aigisthos and Klytaimnestra, or Achilles, hidden by his mother among the maidens on the island of Skyros, confronting the dangers of the Trojan War.

But the third and most important reason for the inherent theatricality of ephebes is precisely the lack, before the late fourth century BCE, of a city-wide ephebate. As David Gilmore has noted, for the modern family of cultures around the Mediterranean basin, the lack of an official rite of passage to manhood makes of that social category a contested and hard-won state, a precarious achievement rather than an automatic status.[21] Where there is no public ceremony to grant and guarantee that the individual youngster is now a man, each youth must locate opportunities for winning that status. He must be watchful of chances to display—and thereby to achieve, in the community's estimation—his *andragathiē*. Thus, in Euripides' *Ion* we see a boy on the verge

20. J. Campbell 1964: 280–81.

21. Gilmore 1987. See also the fundamental work of Winkler 1990a and Gleason 1990.

of manhood whose status is officially altered from slave to citizen-son, and this is celebrated at a banquet, but he does not really acquire *andragathiē* until the dramatic moment of his challenge to Apollo, when he is ready to charge into the temple and confront the god with the evidence of the latter's wrongdoing.[22]

In those cultures where being an *anēr* ("man" in the sense of fully achieved male rather than default "human") is not a programmed, inexorable event dependent on calendar age but a personal act of seizing the moment when it offers, the social actors and audiences become very attuned to inventiveness, spontaneity, and improvisation. (No doubt this was how Konon and his friends viewed his crowing in the Agora—as a stunning theatrical gesture, created on the spur of the moment. One might also cite the act of Kleophon, who went to the Assembly drunk and wearing his breast-plate and insisted on continuing the war with Sparta; Aiskhines says he threatened to cut the throat of anyone who mentioned the word "peace."[23] That was certainly outrageous behavior, and many must have disapproved, but some might also have admired his bold, overstated—and thus theatrical—gesture, either despite or because of its extreme cockiness: after all, it carried the day.) Of course, the sons of citizen parents were acknowledged by their phratry at the age of sixteen and enrolled on the deme register at the age of eighteen, but unlike at Sparta, where the age-classes were carefully organized in a training program for all citizens, Athenian youth, and men in general, had to make it on their own. And this, not the Spartan, is by far the more typical arrangement.[24]

22. Evidence of Ion's physical manhood include: *hōs d'apēndrōthē demas*, "he having matured in form," 53; *ektelē neanian*, "fully grown youth," 780; *neanian . . . ektethrammenon*, "the youth fully grown," 823; Xouthos' birth sacrifices for Ion: 653, 805, 1130. Two other signs of Ion's maturity occur toward the end of the play: he appears before the Delphian leaders, apparently initiating a legal action that concludes with a vote for Kreousa's execution (1219), and he takes up a shield and spear to pursue her (1305). The final confrontation between them therefore looks like a strange parody of the usual iconography on vases of a mother watching her now-grown son assume his ephebic armor.

23. [Arist.], *Ath. Pol.* 34.1; Aiskh. 2.76.

24. Passing the scrutiny (*dokimasia*) and being enrolled at age eighteen entitled a young man to initiate actions in court, a sure sign of membership in the community of adult males. Thus, Demosthenes entered charges against his guardians as soon as he was scrutinized (*euthus . . . dokimastheis*, 30.15)—though the suit was entered two years later—and the speaker of Lysias 10 charged the Thirty with the homicide of his father immediately upon being qualified by passing scrutiny (*epeidē takhista edokimasthōn*, 31). But what is most noteworthy about these instances is that the risky court actions themselves (that is, the decisions to bring them rather than lie low) serve as proofs of the young prosecutors' manhood.

The Drama of Danger

We have learned over recent decades to appreciate the format of zero-sum competition as a ground-plan for personal behavior and value in ancient Greece.[25] According to the zero-sum calculus, a rise in the stock of one person or family or tribe means a fall in the value of others—so long as all the rivals belong to the same social category and are competing for the same thing (thus, men compete for preeminence with other men, not with women, gods, boys, or beasts). The economic metaphor of the market is natural to us but should not mislead: the value for which people, families, or cities compete is *timē* ("honor"), and honor is precisely not something that can be quantified and exchanged like money or goods in a market economy. Rather, it depends on personal assertion, vindication, and negotiation in the intimate forums of a small-scale society. To maintain his personal value in this social setting, a man must always be ready to display his strength or wit or courage before an audience of carefully watching neighbors, who will evaluate his performance and spread their report.[26]

If the first principle of zero-sum competition is that there is a limited amount of honor to go around, such that your loss of it is another's gain, the second principle is a corollary of the first: honor and manhood may always be challenged; they are inherently precarious qualities.[27] That is why, as Herzfeld puts it in describing the Glendiots of Krete, the aim is not simply to be a good man but to be good at being a man.[28] Honor and a reputation for manhood are never given from the start or freely handed out; they are always acquired by personal skill, strength, and courage (also by charm, good humor, and hospitality, of course, but I am leaving those qualities out for the moment because I am emphasizing the crisis mode of manhood). What's more, the acquisition (or loss) of honor and reputation is essentially a public event, since the crucial scene will both have an immediate audience and will be ceaselessly retold, reenacted, and reevaluated from various perspectives, until it has been performed for every relevant member of the community.

25. Gouldner 1965; see also Winkler 1990a: ch. 2.

26. The high stakes and uncertain outcome inherent in the pursuit of *timē* also provoke observations about the value of a quiet life, one that does not challenge the envy of the gods or the political clout of the masses; for the former, see Wehrli 1976 [1931]; for the latter, L. Carter 1986.

27. Aristotle's definition of anger is interesting in this connection: "a desire, accompanied by pain, for a perceived revenge, on account of a perceived slight on the part of people who are not fit to slight one or one's own" (*Rhet.* 2.2.1, 1378a31–33). In other words, anger is a response to a put-down, and it expresses a man's proper resistance to any challenge to his social standing, especially by someone he considers to be below him in the social hierarchy.

28. Herzfeld 1986: 16.

PLATE 1. Red-figure Attic volute-krater, with scenes of a satyric chorus, actors, and musicians (the "Pronomos Vase"), c. 425–375 BCE. From Ruvo di Puglia. National Archaeological Museum, Naples, inv. 81673, H3240. Photo: Album / Art Resource, NY.

PLATE 2. Fragment of an Apulian vase from Taranto, showing an actor, c. 340 BCE. Martin von Wagner Museum, Würzburg, inv. 832, H4600. © Martin von Wagner Museum, The University of Würzburg. Photo credit: C. Kiefer.

PLATE 3. Red-figure bell-krater, showing two actors, one holding a mask, c. 460–450 BCE. National Archaeological Museum, Ferrara, inv. 2299, T. 173C VT. By permission of the Ministry of Culture—Photographic Archive, Regional Directorate of the Museums of Emilia-Romagna (further reproduction or duplication by any means is prohibited).

PLATE 12. Red-figure Paestan bell-krater, showing Hermes, Zeus as an old man with a ladder, and a woman's face at a window. Attributed to Asteas, c. 350–340 BCE. Vatican Museums, Vatican City, inv. 17106. Photo copyright © Governatorate of the Vatican City State—Directorate of the Vatican Museums.

PLATE 13. Red-figure bell-krater, showing a comic version of the *Antigone*, fourth century BCE. Vase in a private collection, reproduced here by permission of the owner.

PLATE 14. Red-figure Apulian bell-krater, showing the birth of Helen from an egg. Painter of Dijon, 375–350 BCE. Archaeological Museum, Bari, inv. 3899. Photo credit: White Images / Scala / Art Resource, NY.

A key term in analyzing the meaning of such performances of manhood is *kindunos*, risk or danger.[29] It is facing danger that defines manhood. The supreme instance is to face without flinching an enemy's spear aimed at your chest in battle.[30] The *dokimasia* procedure, in which a candidate for office was challenged and scrutinized, has left us a valuable set of documents that bring out the often latent ideology of citizenship and its close dependence on acts of bravery and personal risk undertaken for the common good.[31] Thus Mantitheos, whose fitness to be a Councilor has been challenged, defends himself by listing the campaigns he has fought in for the city and the dangers (*kindunoi*) he has faced (Lys. 16.12). Other men, he remarks, transferred to the cavalry when they thought there would be less *kindunos* there in the coming battle at Haliartos, but he asked the general to register him as a hoplite instead of a cavalryman, ready to face danger (*kinduneuein*) with his fellow-citizens (13). The chief charge brought against a certain Philo at his *dokimasia* is that "he set more value on his private safety than on the common danger of the *polis* and he preferred to lead his own life without danger [*akindunōs*], rather than save the city by facing risks [*kinduneuein*] alongside his fellow-citizens" (Lys. 31.7).

All that is or ever was best in the city is summed up in that moment of risk. Demosthenes alludes to the privilege experienced by those Athenians who fought at Marathon and confronted danger, in the form of the invading Persian army, on behalf of all other imperiled Greeks (*prokinduneusantas*, 18.208): they had the chance (*kairos*) to do something glorious and they seized that opportune moment (19.269). Athenians now, he says, should imitate those ancestors, "and if the opportunity for glory does not arise in the form of battles or campaigns or dangers [*kindunoi*], at least you can imitate their good judgment" (19.269). In many trial speeches, defendants appeal to the jury by standing on their record of service, noting how many public events they have financed and how many dangers they have undergone (*egō pollous kindunous kekinduneuka kai pollas lēitourgias lelēitourgēka*, "I have risked many risks and I have endowed many endowments [i.e., 'liturgies']" [Lys. 3.47; cf. Lys. 10.27]). No wonder that cockfighting—a supremely clear representation of zero-sum competition in the mode of do or die—provided such a convenient and recurrent symbol for combative manliness in the face of risk.

The focus on risk as the defining moment of manhood, together with the absence of any status-changing ceremony that would display and guarantee a citizen's manhood once and for all, led to a multiplication of venues in ancient

29. *Hoi andreioi kindunoi* according to a formulation in Plato, *Laws* 12.945A.

30. Bassi 2003 provides a comprehensive discussion of the term *andreia*, "manliness, courage," from the Archaic period through Plato and argues that in its earliest appearance the term has a specific martial context: to be "manly" means to hold one's place in battle.

31. For a general discussion of the Athenian *dokimasia*, see Robertson 2000.

Greece for the staging and observation of scenarios of risk: athletic competition, trophy warfare (as opposed to mass murder and territorial conquest), and game hunting. Xenophon, in his *Kynēgetikos*, analyzes the types of sport hunting according to how well each displays the manhood of the hunter—that is, according to the degree of risk involved.[32] Rabbits are on the low end of the scale, but lions are too high. Wild boars are just right, since the pursuit may turn into a battle whose outcome could go either way (10). A boar can kill you when it charges, but if you stay alert and hold your spear ready, you may be able to kill it before it gores you—most of the time.

In addition to hunting, athletics, and war, there were two other venues available for mounting scenarios of risk—scenarios even more complex than those afforded by sports or combat—namely, jury trials and drama. The remainder of this chapter will serve to bring out the correspondences between the two. For both trials and drama stage critical, spectacular moments of confrontation with danger. Such moments afford ready vehicles for exposing to public scrutiny the cockiness of the various contestants as they play, often for keeps, a high-stakes, zero-sum game that tests their mettle and displays the temper of their manly excellence.

Trials of Manhood

The very word *kinduneuein* has the specialized meaning "to be on trial,"[33] since both parties are putting their honor on the chopping block (as Dikaiopolis does in the *Akharnians*). The antagonists stand to lose not just money or even life but a more precious part of the self: honor, reputation, face. Those are qualities that survive death and continue to affect the fortunes of one's family.[34]

It is illuminating to compare jury trials and drama as venues for self-definition and for an audience's judgment of a man's success at being a man.[35] The basic similarity is that a citizen-audience, acting in its capacity as

32. The unity, authorship, and parainetic form of Xenophon's *Kynēgetikos* are discussed by Gray 1985.

33. Worthington 1985.

34. Andokides 1.141 presents his ancestors' services to the city as a kind of savings account which they set aside for the emergency needs of their descendants: "[I]n order that, if ever any danger [*kindunos*] or distress fell upon them or any of their descendants, they would be saved [*sōizointo*] by winning your sympathy."

35. Some similarities of procedure, argumentation, and tone between tragedies and trials are developed by Garner 1987: ch. 4. He notes that the rapid expansion of popular courts after Ephialtes parallels the entry of forensic debates into tragedy, largely absent from Aiskhylos (pp. 96–97). See now the useful discussion of D. Carter 2011a, who uses Plato's *Gorgias* to bring out the homologies between theater and the Assembly; he observes, "Plato's assimilation of dramatic and political rhetoric serves if anything to underline that attending the theatre could be as political an act as attending the *ekklēsia*" (52).

representative of the *polis*, is presented with a series of events and perspectives and rationales that touch on crucial issues in the assessment of *andragathiē*. Furthermore, the crisis is concentrated in time and must be resolved within a single day. An index of the comparative urgency of Attic trials is the fact that once a man was convicted of capital charges, execution was instant and appeals were not possible. (Sokrates' delayed execution, for religious reasons, was not the rule.) That urgency is often reflected in drama, for instance in Euripides' *Orestes*, where the Argive assembly decides that Orestes and Elektra must be put to death "today" (858), and Orestes begs his uncle Menelaos to stand up as their savior and exert himself for a single day—a day's effort being a small recompense for the ten years that their father Agamemnon spent fighting at Troy in Menelaos' cause (655–57).[36]

Trials, like plays, can also be seen as showcases, as exemplary occasions on which the city represents itself to itself and reaches a decision that adjudicates between competing aspects of the civic value system. As Demosthenes says in one case, it is a serious matter to reach the proper verdict. For the audience of judges, in examining the two sides presented by the competitors, has to balance the concerns of sympathy and rigor (he almost says, of pity and fear). This is not just for the sake of abstract justice but as an example displayed to younger citizens, so that they will learn maturity and sound judgment (*sōphrosunē*): "By Zeus, our young men [*hoi neoi*] will become better as a result of that contest [*agōn*]."[37] Judicial proceedings are, among other things, a kind of spectacle designed to educate the young.

The issues at stake in such spectacles extend, of course, from heads of household, who regard themselves as the central protagonists, to include all the population—women, children, seniors, foreigners, slaves—who find themselves implicated in the outcome. Thus, both trials and drama may expose the inner tensions of families, usually concealed from the community, to public view (as in the inheritance trials of Isaios). By focusing on contests of manhood as the fundamental plan informing trials and drama, I may seem to slight these other classes of the population, but in fact they are thoroughly caught up in such conflicts. Though the duel model—man on man, army on army—is central, most situations not only reach out to affect wives and slaves and foreigners, but often the disputed issue turns on a question of whether a man has behaved in a way appropriate to an *anēr* or to someone who belongs to one of these other classes. A spectator at the trial of Konon, for instance, might judge that Ariston was a sissy, behaving more like a woman or a slave in not defending himself better.

36. In Sophokles' *Philoktetes* 83–85, Odysseus tries to persuade Neoptolemos to bend his principles and participate in the intrigue that constitutes the dramatic action of the play for "a short, shameless portion of a day."

37. Dem. 19.285.

The wide-ranging stakes for the whole community that are manifest in trials of manhood can be illustrated in their simplest terms by recalling the plot of Aiskhylos' *Persians*. The old men of the kingdom and Xerxes' mother wait anxiously for the news of the vast Persian army, to find out whether it has successfully fought the Greeks. As the news of one defeat after another comes in, their attention turns from the question of what has happened to the issue of why. Various factors are mentioned: the messenger blames Greek trickery and divine "envy" (*phthonos*); the ghost of Dareios, Xerxes' dead father, asserts that some god made Xerxes misjudge (725). But the explanation deemed most just is reached by the Queen and Dareios together (739–86). Dareios realizes that his son Xerxes made a mistake in treating the divine Bosporos as a slave, by shackling it with a bridge for his army to cross; he knows too that this was an act of specifically youthful bravado (*neon thrasos*, 744), but he still goes on to wonder what could have prompted Xerxes to do it. The Queen then tells him what happened after he, Dareios, died: Xerxes listened to bad men and accepted their opinion that it was cowardly—literally "unmanly" (*anandrias hupo*, 755)—of him not to extend his kingdom beyond the boundaries won by his father. Feeling the shame of that reproach and internalizing that false perspective, Xerxes had mounted his disastrous expedition to Greece.

This is a fairly straightforward example (though a negative and cautionary one) of the calculus of the social responsibilities of manhood and their consequences for others, presented in a plain didactic mode. It is the sort of thing that one can find often enough in the orators, who frequently instance old tales and the texts of drama when making a point about the right way for a man or a city to behave in the face of conflicting values.[38] Lykourgos, for instance, tells the melodramatic story of King Kodros (1.83–87) and recites long passages from Euripides' *Erekhtheus* in praise of patriotism and self-sacrifice (1.98–101). The orator Thrasymakhos quotes a line from Euripides' lost play the *Telephos* in order to argue against submission to King Arkhelaos of Makedon.[39] Aiskhines engages in a veritable all-you-can-read buffet in justifying the proper method of paederastic love—that is, his own—as opposed to the improper method exemplified by his enemies Timarkhos and Demosthenes. Not only does he invoke several passages from Homer, citing Achilles and Patroklos as ideal lovers, but he goes on to quote Euripides' plays (now lost): first, the *Stheneboia*,[40] to show that Euripides approved of the right kind of love, and then the *Phoinix*,[41] to make an argument about what should

38. Arist., *Rhet.* 1.15.13 includes the old poets among the potential witnesses at a trial, since they can sometimes be quoted to provide evidence in support of a cause.

39. Thrasymakhos, fr. B2 (Diels-Kranz), quoting one of the Greek leaders—possibly Achilles—in the *Telephos* (Eur., fr. 719 [Nauck]). For discussion, see White 1995: 318–19.

40. Eur., fr. 672 (Nauck), quoted at Aiskh. 1.151.

41. Eur., fr. 812 (Nauck), quoted at Aiskh. 1.152.

constitute appropriate evidence in such a case. Demosthenes, for his part, quotes a speech of Kreon in Sophokles' *Antigone* as if it were straight political advice.[42] Which it is, of course. But most plays and trials are rather more complicated than the *Persians* or the various didactic passages from tragedy cited by orators.

Most dramas are about conflicts of feeling and allegiance and value, conflicts in which both sides have a plausible rationale and can justify their position, whether it is Kreon vs. Antigone, Medeia vs. Jason, or Apollo vs. the Furies. Drama, like trial by jury, often serves to deepen the complexity of such conflicts. I would like to suggest, accordingly, that we take a forensic approach to the conflict of societal issues that Athenian drama loves to stage in its quasi-judicial effort to arbitrate among competing aspects of the civic value system and competing models of *andragathiē*.

Let me highlight for that purpose a common scheme of thought, one that can be found in legal debates as well as in the scripts of the plays. Take, for instance, a dramatic passage in Plato's *Laws* (12.943E–944A). Plato is discussing that most heinous of crimes, desertion from the ranks in battle. While the fundamental issue is clear—namely, that cowardice in such conditions is inexcusable and should be punished with unending shame—Plato acknowledges that it may not be easy to decide in a particular case whether a man involved in a rout has shown personal cowardice or merely been caught in a circumstance that no man could withstand. What if, he continues, Patroklos had been carried off the field of battle after being vanquished by Hektor and stripped of his arms, and then had recovered in his tent? It would theoretically be possible for some base fellow in Homeric times to have accused Patroklos of abandoning his arms. The technical name for Plato's procedure here is casuistry—the proposing of interesting, and sometimes fanciful, cases that illustrate conflicts in the law and that might be judged in various ways.

A more developed instance is found in the pair of speeches that Antisthenes composed in a rhetorical mode for Aias and Odysseus, each of the heroes claiming the right to inherit Achilles' arms.[43] Aias is characterized as no orator at all; his speech is short, repetitive, and consists mainly of the assertion that there really isn't much to say: his deeds should speak louder than any words. Odysseus, by contrast, eloquently defends his unique role in winning the Trojan War by stealing the Palladion—an act itself of questionable virtue, for though it was essential to the Greek victory and involved a high degree of *kindunos*, it was also an act of stealth, undertaken in disguise and under cover of night. As a genre, a form of rhetorical composition, Antisthenes' speeches fall exactly midway between jury trials and drama: they are

42. Dem. 19.247–48, quoting Soph., *Ant.* 175–90.

43. Text is in Blass 1908: 175–82.

historical recreations of how an issue of *andreia* could have been debated in myth-historical times.

Many tragedies—one should never say all—can be viewed in this quasi-judicial light as the casuistry of the civic ideology.[44] Trials of manhood are ideal vehicles for this exercise. Consider Sophokles' *Aias*. What if the most valiant soldier went temporarily insane after his honor was unjustly slighted and thought he was wreaking havoc on those who had wronged him? Would it be honorable for such a man, upon later discovering his error, to commit suicide, and, if he did, should he be honored or dishonored by the community? Or take this real-life parallel to Medeia: [Andokides'] speech against Alkibiades describes how the latter brought a Melian woman home as his mistress and what extreme intrafamilial tension and enmity arose from that act. The speaker actually compares the situation to a tragedy but says that it should be taken more seriously, since "you do not know whether [events in a tragedy] actually happened as the poet presents them or whether they have been made up" (4.22–23). Clearly this speaker, in even cautiously questioning the historical reality of tragedy, takes it much more seriously than we do as a test case of human conduct.

One merit of this forensic approach to tragic scripts and to their ways of dramatizing ideological conflicts among competing societal values is that it allows us to arrive at an appropriate balance in weighing those scripts' emotional impact against their intellectual content, the latter being compounded of significant clichés, shown clashing on the rocks of particularity. As in trial speeches, the basic truths are familiar ones, but their combination and conflicting applications offer much to ponder. Such casuistry—or designing of cases—is a way of representing the complexities of social identity and action that is both inherently moving and intellectually charged, for it is alive to the fundamental insecurity, competitive spirit, and self-dramatization that were characteristic of life, especially male life, in the Classical *polis*. And of course such casuistry works even better in comedy, where current political issues not only get represented in a fun-house mirror mode, but where the poet also gets to do some outright editorializing about the issues of the day when he steps forward boldly to advise the city, risking his reputation to speak the often unpopular truth.[45]

44. See Peter Burian's discussion of Euripides' *Suppliants* and its enactment of debates about democratic discourse: Burian 2011: 104–7.

45. For example, *Knights* 510: our poet dares to say what is just. Helene Foley argues that Aristophanes stages his own peril in a conflict with Kleon through the character of Dikaiopolis in the *Akharnians*; significantly, Dikaiopolis' central defense involves a parody of Euripides' lost play the *Telephos*, thus appropriating "tragedy's mode of making social criticism safely distanced and disguised through myth" (Foley 1988: 39).

The Ephebe of All Ephebes

At this point it might seem appropriate to settle down to reading some dramatic texts in this forensic fashion, as lessons in the difficulty of resolving tensions among basic Athenian values in specific, practical, emotionally fraught situations. But authors like Brian Vickers in *Towards Greek Tragedy* have already done that very well for the plays where the social conflicts, along with the anxiety and necessity of competition, are presented literally. Instead, I would like to turn to a type of play where we can see the scenario of risk aestheticized into a form whose extrapolation from Athenian social life is less recognizable. For while I have been insisting on the social meanings of the material and physical components of Athenian drama, I do not want to underestimate drama's aesthetic autonomy, the degree to which drama may leave the recognizable realities of social life behind, creating through song and narrative and spectacle an aesthetic display that, like Medeia's dragon chariot, outstrips the banalities of daily life, even as it elicits realms of inner feeling so powerful that we would usually rather avoid them. Whatever ephebo-centric qualities we may detect in the elementary components of drama, we should not downplay the fact that in the course of the fifth century, with the export of drama from Athens and its reperformance in other cities, the scope of tragic and also comic scripts expanded far beyond the localized topoi of Athenian culture.[46]

For an instance of such a play, which might seem to have little to do with the typical issues of Athenian *andreia* as they would be presented and debated in jury trials, consider Euripides' *Iphigeneia among the Taurians* (or *IT*). Like his *Helen*, Euripides' *IT* is set in a far-off land where monstrous people live and where one's very identity as a Greek is in peril.

Here is the story. Orestes, still pursued by the Furies, makes landfall among the Taurians in what is roughly the Crimean Peninsula today, the farthest limit of Greek trading colonies in historical times. There, unbeknownst to him and his good friend Pylades, who accompanies him, his sister Iphigeneia, rescued from human sacrifice at the hands of the Greek army by divine intervention years before, now officiates at the sacrifice of all strangers. For such is the brutal custom in that land: not a pleasant job, but someone's got to do it. In fact, as Iphigeneia tells us, she hates all Greeks for what they almost did to her, excepting only her beloved brother, who is the one person she still longs to see. So much does she want to make contact with her brother that she decides to let one of the two new victims escape, if he will promise to take a letter from

46. Stewart 2017. See also Anne Duncan's discussion of tragedies at the courts of tyrants (Duncan 2011) in Carter 2011b. Wilson's piece in the same volume (Wilson 2011) provides a useful and comprehensive discussion of the ways that the institution of theater was central to, and enabled by, the newly emerged Athenian democracy.

her back to her brother in Argos, whom Iphigeneia never names. Pylades is chosen for the job and is handed the sealed letter, leaving Orestes to be sacrificed. But wait! What if, she shrewdly wonders, Pylades' ship goes down but he survives? There's no help for it: he will have to memorize the letter, so that he can recite it when he reaches her brother at home. And so Iphigeneia reveals the contents of the letter, beginning with "Dear Orestes." Shock all around. As brother and sister recognize each other and are at last reunited, they suddenly realize not only what a terrible situation they have just avoided but also what a pickle they are still in, for now they must all three try to escape. They manage to do this cleverly and courageously with a false story about Orestes' pollution, based on the fact that he still has occasional fits of madness, which allows them to get down to the seashore and near his boat, where they do battle with the King's guards.

It is a stirring, adventurous, one might even say melodramatic play. But even those who, like Vickers, appreciate the social resonance of most extant tragedies have trouble incorporating the *IT* (and other plays by Euripides, such as the *Helen*) into their view of Attic drama. Nonetheless, one can see with unusual clarity in the *IT* both the scenario of risk, specifically of a young warrior who undergoes trials and refuses to be faint-hearted in the face of extremest peril, and the somewhat fanciful elaboration of that ground plan into an imaginatively free form, with a terrain of distant danger and an unforeseen intersection of divine plots—Artemis' to save Iphigeneia, Apollo's to restore Orestes to his sister. Despite all those imaginative elements, and despite the extent to which the plot is wildly extrapolated from any recognizable scenario of risk and salvation that one might encounter on the streets or in the courtrooms of Athens, it is surely no accident that the *IT* tellingly concludes by labeling Orestes the ephebe of all ephebes: the play seems to propose the young man's encounter with extreme peril as a model for self-definition on the part of men and women alike.[47] Even this distant fable, then, can be seen to reflect the importance of the *kindunos* plot in shaping and informing both social life and civic ideology in classical Athens.

In the concluding scene, Athena appears and gives her interpretation of the play's significance in a set of three aetiologies.[48] The adventure of Orestes among the Taurians will be told in future time to explain three recurring events in Attic culture.

(1) First, at Halai, a place at the farthest boundaries of Attika (1450–51), Orestes will build a temple and put in it the statue of Artemis he has stolen from the Taurians. From now on, Artemis in that location will be known as Artemis Tauropolos, a word recalling in its two parts the ephebic story of Orestes: "named for the Taurian land and for the toils you underwent roaming

47. Cf. Belpassi 1988.
48. See Wolff 1992 for a detailed analysis.

[or, circumambulating] Greece [*peripolōn kat' Hellada*], stung by the Furies" (1454–56). In Athena's dictionary, the *pol-* in Tauropolos is derived from *peripolos*, the late-fifth-century word for ephebe, he who "patrols" the borderlands of Attika. By superimposing a map of Attika onto a map of the known world, Athena draws an analogy between Orestes wandering at the farthest edges of "civilization" and the *peripoloi* going out from Athens itself to patrol the wilder hill country and its borders.

Athena goes on to say that a public festival at that temple will feature, in addition to the usual animal sacrifices, a mock human sacrifice: "[W]hen my people celebrate a feast day there, in token of your slaughter let them place a sword against a man's neck and let blood flow forth, for holiness and for the honor of the goddess" (1458–61). Some take this to mean that, for a while at least, human sacrifice was practiced (that is, was thought to have been practiced) at Halai. That is not to be ruled out automatically. But what is more interesting is that Athena does not quite say that. Her language here comes very close to saying—but avoids saying—that a man will be decapitated. The most plausible reading is that the festival at Halai in Euripides' day included a mock human sacrifice, in which a sword placed against a man's neck was made to draw a line of blood but not to kill him. This presumably was thought to be a remnant of human sacrifice once practiced there. Such an interpretation is supported by the analogy with Iphigeneia. She and Orestes undergo parallel experiences, both coming within a millimeter of death by the sword in a ritual presided over by a family member—Agamemnon in her case, she in the case of Orestes.

(2) According to Athena's second aetiology, Iphigeneia herself will go to another Attic temple of Artemis, the one at Brauron, where she will continue to be a priestess until her death and burial there. The way in which future generations will memorialize her is as follows: "[T]hey will dedicate to you well-woven robes, left at home by women whose soul is ripped in childbirth" (1464–66). The usual interpretation, not to be entirely ruled out, is that this refers exclusively to the clothing of women who died in childbirth. "Left at home" tends to support that, but there is a certain ambiguity in the entire expression. A woman need not actually die in order to justify the designation of birthing as a soul-shattering experience. In any case, this second aetiology refers to a moment of ultimate risk in the life experience of women, seen as parallel to those trials by *kindunos* that men typically undergo.[49]

So far we have two aetiologies of Attic ritual actions—the first an enactment of risk for a man at a public festival, the second a testimonial for an ordinary, real-life experience of *kindunos* undergone by women. Now Athena gives a third aetiology, a third use of the Orestes story in Athenian culture.

49. Euripides' Medeia makes the parallel explicit when she says that she would rather fight in battle three times than give birth once (250–51).

(3) Whenever a man is on trial and the votes are equal, the rule for all time will be that the defendant will win. (Note the characteristic expression: the acquitted defendant does not, as we would say, go free; he *wins* the contest.) Orestes' saga will thus be present at every jury trial as a founding cultural pattern, as one of the stories all participants have stocked in their minds as they render their verdict. The story refers literally to Orestes' trial before the Council of the Areopagos, but the effect of this aetiology coming third in the series is to bring out an aspect of all judicial proceedings at Athens, namely that they were closely watched rituals of risk, public spectacles in which one person's manhood was tested in a duel with his enemies, often with his life hanging in the balance.[50]

Thus it is that Athena herself, *dea ex machina*, swaying gently in her cables over the stage, declares the meaning for all time of these perilous events just enacted. For her, for Euripides, and for the audience, Orestes' bold, death-defying and death-approximating voyage to the borders of Hellenic cultural space traces a fundamental schema of personal excellence, defined for all socially significant actors in Athens through scenarios of risk, and most appropriately acted out by the paradigmatic ephebe Orestes and his smarter sister.

In the next and final chapter, I will continue this analysis by asking the question, "Why was *Iphigeneia among the Taurians* Aristotle's favorite tragedy?"

50. We might recall at this point that, in the conventional language for describing trials and battles, the co-term to *kindunos* is *sōtēria*, salvation, and that the Greeks' perception of trials is quite a few notches more melodramatic than ours. Thus, Andokides 1.137–39 compares his escape (*sōtēria*) from the danger (*kindunos*) of a winter storm at sea with the dangers of his present trial.

CHAPTER FOUR

An Oscar for Iphigeneia

THE CANON ACCORDING TO ARISTOTLE

SOMETIME IN THE 330s BCE an Academy Award for "Best Tragedy" was given to a play that many people still regard as a strange choice, so strange that there has been a sort of unspoken agreement to ignore the award. The play was Euripides' *Iphigeneia among the Taurians*, the academy in question was Aristotle's, and the award was bestowed in chapter 14 of the *Poetics*. In this play (which classicists call the *IT*, for short), Iphigeneia recognizes her brother Orestes shortly before she is about to officiate at his sacrifice at the hands of the Taurians; by a combination of ruse, bravado, and divine intervention, the pair manage to escape from that barbarous kingdom. Aristotle uses two plays throughout the *Poetics* as touchstones for the various kinds of tragic excellence—namely, Sophokles' *Oidipous Tyrannos* (or *OT*) and Euripides' *IT*—but when he comes in chapter 14 to rank plays according to their most important feature, their plot organization, he places the *IT* in the top class, the *OT* only in the second class.[1]

1. Could Aristotle have seen a performance of Euripides' *IT*? One of the Iphigeneia plays by Euripides was staged in the spring of 341 by Neoptolemos. See *IG* II^2 2320, fr. a col. 2, lines 1–3; the inscription dates to the archonship of Nikomakhos, i.e., 341.

[In the years since Winkler wrote this chapter, which he also delivered several times as a public lecture, a number of scholars, most notably Stephen White and Elizabeth Belfiore, have gone on to pay careful attention to Aristotle's apparently contradictory rankings of tragedies in chapters 13 and 14 of the *Poetics*. White 1992 argues that Aristotle places both the *OT* and the *IT* in the class of the "best" (*kallistē*) kind of tragedy, but that he ranks the *IT* as an instance of the "most powerful" (*kratiston*, which is often translated here as "best"), because it appeals to the audience's sense of fairness. Belfiore 1992 advances an interpretation closer to Winkler's. She suggests that the qualities that modern audiences consider central to the definition of a good tragedy—notably, character development and psychology—were of little importance to Aristotle, who saw plot as the "soul" of tragedy. In these terms, Belfiore argues, the *IT* is an excellent tragedy: "[A] drama that is concerned

We are not used to thinking of Sophokles' *Oidipous* as a B– tragedy (though it did originally place second in competition to a play by one Philokles). And as for giving the *IT* pride of place as a paradigm of what the genre of tragedy should aspire to—well, that's like giving an Oscar for Best Actress to Joan Collins.

There is a fascinating problem here—a problem that has relatively little to do, contrary to scholarly opinion, with the history of taste. An appeal to the oddness of Aristotle's taste, or that of the fourth-century public in Athens,[2] is the first remedy applied by critics who would like to neutralize the upsetting evidence that the *IT* was not only Aristotle's Academy Award winner but was also, to judge from the evidence of Greek vase-paintings, one of the most popular of all the ancient plays in reperformance.

The problem is rather to be located in the literary and academic traditions that already tell us what Greek tragedies are before we ever start reading them or going to the theater. The current usage of the word "tragedy," the ancient and modern artworks grouped together under that designation, their strategic use in both formal and informal education—all of this shapes our approach to Greek drama. We have an institutionalized common sense that teaches us to recognize a tragedy when we see one and to value Sophokles' *Oidipous Tyrannos* in particular. The *IT*, which automatically seems to many readers to be a variety of romantic comedy,[3] falls into a kind of blind spot in our institutional vision. I take this blind spot to be one of the unnoticed culprits in our persistent misprision of the full meaning of Attic tragedy to its original audience.

Modern institutionalized habits of thought have been long in the fabrication, as different national and personal styles of tragedy have succeeded the Attic—Senecan, Elizabethan, French neoclassical, German romantic, Italian

with terrible events that threaten our very humanity is essentially serious, important, 'tragic'" (367). Belfiore indicates that she was aware of Winkler's argument from his Martin Classical Lectures (see her note 7). Neither White nor Belfiore seeks to explain Aristotle's judgment precisely in the way that Winkler does—i.e., by identifying Aristotle's favorite type of tragic plot according to the criteria that Winkler lays out in this chapter. Scott 2018 devotes an entire study to the very problem raised here: he zeroes in on Aristotle's surprising and often neglected demotion of the *OT* in favor of tragedies with happy endings like the *IT*, but his explanation, which focuses on Aristotle's theory of the emotions, is very different from Winkler's.]

2. Webster 1954; Kitto 1966. Another response to the problem is to insist that the *Poetics* is a purely theoretical analysis with no relation to any playwright's practice: so Radt 1976.

3. Even B. Vickers 1973, whose account of the field is one of the least mystified by post-Senecan notions of "the tragic," resorts to reclassifying the *IT* together with the *Ion* and the *Helen*, all of them supposed examples of "tragicomedies" or "romances." See Belfiore 1992: 360–61 for an analysis of how Aristotle sees the *IT* as fundamentally different from the *Helen*, often viewed by modern scholars as a similar play.

operatic, American realist. Each of these broad styles has offered at least nominal homage to Attic tragedy, but for the cultural archaeologist, trying to excavate the original meanings of ancient Greek drama, those later developments are more a hindrance than a help.[4]

What I have been trying to do in the preceding three chapters, accordingly, is to bracket the assumptions we usually bring to the study of Athenian drama, to erase the historically and institutionally shaped knowledge of what tragedy and comedy are and why they are important. Instead, I have been exploring the performance of drama in Athens as might an anthropologist, visiting a culture whose strangeness and untranslatable difference are assumed to be at least as interesting as its recognizably human familiarity. Wandering like a stranger into the outdoor auditorium on festival day, I have been observing the physical and material components of Attic drama (including the gender and age of the participants), noting the conditions of production (the seating and composition of the audience as well as the costuming of the players), and focusing particularly on the social meanings attached to each of those features. The systems of aesthetic, moral, and emotional value built into the various elements of ancient dramatic performance seem to have rather different emphases from the systems of value that inform modern dramatic performances, and the differences appear most notably in relation to themes of male conduct: Athenian dramatic festivals are evidently given to rehearsing the sometimes problematic behavior of men whose civic and personal virtue is intimately linked to their ability as warriors, who are caught in situations of conflict, and who enact scenarios of risk.

In this chapter, I want to consider a later institutional factor that has in large measure determined for us what Attic tragedy means and that has, in the process of constituting the field of tragedy for us, bent and warped it. I speak of canon formation, which involves two phases: the selection of the "best" texts for preservation and for commentary, and the devising of theoretical justifications for their "bestness." What has happened in the case of Attic *tragōidiai* is that we have an ancient but post-Classical selection of best plays (made, it would seem, for academic and educational purposes), and in Aristotle's *Poetics* we have a theory of what is required to compose "a best play" (*hē kallistē tragōidia*, not tragedy in general). Since the Renaissance, these two have been used together, inconsistently, to fabricate a notion of tragedy derived partly from the surviving plays (some of them, that is) and partly from the theoretical pronouncements of the *Poetics*. What I would like to demonstrate is that Aristotle's arguments for dramatic excellence imply a very different canon from the actual selection of plays that remains to us, that his best type of play

4. See now Marx 2012, who provides a comprehensive argument that our modern notion of "tragedy" has been overwhelmingly shaped by nineteenth-century German romanticism, to the detriment of ancient Attic understandings of the tragic genre.

roughly coincides with what I have called the scenario of risk, and that his formal criteria for tragic plot construction are determined by social considerations that mesh very closely with the perspectives I have outlined in the previous three chapters.

Aristotle's General Theory of Narrativity

The dissection of Aristotle's argument and theoretical principles requires the exploration of some larger issues in the *Poetics*, particularly its emphasis on the story line or plot. Aristotle's *Poetics* may quite literally be described as a narratological analysis of serious drama: it is centrally concerned with the construction and aesthetic impact of dramatic narrative (or story-telling). In the course of this exploration, I will also have a good deal to say about comedy, whose boundary with tragedy has periodically been contested and redrawn in significant ways. From Aristotle's point of view, as I will try to show, the best tragedies were those whose story line and structure of events could come very close to producing a comedy of errors. Thus, to analyze his argument in this stretch of the *Poetics* is to come face to face with that mysterious aspect of Aristotle's literary criticism—his theory of comedy—for which . . . monks have died.[5]

The basis for my approach, which some may find unduly mischievous, has in fact already been laid in stimulating rereadings of the *Poetics* and of Greek tragedy by Gerald Else 1957, John Jones 1962, Richmond Lattimore 1964, Anne Pippin Burnett 1971, and Brian Vickers 1973. Before those relatively recent advances, the typical accounts of Attic *tragōidiai* were deeply anachronistic, containing fundamental misrepresentations of serious Dionysian drama in ancient Athens. The specifically modern orientation of that recently outmoded outlook on tragedy frequently emerges—to mention but a single symptom—in its characteristic vocabulary: "profound" is perhaps the most favored word, followed closely by "destiny," "grappling," "questions," "cosmos," and their synonyms. These cue cards can be flashed in almost any order, such as "In the *Prometheus Bound* Aiskhylos is wrestling with profound questions of fate and freedom," or "Sophokles shows us a man grappling with the cosmic issues of human destiny." Wrestling, to be sure, was a favorite Greek sport, but men never wrestled with issues, certainly not with cosmic issues. They wrestled with other men. In all areas of social interaction, they engaged in what was, by our standards, very fierce competition. The older, anachronistic

5. [Since this joke will be lost on those readers who don't get the allusion, now less evident than it was when Winkler was writing, it may be worth pointing out that Winkler is referring to Umberto Eco's mediaeval murder mystery, *The Name of the Rose* (1980), set in a Benedictine monastery; the book held a special charm for Winkler, beyond its learned gamesmanship, since Winkler had for more than half a dozen years been a Benedictine monk himself.]

interpretations of Attic tragedy systematically rewrote social competition, which was of overwhelming interest to the audiences of the Greek festivals, in terms of abstract entities—issues and questions. I think of this tendency globally as the "Fate and Freedom" interpretation of Greek tragedy.

Critical fantasies, to be sure, like movie monsters, die hard and often rise from their graves to walk again. But though the news of their demise may be premature, greatly exaggerated, and may even, at times, be slow in getting reported at all, it is now no novelty to assert that Greek tragedy is at least as much about family complications as it is about the careers of great soloists ("tragic heroes"), that the crucial complication is quite frequently a matter of mistaken identity rather than of moral failure, and that the ethical energy in the plays is more likely to be centered on concrete, conflicting social norms than on abstract metaphysical issues such as fate and free will.[6]

Let us begin with chapter 14 of the *Poetics*, where Aristotle gives his award for best play at the end of a clear and forceful argument in favor of *tragōidiai* with happy endings.[7] Here Aristotle expands on what I would call his general theory of narrativity—that is, a somewhat peculiar insistence that *muthos*, as he calls it (meaning "story" or "plot"),[8] is the primary element of a serious drama, the "soul" (6.50a38) of the play.[9] At least that insistence becomes peculiar to us when Aristotle goes so far as to dismiss the contribution of staging and actors altogether: "[W]ithout a performance [*agōn*] or actors [*hupokritai*] you still have the essence [*dunamis*] of the play" (6.50b18–19).

6. [Since Winkler wrote these words, readings of Greek tragedy that focus on social issues have become too numerous to record. Among many others, see Griffith 1995, Zeitlin 1996, Wohl 1998, Foley 2001, and the essays in McCoskey and Zakin 2009 and D. Carter 2011b. The essays in Ormand 2012 highlight the connections between Sophokles' plays and contemporary Athenian social and political concerns. The essays collected in Harris, Leão, and Rhodes 2010 focus on the relation of Greek tragedies to Athenian Law. Both White 1992: 232; and Belfiore 1992: 366–67 point out Aristotle's emphasis on conflicts within families (that is, within ties of *philia*).]

7. See White 1992 and Belfiore 1992 for complementary arguments demonstrating that tragedies need not end unhappily to engage seriously with moral concerns.

8. "Although there are some general references to poetic *muthologia* (e.g., *EE* 1230a3), I cannot find the *Poetics*' special sense of *muthos* anywhere else in the corpus. What this means is that Aristotle has taken a term with the senses of story-fable-legend-myth, and without erasing these altogether (they can be seen within the *Poetics* itself at 51b24, 53a18, 37, 53b22) he has given the word a new critical edge and significance" (Halliwell 1986: 57 n. 16). See Belfiore 1992 for an argument that *muthos*, plot, is more important to Aristotle than to most modern viewers of tragedy.

9. The *Poetics* will be cited by chapter number (followed by a period) and then by Bekker page/column/line(s). Inasmuch as the Bekker pages for the *Poetics* run from 1447 to 1462, the first two digits (14-) will be omitted throughout (14.54a4–8 thus refers to chapter 14 of the *Poetics*, Bekker page 1454, column a, lines 4–8). The text I have used is that of D. W. Lucas, *Aristotle*: Poetics (Oxford: Clarendon Press, 1981).

In other words, our emotions of alarm and sympathy should be engaged by the very structure of the story, by "the actual arrangement of the events," not by the diction or the actors' abilities or the many effects of costume and staging (14.53b1–5). "The plot should be so constructed that, without seeing anything take place but just from hearing what occurred, the listener will be moved to feel fear and pity, which is what would happen to anyone who simply heard the story of Oidipous" (or, conceivably, "who simply listened to the text of *Oidipous*") (14.53b3–6). Using this criterion to rank the plots of some existing Classical tragedies, Aristotle goes on to consider the relative merits of different sorts of tragic story lines and to indicate which are better and worse (14.53b26–54a8).

For example, he says that the worst worst-case scenario—the least-tragic tragic plot—is the murder of a family member consciously planned but not executed. Such a scenario can be found, at least in outline, at the end of Sophokles' *Antigone*, when Haimon thinks of killing his father Kreon, lunging at him with his sword but missing him and giving up (14.53b37–54a2). More effective is a deliberate family murder, planned and executed, such as Medeia's slaughter of her children (14.53b27–29).[10] But it is still better to have someone (Oidipous, for example) kill or rape a family member in ignorance of his or her identity and only afterwards realize what they have done. Best of all, however, is the scenario mentioned last, in which someone is "about to commit an irreparable act through ignorance but recognizes the truth before going through with the deed" (14.53b34–36). Aristotle elaborates as follows: "The last possibility is the best [*kratiston*], I mean for instance in the *Kresphontes* when Merope is about to kill her son, but she recognizes him and doesn't kill him, and in the *Iphigeneia* where the same thing happens to sister and brother, and in the *Helle* where the son is about to hand over his mother but recognizes her in time" (14.54a4–8).[11]

To set the stage for this discussion of the best tragic plot, let us return to the spring of the year 425 BCE or shortly before, when Euripides presented his play *Kresphontes*. The subject of two modern commentaries, the *Kresphontes* is one of the best known of Euripides' lost plays.[12] It told how the Her-

10. There is some debate over whether the plot designated here is "next worst" or "second best"; see the useful discussion at White 1992: 233.

11. *Kratiston*, the word translated here as "best," literally means "strongest." There are good reasons to translate it as "best" in this passage, as it has that meaning elsewhere in the *Poetics*, but, as White 1992: 234 notes, Aristotle's practice of shifting between *kratistos* and *kallistos* "risk[s] misunderstanding by varying his terms." On Aristotle's declared preference for the *Kresphontes*, see Scott 2018.

12. Musso 1974; Harder 1985; also, Webster 1967: 136–43. For a general account of Euripidean fragments, see Van Looy 1963. There are fragments as late as the fifth century CE of Euripides' *Melanippe Desmotis* (fragment 495 in Nauck 1964) and of his *Phaithon* (Diggle 1970).

aklid Kresphontes, ruler of Messenia, and two of his sons were assassinated by his brother Polyphontes, who not only assumed the throne but also took Kresphontes' wife Merope as his own. Merope, however, managed to send her baby son, also named Kresphontes, out of the country. He grew up in Aitolia, his life always in danger because Polyphontes, his wicked uncle, had put a price on his head. When he is fully grown, he returns to Messenia and, in order to get into the palace, claims that he has killed Kresphontes Jr. and is entitled to the reward. While King Polyphontes is investigating his story and Kresphontes is waiting in a guest room, Merope's faithful old servant arrives with the news that young Kresphontes has disappeared from Aitolia. Merope then believes that the pretended assassin has told the truth and she heads for his bedchamber with an ax to do him in.

Just as she has raised the ax above her head to deal the blow, the old servant rushes in and stops her. We know what electricity was generated by this scene in performance, because Plutarch says, "Consider Merope in the drama, raising the ax against her son in the belief that he is the one who killed her son, and saying, 'I render you this costly blow'—what a commotion it causes in the theater, bringing everyone to their feet as one, in fear lest she wound the boy before the old man grabs her arm" (Plut., *Moralia* 998E).

We should meditate long and hard on this theatrical moment, inasmuch as Aristotle has singled it out for special praise in the *Poetics* (14.54a4–7, quoted above) and refers to it again in the *Nikomakhean Ethics* (3.1.1111a11). Melodramatic, I think, is not too strong a word to describe it, though we should be careful of the pejorative associations of the term. A key issue with what is loosely called melodrama is the delicate balance it creates between the thrilling and the incredible, a balance that is easily upset.

But when that happens, the result is laughter. Like other memorably melodramatic scenes in Euripides, such as Telephos' threat to kill the baby Orestes, Merope's narrowly averted murder of her son appears to have had its comic take-off, though we cannot identify the author or the play. On an Apulian bell-krater in Bari dated to the second quarter of the fourth century BCE, we find an old man with a huge ax raised over his head, just about to smash an enormous and ominous egg, swaddled in a baby blanket; a servant gestures to him to stop, and out of the egg pops a beautiful female child (plate 14). The baby is usually and obviously identified as Helen; if the old man is Tyndareus and the servant is one who knows the secret of the egg's origin, then we have a scene of family-murder averted at the last minute, based on the *Kresphontes* and cast in a comic mode—as is clear from the dress and padding and masks of the characters.[13] For the overall comic effect, compare Gary Larson's brilliant

13. The vase in question, which has been much discussed, is Bari, Archaeological Museum, inv. 3899; *IGD* IV 26. Porter 1990: 272–73 reads the vase as showing a comedy that parodies the *Kresphontes*. He also suggests that the story here might be a parody of the

cartoon from *The Far Side* series, which depicts an elderly, implacable farmer holding down a chicken on the chopping-block with one hand and raising an ax high over his head with the other: the caption reads, "Seconds before his ax fell, Farmer Dale suddenly noticed the chicken's tattoo—the tattoo that marked them both as brothers of an ancient Tibetan order sworn to loyalty and mutual aid" (the tattoos are, fittingly, quite visible in the drawing).[14]

The plot of Euripides' play continues with the conspiracy of Merope and Kresphontes to assassinate the usurper. She pretends that at long last she will accept his authority, now that her son is dead, and he arranges a joyful celebration. While the sacrifice is being conducted, Kresphontes is assigned to kill the animal-victim but instead strikes down the king.

In rehearsing the plot of the *Kresphontes*, I have applied Aristotle's test of narratability, his general theory of narrativity, as laid out originally in chapter 6 of the *Poetics*, but also put forth, with vivid illustrations, in chapter 14. Does the story of Kresphontes itself engage our emotions of sympathy and alarm? Are we moved to feel fear and pity, just from hearing about the events that occurred? Well, if you find nothing about the plot of Euripides' *Kresphontes* particularly exciting when it is told to you, you probably won't get a lot of thrills or chills from seeing the play performed onstage, or so Aristotle's general theory of narrativity implies.

Aristotle's Special Theory of Narrativity

One of the effects of Aristotle's decision to give so much primacy to plot is that it enables us to have some idea of what he would have made of certain lost plays whose plots we know. This of course takes us into the treacherous waters of the *Hupotheseis Euripidou* ("Tales from Euripides")—which Sextus Empiricus (*Adv. Math.* 3.3) refers to as the "Tales from Euripides and Sophokles," though only portions relating to Euripides have been found[15]—and into the even more risky terrain of Hyginus' *Fabulae*. At least one alphabetized collection of tragic plot summaries is known to have circulated as a work of the great Peripatetic

birth of Athena (273–74). For its relation to the *Kresphontes*, see also Harder 1985: 114–18. Taplin 1993: 82–83 suggests that the vase shows a comedy about the birth of Helen and points out that in Kratinos' *Nemesis* the egg out of which Helen was born was shown on stage. Marshall 2014: 68 sees the vase as evidence for a comedy about the birth of Helen.

14. [We were, unfortunately, unable to obtain permission from Andrews McMeel Syndication, which manages the rights to Mr. Larson's work, to publish the cartoon.]

15. To date, eight or nine copies of this work (or works) have been identified: *P. Oxy.* 2457 (*Alexandros, Alkestis, Aiolos*); *P. Colon.* inv. 264 (*Auge*); *P. Oxy.* 420 (*Elektra*); *P. IFAO, PSP* 248 (*Medeia*); *P. Amst.* inv. 35 (*Peliades*); *P. Oxy.* 2455 (*Orestes, Sisyphos, Temenos, Telephos* [?], *Troiades, Temenidai, Tennes, Philoktetes, Phrixos II, Phoinissai, Khrysippos*, and on another piece of the same copy [*P. Strasbourg Gr.* 2676 A a] *Syleus*); *PSI* 1286 (*Rhesos, Rhadamanthus, Skirioi*); *P. Mich.* inv. 1319 (*Temenidai*). Austin 1968, appendix II.

scholar Dikaiarkhos. But Jeffrey Rusten has argued that, inasmuch as alphabetization is a post-Dikaiarkhan development in the technology of scholarship, this collection is likely in fact to be pseudonymous.[16] The same seems to be true for an even more important source of information about Classical plays: Hyginus' *Fabulae* (ed. H. J. Rose, 1933). The real Hyginus was a learned Greek in charge of the emperor Augustus' library; the mythological handbook that survives under his name is a Latin translation of a Greek original and is probably by someone other than the famous Hyginus.

In any case, two of the chapters in "Hyginus" are explicitly titled *Euripidis*, "of Euripides." Most scholars admit Hyginus' *Fabulae* to the front ranks of informative testimony about the content of lost plays, not only because of the patently theatrical quality of many of the narratives, but also because of the close correspondence between the topics treated in the *Fabulae* and the known list of Classical tragedies. One may quibble about points of detail: for example, whose *Elektra* or whose *Thyestes* is Hyginus summarizing? Since playwrights continuously recycled the same finite set of myth-historical situations, it is quite conceivable that some of the tragic plots that I will retail derive not from Euripides or Sophokles but from little-known poets. For my purposes, however, it matters only that Hyginus' material be derived from some Classical play composed between 534 and c. 330 BCE.[17]

With appropriate caution I would venture to say that among the lost plays of both Euripides and Sophokles, tentatively reconstructed from many such sources, there are a fair number that answer to the exact requirements of what I call Aristotle's special theory of narrativity: that is, his doctrine that there is one type of plot beyond all others that makes for an excellent tragedy—namely, one in which someone actually, or nearly, rapes or murders an unsuspected family member before going on to discover that person's true identity. The Greek plays that once exemplified Aristotle's favorite plot type may have been gradually weeded out of the canon of Classical tragedy by post-Classical selectors, and they may now be rarities in the corpus of surviving tragedies, but the evidence of ancient plot summaries indicates that they were not necessarily untypical of *tragōidiai* produced in the fifth and fourth centuries BCE. The key features of the plot type of this "best tragedy," *hē kallistē tragōidia*, which

16. Rusten 1982. Several papyrus fragments of ps.-Dikaiarkhos survive, and they appear to be the common source for plot summaries in various mythographic works and scholia; the work seems to have contained only plot summaries of Euripides' plays and "no critical comments or didascalic information" (Rusten 1982: 358).

17. The scorecard on Hyginus' accuracy keeps changing: *P. Oxy.* 2455 shows that his version of Phrixos' story is that of Euripides' *Phrixos II*; but his version of Alexandros' exposure and recognition, though it follows the same lines as Euripides' *Alexandros*, differs in the motive for Alexandros' return and in the identity of his would-be murderer (Coles 1974).

Aristotle devotes most of his time and attention in the *Poetics* to delineating, are set out in chapters 7–14 of that treatise.

Tragic plots, Aristotle tells us, may be either simple or complex (10.52a12). The succession of events in a story may be a simple, linear one. For instance, the tyrant declares he will murder the children of Herakles, the chorus and other characters beg him not to do it, he stands firm, and eventually a messenger arrives and announces that he has done it. The End. Such a plot type, obviously enough, does not pass Aristotle's test of narratability, as stipulated in his general theory of narrativity. It would not be unfair to the achievements of Aiskhylos to note that the *Persians*, *Seven against Thebes*, and *Suppliant Women*, for all their many excellences, do not have plots that can grip an audience's attention in the retelling.[18] To do that, an author needs to introduce two kinds of unexpected change: *peripeteia*/Reversal (Herakles appears, kills the tyrant, and saves his children) and *anagnōrisis*/Recognition (Herakles appears, kills the tyrant, and saves his children; then an old shepherd wanders in and tells him that the tyrant was actually Herakles' long-lost brother).

Euripides' *Ino* (= Hyginus 4), like the *Kresphontes* a relatively early play, will illustrate the type. Ino, the wife of the Thessalian king Athamas, by whom she has two sons, goes off with other women to join the Bacchic rout of Dionysos. Athamas, believing that she is dead, takes a second wife, named Themisto, and has two children by her too. Later, he learns that Ino is still alive on Mount Parnassos. He sends for her, but he hides her identity from his second wife and passes her off as a new nursemaid for the four children. Themisto, true to her role as stepmother, decides to do away with the two older children. She tells the nurse to cover Ino's children with black covers when they go to bed and her own children with white covers. Ino reverses the blankets, and Themisto ends up killing her own children. No one comes to a good end in this play: Themisto commits suicide; Athamas goes mad and kills one of his other children; Ino jumps off a cliff and becomes a sea-goddess.

While we are still on the topic of infanticide, let us consider a series of events late in the Medeia saga, as told in what is probably another Classical tragedy, this one answering to Aristotle's preference for happy endings (Hyginus 27). Medeia, having murdered her children, flees to Athens, where she is received by King Aigeus and has a son by him called Medus. (Both Sophokles and Euripides composed plays with the title of *Aigeus* that touched on Medeia's sojourn in Athens.[19]) Exiled from Athens in turn for additional bad behavior, Medeia returns to her native Kolkhis, now ruled by Perses, her uncle, who has been warned by an oracle to fear for his life from his brother's

18. "The structure of his dramas does not contain many reversals and complications, as do those of the younger dramatists" (according to an ancient "Life of Aiskhylos": Page 1972: 331, line 16).

19. See Collard and Cropp 2008: 3–5.

descendants (Medeia and her line). Medus follows his mother to Kolkhis, gets caught in a storm, and after being washed up on shore falls into the king's hands. Aware of the danger he is in, Medus pretends to be Hippotes, son of Kreon, the Korinthian king whom Medeia had murdered. Perses imprisons him while looking into the matter. Meanwhile Medeia, thinking Medus really is Hippotes and has come to Kolkhis in order to avenge his father by killing her, persuades Perses that his prisoner is actually Medus (which is indeed the case, though Medeia doesn't know it), who has been sent by Aigeus to kill the king. Having thus outed her son to Perses, though unwittingly, Medeia then persuades Perses to hand Medus over to her, so she can kill him (in what would be a reprise of her infanticide). Just when Medus is about to be killed by his mother for impersonating Hippotes, Medeia recognizes him, gets him alone, gives him a sword, and arranges for him to kill Perses and to rule the kingdom, now called Media ("Persia"). Recognition and Reversal win the day. The thrill produced by their close proximity vindicates Aristotle's claim that, in the best sort of plays, *peripeteia* and *anagnōrisis* happen at the same moment (11.52a32–33).[20] That is what we find in the *Kresphontes* and, of course, in *Iphigeneia among the Taurians*.

Let me also cite an example from Sophokles, since Euripides and his ilk should not be allowed to hog center stage. As everyone knows, there are two surviving Iphigeneia plays, both of them by Euripides. What everyone may not know, however, is that in addition to Euripides' *Iphigeneia at Aulis* and *Iphigeneia among the Taurians*, there was also Sophokles' *Khryses* ("Iphigeneia Part Three") and his *Aletes* ("Iphigeneia Part Four").[21] Sophokles' *Khryses* (= Hyginus 121) picks up the continuing story of Orestes from the point when Iphigeneia, Orestes, and Pylades are fleeing from the Taurians with King Thoas hot on their trail. They stop over at the island of Sminthē, home of Apollo's priest Khryses, whose daughter Khryseis (as we know from the first book of Homer's *Iliad*) had been carried off by Agamemnon to be his mistress when the Greeks sacked the island on their way to Troy. According to Sophokles' play, when Agamemnon gave Khryseis back to her father, she swore that he had not slept with her, but she was lying. When she had Agamemnon's baby, she told Khryses that Apollo was the father. That son, also named Khryses, who is in fact Iphigeneia's and Orestes' half-brother, is now king of the island, and obviously he is no friend to traveling Greeks. When Iphigeneia and company land, he captures them and holds them, intending to turn them over to Thoas. But his mother hears the strangers

20. See Belfiore 1992: 366–68.

21. The case for attributing Hyginus' chapters entitled "Chryses" and "Aletes" (121, 122) to Sophokles' plays of the same name is not quite as iron-clad as it was for attributing to Euripides' *Kresphontes* and *Ino* the corresponding chapters in Hyginus, but the probability is still very high. See Pearson 1917: vol. 2, pp. 327–30; vol. 1, pp. 62–67.

say that they are the children of Agamemnon, and she reveals to her son that they are his brother and sister. He therefore takes their side and conspires with them to kill Thoas. The Recognition quickly leads to a Reversal and averts the catastrophe, and the characters with whom we sympathize have a happy ending.

There are other plays of Sophokles that fit the same "melodramatic" plot type—such as the *Aletes* (= Hyginus 122), which follows Orestes and Iphigeneia back to Argos. Elektra has received a false message arranged by Aigisthos' son, Aletes, to the effect that Orestes has been killed by the Taurians. So she goes to the oracle of Apollo at Delphi, the scene of the play, in order to verify the report by asking the god. She arrives there on the very same day as Iphigeneia and friends, and the same deceitful messenger tells her that the strange woman who has just arrived from the Taurians is the very one who killed her brother. Elektra grabs a flaming torch from the altar and tries to put out Iphigeneia's eyes, but Orestes stops her, the Recognition occurs, and together they head back to Mykenai and assassinate Aletes. Orestes wants to kill Aletes' sister, too, but Artemis snatches her away and makes her a priestess in Athens.[22]

I called these plays sequels, but the truth is more interesting. *Aletes* cannot be dated with certainty, but *Khryses* must have been produced before the year 414, because Aristophanes parodies it in the *Birds*. *Iphigeneia among the Taurians* was probably performed around 412; *Iphigeneia at Aulis* was produced after Euripides' death in 406 (Sophokles also wrote a play on that subject, but its date is not known). If this chronology is correct, we are most likely confronted by the unlikely phenomenon of a four-part saga written in reverse order, which suggests that the Iphigeneia material was well enough known that playwrights could dip into it at whatever point in the story they wished.

22. Scholars like Wilamowitz and Rose refuse to believe that the plot summaries of *Khryses* and *Aletes* in Hyginus, both of which are clearly theatrical in nature, can go back to Sophokles, because Sophokles just didn't do that kind of thing: Wilamowitz, aware that Pacuvius wrote a play called the *Chryses*, assumes that his source could not have been Sophokles, but must have been a post-Euripidean drama (Wilamowitz-Moellendorf 1883: 257; cited in Pearson 1917: vol. 2, p. 335). Rose 1933 *ad* Hyginus 122 (p. 87) comments (in Latin), "For if anyone wishes to believe that the material from this chapter and the one above it comes from the *Aletes* and *Khryses* of Sophokles, let him believe it for all I care, but let him note that there is no evidence for this, nor is any support provided for the proof of the matter from the smallest fragments [of Sophokles] that remain." Wilamowitz insists that the plot of Euripides' *Iphigeneia among the Taurians* is a novelty, a free fantasy of the playwright's own creation, which had no basis in tradition. There is no supporting argument for this view: it is just an opinion based on the premises that Classical *tragōidiai* were consistently "tragic" and that Euripides was something of a scamp.

Loose Canons

There are other plays of Sophokles that fit the "melodramatic" plot type. Among the lost plays, for example, is the marvelous *Thyestes in Sikyon*, a Verdiesque grand opera if there ever was one: I'll return to it at the conclusion of this chapter. Among Sophokles' extant plays, however, only the *OT* really fits Aristotle's special theory of narrativity, his narrow preference for family dramas of mistaken identity that combine Reversal and Recognition. This raises an interesting question. If we had a random sample of fifth-century plays, would they confirm Aristotle's taste and principles or not?

As it happens, we can formulate a tentative answer to that question—in the affirmative.[23] Conveniently enough for our purposes, the extant plays of Euripides fall into two traditions: there are the ten that were selected for commentary,[24] like the seven (out of seventy) of Aiskhylos and the seven (out of ninety plus) of Sophokles that were similarly selected; there are also nine others that survived by accident from an alphabetically arranged collection of Euripides' complete works. It is to the latter happy twist of *tukhē* that we owe the plays whose titles begin with *E, H, I,* and *K*.[25] Among them are the *Helen*, the *Ion*, and the *Iphigeneia among the Taurians*. Now, whole books have been written about Greek tragedy that do not mention these three *tragōidiai*, since they are not particularly "tragic" in the loose—and, I would argue, post-Classical—sense of the term. Perhaps the chief methodological ineptitude of modern discussions of Attic *tragōidiai* is their blinkered concentration on the canonical selection and the implicit equation of that selection with the whole field of tragedy. Even the most meticulous scholars lapse into the mistake of treating the thirty-two extant *tragōidiai* as if they constituted Greek Tragedy as a whole. "The number of Greek tragedies [to which Else's notion of *hamartia* ("tragic error") applies] does not exceed one," says the ever-acidulous R. D. Dawe.[26]

The survival of Euripides' "alphabetical" plays was an accident, but it is no accident that Aristotle's special theory of narrativity, his definition of the best

23. See, now, Marx 2012, who elaborates this argument independently, having had no previous access to this chapter.

24. The pattern of papyrus discoveries indicates both that the selected plays were among the most popular of all times and that the other plays, those outside the select group, were still available to readers in later centuries.

25. *Helen, Elektra, Herakles, Herakleidai, Hiketides, IA, IT, Ion, Kyklops*. See Zuntz 1965, chapter 6; Page 1934, chapter 1; Barrett 1964: 45–53. The ten selected plays are *Hekabe, Orestes, Phoinissai, Hippolytos, Medeia, Andromakhe, Alkestis, Rhesos, Troiades*, and *Bakkhai*. These ten plays (except the *Bakkhai*) are accompanied by ancient scholia and show a manuscript tradition distinct from the other nine. The nine plays outside the selection have no scholia.

26. Dawe 1968: 91.

sort of tragic plot, is most fully exemplified by some of those plays. For Aristotle's analysis was aimed at a particular type of *tragōidia*, one that was admired in its time but that came to seem peculiarly untragic by later, post-Aristotelian standards. As a result, this type of *tragōidia* is seriously underrepresented in our canon of Greek tragedy—and, therefore, in our theories of tragedy as well. Moreover, the core of the plot of Aristotle's favorite type of tragedy is what I have called a scenario of risk: it features a peril (*kindunos*) of unexpected complexity that threatens to overwhelm the protagonists, but from which they sometimes manage to escape (like Iphigeneia and Orestes) and at other times do not (like Oidipous).[27]

Aristotle on the Social Classes of Literature

Modern white-collar folk are no longer attuned, for the most part, to the cultural significance that *kindunos* held for the Classical Greeks. We tend not to have such a powerful sense of how moments of peril faced are supremely self-defining for those who face them, both in their own eyes and in the eyes of those who may be present to witness the spectacle. Nor do we often have occasion to conceive, in Mediterranean fashion, of ordinary, daily personal life as a theater of excellence in which people of real (though not perfect) virtue show their neighbors what they are made of—most of all in moments of crisis, when they find themselves threatened by the encircling coils of malice and their own mistakes. In fact, such a cultural style of dramatizing characters and events can easily seem to us to be melodramatic.

We may be tempted to smile at the sort of situations called for by Aristotle's criteria for the best tragic plot: long-lost relatives who do not recognize one another and who are involved in situations where rape, incest, and murder either have occurred or are just on the verge of occurring. In our world, there are several art forms in which the plots favored by Aristotle still abound, but those art forms tend to be relegated to the special regions of very high or very low culture—namely, grand opera and soap opera. In order to appreciate both the pleasure such tales afforded Athenian (and more generally Greek) audiences and the cultural wisdom they seemed to embody, not only must we carefully bracket our aesthetic feelings about "melodramatic" plots, but also, most especially, we need to suspend the assumptions of our own society about civic and personal identity, proper bearing in public and in private, as well as social relations in the family and in the marketplace.

27. White 1992 argues, similarly, that Aristotle's "best" tragedies all involve admirable responses to instances of "moral luck," i.e., circumstances that are out of the control of the characters in question. Whether the end result of the play is happy or unhappy is, in White's view, less important than the way in which the characters respond to these situations. See especially White 1992: 222–25.

Now it might seem that Aristotle himself has made a major contribution to the misunderstanding of the immediate social impact of such *kindunos* plots on their public by analyzing them in sheerly formalist or structural terms. According to a facile reading of the *Poetics*, the easiest way to tell a superb tragedy from a mediocre one is simply to look at its plot and see whether that plot contains a Reversal and a Recognition. But such a formalist reading misses the degree to which the criteria of dramatic excellence in the *Poetics* are dependent on and supported by overriding considerations of social value. In what follows, I will try to show that what might at first appear to be Aristotle's purely structural checklist for the essential elements of a successful tragic plot is in fact the expression of a set of specifically social concerns, and that his literary analysis is often motivated by preoccupations of a social nature.

The full extent of Aristotle's social preoccupations in the *Poetics* ought to be evident from a glance at the text's opening pages, which are a kind of meditation on how to cut up the field of literature. Shall we do it by formal differences, such as musical vs. nonmusical, prose vs. verse? No, because some important genres, such as tragedy and comedy, are both musical and nonmusical and employ various kinds of verse and dance rhythms.

Shall we then segregate the genres according to the kinds of characters in them? That would entail drawing a major boundary on the map of literature in accordance with the social division between better and worse sorts of human behavior—that is, a boundary separating those literary characters who pursue social and personal excellence from the irresponsible clowns who don't. Aristotle's words for these two broad social types are *spoudaios* and *phaulos*. *Spoudaioi* characters are those who cultivate *aretē* ("excellence"); *phauloi* do not. *Phauloi* are not players on the competitive gameboard that is *polis* society;[28] the literary world they inhabit is called "comedy." As Aristotle says, "[T]his is precisely the difference between tragedy and comedy" (2.48a16–17). So a decision to privilege this specifically social principle of categorization would have the effect of keeping tragedy and comedy at a great distance from each other. Such a method of distinguishing tragedy and comedy would not make use of any formal considerations, but would focus on the comparative virtue of the characters, on their respective styles of behavior and degrees of social reputability.

Without yet announcing a decision, Aristotle moves on to a third possibility. We might classify literature by its mode of presentation, separating those kinds of literature that are recited or narrated by a single person, who may take many parts, from those enacted by a company of costumed performers (3.48a19–23; such a scheme of literary classification, in fact, had already

28. "The more dignified performers represented decent behavior and decent people, the commoner sort represented the behavior of good-for-nothing people [*phauloi*]" (5.48b25–26).

been proposed by Sokrates in the third book of Plato's *Republic*). Aristotle's one comment on the consequences of this division, which I read as a devastating objection in his mind (and a straw in the wind indicating the general drift of his thought), is that it would result in classing Sophokles with Aristophanes, tragedy with comedy: the dominant category, in short, would simply be "drama." The previous alternative, a categorization of literature by social behavior—by the relative value attaching to the pursuits of the characters featured in it—would result (he says) in classing Sophokles with Homer, since both portray *spoudaioi*, men in pursuit of excellence, rather than *phauloi* (3.48a25–27). The alternatives are clearly set out: shall we let our literary map be determined by the categories of social behavior or by the difference in mode of presentation between narrative and drama?

The answer, though not made explicit, comes through loud and clear in the rest of the *Poetics*. Aristotle frequently illustrates the excellence of tragedy with examples drawn from Homer, without betraying any awareness that he has crossed a categorial boundary separating drama from narrative (or epic).[29] Furthermore, his overall insistence throughout the *Poetics* on considering the plot before anything else is of a piece with his antidramatic bias, his de-emphasis of the mode of presentation as a basis for literary classification, his denigration of spectacle, and his constant appeal to degrees of social value for taxonomic purposes.

This is especially clear in his treatment of tragedy. Aristotle's rejection of the dramatic mode of presentation, and of performance itself, in favor of plot as the essence of tragedy reflects his sense that social criteria matter for literary classification. For if Aristotle is hesitant to treat drama as a unitary category defined by its mode of presentation, à la Plato, that is at least partly because such a definition of drama would comprehend both tragedy and comedy without making sufficient allowance for the social distance between the kinds of literary characters featured in them.[30] An emphasis on plot, by contrast, allows for the possibility of classifying stories according to the relative worth or seriousness of their main characters.

In order to grasp this, and to understand how such a commitment to social distinctions animates Aristotle's insistence on the primacy of plot, we'll need to look more closely at the confrontation Aristotle has engineered between *muthos* and *opsis*, between "plot" and "spectacle." One of the three axes along

29. 16.54b25–30; 55a2–4; 17.55b16–23; 24.60a25–26, 34–36. As Rosenmeyer 1985: 79 puts it, "The handling of the epic in the *Poetics* might justifiably lead to the conclusion that, in important respects, for Aristotle the epic is as much a subcategory of drama as an independent entity."

30. See L. Golden 1992 on the distinction between comic and tragic mimesis in Aristotle's discussions. Golden argues that the quality of mimesis and the pleasure it produces are not distinct in comedy and tragedy, but that "these differences evoke contrasting emotional responses because the object of the *mimesis* in each case is radically different" (65).

which kinds of literature may be classified, according to Aristotle, is the "manner" (*hōs*: 1.47a16–18, 3.48a19–24)—in other words, the mode of presentation. The choice of manner or mode of presentation spells the difference, as we have seen, between (1) a story that is narrated, whether in the narrator's own voice or in the voices of other people (fictional characters), whom the narrator impersonates by quoting their words, as Homer does, and (2) a story that is acted out without a narrator by several persons who pretend to be the characters.[31] Our words for this distinction are simply "narrative" and "drama," but Aristotle's habit in speaking of his distinction of "manner" is to call the second of these two modes of presentation—the fully enacted, narrator-less mode or manner—the "spectacle" (*opsis*). Thus, at 6.49b31–33 he says, "Since the imitation is being presented as a performance by actors [rather than by a narrator], mounting a spectacle [*opsis*] is obviously one of the primary elements of a tragedy."

Aristotle makes the same point again at 6.50a7–12, where the three *ways* of distinguishing kinds of literature are coordinated with the six "parts" of any tragedy: the *means* of imitation in tragedy comprise (1) "speech," (2) "thought," and (3) "music"; the *objects* of imitation are (4) "action" and (5) "character"; the *manner* of imitation is simply called (6) "spectacle." "Spectacle," in some passages then, is Aristotle's name for the factor that differentiates a dramatic presentation from a narrative presentation, such as a Homeric epic or any other narrative. *Opsis* can thus be used both in a narrow sense, which focuses on the scenery, costumes, and staging of a play, and in a more global sense, which includes everything dramatically enacted as opposed to narrated. *Opsis*, that is, can refer to the dramatic mode of presentation itself.

Aristotle's derogation of *opsis* is insistent and repeated. "Spectacle is entertaining, to be sure, but it requires no expertise and is quite irrelevant to the work itself" (6.50b16–17). "The contrivance of spectacle is more the province of the prop-man [or 'costume designer'] than of the poet" (6.50b19–20). "An author may contrive to send tremors of pity and fear through the audience by spectacle alone, but [compared to the emotions generated by the plot] these are mindless effects which money can buy" (14.53b1–11, paraphrased).

Aristotle's glossing of *opsis* as the work of the prop-man or costume designer has allowed some readers to think that the word *opsis*, according to Aristotle's usage, is restricted to those material accessories and not to notice that the term can also include acting and indeed the dramatic mode of presentation as such. But, in fact, *opsis* is defined in such a way that it becomes Aristotle's global word for enactment by role-playing performers as opposed to recital by a single narrator. To banish all doubt, in the same sentence that

31. 3.48a21–24. This difficult passage may also be construed as setting out a threefold division, similar to that in Plato, *Republic* 392D–394D. See Lucas' commentary ad loc. (Lucas 1981).

glosses *opsis* as sets and costumes, Aristotle, as we have seen, also dismisses performance and actors as inessential to tragedy: "without a performance [*agōn*] or actors [*hupokritai*] you still have the essence [*dunamis*] of the play" (6.50b18–19).

Modern readers may find it perverse that Aristotle should, both in his explicit pronouncements and in his choice of category names, reduce all that pertains to the performance of a story by actors (rather than by a narrator) to a single, slightly contemptuous word: *opsis*. But the reduction is a deliberate and well-motivated strategy. It flows from Aristotle's sense that it is more meaningful to compare tragedians to Homer than to Aristophanes: "Sophokles can on one arrangement be classed with Homer, for both portray serious personages, but on another arrangement Sophokles would be classed with Aristophanes, for both of them put actors and performers before us" (3.48a25–27, paraphrased). We do not find it upsetting to group Sophokles and Aristophanes together, for both are—in our perception—dramatists, or playwrights, whose works exhibit a shared mode of presentation. We are therefore perfectly comfortable with a theory of literature that includes comedy along with tragedy in a single, unitary category called drama. But Aristotle balks at any proposition that would allow tragedy and comedy to be yoked together. Because Sophokles and Aristophanes share the same poetic "manner" or mode of presentation, *viz.* use of actors and stage equipment, and because it seems to Aristotle profoundly wrong, even slightly disgusting, to treat them as if they were somehow versions of the same thing, Aristotle systematically demeans what they have in common—namely, *opsis*: spectacle, theatrical enactment—and exalts instead the element that differentiates them, the element that serious playwrights share with Homer—namely, *muthos*: plot.[32] For plot makes reference to the personages who figure in the story and specifies the social ranks they occupy, whereas the difference of "manner" between narrative and drama is blind to social distinctions among the protagonists and inattentive to the contrasts between serious and trivial characters.

In other words, Aristotle's reluctance to categorize tragedy together with comedy—as if they were both species of a single generic class of literature, called "drama"—motivates his tendency to play down the importance of that which is at once unique and common to all forms of drama, whether tragic or comic: namely, the dramatic mode of presentation itself. What gives rise to Aristotle's notorious animus against spectacle—his view (so surprising to us) that staging is inessential to the success of a properly constructed tragedy (what, in short, I have called his general theory of narrativity)—is his desire to preserve the distinction between the better and the worse sorts of human

32. See L. Golden 1992: 63–104 for a sustained discussion of the distinction between comic and tragic mimesis.

behavior as a basis for literary classification and to give that distinction a decisive role in literary analysis.

The acutely trained social sensitivity to matters of dignity and propriety that informs Aristotle's way of constructing of literary classes, and motivates in particular his segregation of Aristophanes from Sophokles, makes itself felt very clearly in chapter 26, where the discussion concerns whether epic is superior to tragedy. The *prima facie* case against tragedy comes down to what is regarded as its "obvious" failing: "[I]t is obvious [*dēlon*] that the art which acts everything out is eminently *phortikē*"—a word whose sense is almost that of "proletarian" (26.61b28–29). The very fact that tragedy employs persons acting out all the events of a plot, instead of employing narrators to convey a simple statement of those events, is acknowledged to be a sign that it is aimed at a lower class of audience. The argument is that commoners (*phauloi*) need more than a verbal account to comprehend what is being communicated. Spectators who are dignified and suitably educated (*epieikeis*) do not need (*deontai*) the additional gestures and movement and so forth (26.62a2–4).

Nevertheless, Aristotle ultimately refuses to consider tragedy inferior to epic on the basis of its intended audience and the social implications of its dramatic mode. Aristotle does allow that such an objection against tragedy is a valid one, but he goes on to argue that the concentrated, tight-knit plots in good tragedies are to be preferred to the looser narratives of epic. For even good epics are so sprawling that they contain enough stories to generate the plots of many tragedies; they don't have the ruthlessly pared-down, unified plots that good tragedies do. Aristotle elevates tragedy over epic, then, not *qua* drama or acting but *qua* plot. It is the superiority of tragic to epic plots that settles the question of the relative value of the two genres.[33] Aristotle's answer to the charge that tragedy, *qua* drama, is intrinsically directed at the lower classes is that it is possible to have restrained performances, which minimize the movement, the gestures, the props, and the acting out, just as there can be Homeric reciters who overact—that is, who act.

The distinction is important. It is acting itself that Aristotle dislikes. Aristotle is not just criticizing crowd-pleasing spectacles: he is downplaying the dramatic mode of presentation as such. He is not merely repudiating what stuffy critics nowadays might regard as the Broadway Musical style of Greek drama—he is not simply recoiling from obviously vulgar performances in which physical movement, material lavishness, and exotic music overwhelm the words—so as to contrive a more defensible brief for Serious Theater; he

33. Aristotle does add, almost as an afterthought, that tragedy improves on epic insofar as tragedy includes, as a kind of bonus, music and visual effects (*tas opseis*) (26.62a15–17). Modern editors of the *Poetics* tend to athetize *tas opseis* for the sake of consistency, but see Konstan 2013, who argues that it is not necessary to banish any reference to spectacle from this passage, so long as we understand that Aristotle regards spectacle as entirely subordinate to plot.

is not attempting to set apart high-toned verbal drama ("acting") from showy extravaganzas ("overacting"). Because it would go against all our expectations that the first organized theory of drama, which is what we take the *Poetics* to be, should have no use for the stage or for actors, modern readers of Aristotle's text have not noted what is literally there—*viz.* that in derogating *opsis* Aristotle is dismissing the importance of dramatic enactment *per se*. But that is precisely what Aristotle is doing.

However counterintuitive to us it may seem that a supposed theory of drama like the *Poetics* would place so little value on theater people—actors and costumers and set designers—and on theatrical representation itself, we should not presume that Aristotle's disparagement of live performance reflects the bookish prejudice of the writer or the professional intellectual. We should rather discern in it a considered philosophical position. What the audience of a tragedy will be most deeply engaged and moved by, Aristotle reasons, are the changing fortunes of social actors caught in situations that replicate the malice, irony, and strife of life itself—scenarios of risk featuring serious personages playing competitive games for high stakes—not mere stage effects or the pumped-up emotionalism of professional actors who play to the crowd. That is why the better sort of tragedian, in composing a tragedy, will concentrate above all on "the actual arrangement of the events [*ta pragmata*]."[34]

By a curious pincer movement, what seemed to be Aristotle's fondness for "melodrama" is countered by his insistence on restraint in presentation. He wants maximum tension (in the plot or narrative) with minimum histrionics (in the performance). His criterion here is exactly that which he applies to the subject of speaking before a jury. It is possible, he notes in the *Rhetoric* (3.1.3–5), to employ certain techniques of overwrought delivery and to sway some votes by blind emotion rather than by presenting the facts of the case. Aristotle's word for "delivery" is *hupokrisis*, literally "acting." *Hupokrisis* may well be effective, but it exceeds the strict demands of justice, which require only reference to the basic facts. Just as in a serious trial, then, you should rely on "the events themselves," *auta ta pragmata*, to make your case (*Rhetoric* 3.1.3), so in composing a serious drama you should focus your main efforts on "the actual arrangement of the events," *ta pragmata* (*Poetics* 14.53b1–3)—that is, the plot.[35]

34. Arist., *Poet.* 14.53b1–3: "[I]t is possible, to be sure, for what is frightening and pitiable to arise from the spectacle [*opsis*], but it is also possible for it to arise from the actual arrangement of the events [*ex autēs tēs sustaseōs tōn pragmatōn*], which is prior and pertains to the better poet." Aristotle insists again on the crucial role of *ta pragmata* ("the events") a few lines later at 14.53b5. Konstan 2013 argues that Aristotle does not wholly despise the kinds of effects brought about by spectacle, merely that he regards spectacle as inferior to plot structure as a method for producing an emotional impact.

35. Harris 2017 provides an excellent study of the way that litigants were expected to behave in Athenian court trials in comparison to the rhetorical modes of characters in

Aristotle's decision to analyze dramatic excellence in terms of narrative rather than properly dramatic techniques goes hand in glove with his focus on the social meanings of the stage. His emphasis on narrative plot is consistent with his commitment to a reading of tragedy in terms of *aretē*—the better and worse in human behavior—and to the priority of social criteria for classifying dramatic presentations in general. That double bias—for plot and against clowns—not only shapes his choice of basic terms and categories. It also determines what problems seem interesting to him. It informs the *Poetics* as a whole.

Aristotle on Comedy

Now at last I come to Aristotle's theory of comedy. In the previous section, I acknowledged that we are tempted to smile at melodramatic plot complications involving long-lost relatives (complications of the sort that Aristotle's special theory of narrativity prescribes for tragedy and that *kindunos* plots in general tend to feature). We may smile, but so did the Athenians, and they had been smiling at such plots for a generation or two before Aristotle's *Poetics*. That much we can gather from the remains of fourth-century Attic comedy. Aristophanes' *Kokalos*, for example, produced shortly after 388, contained a rape and a recognition like those in Euripides' *Ion*. Such features went on to become standard in New Comedy.[36] But the complex emplotment of Athenian comedy that is fully visible to us in Menander, our most complete example of New Comedy, was nothing new. It had been a fact of dramatic life in Athens long before Aristotle moved there.

Most modern accounts of the development of Attic comedy emphasize that Old Comedy is relatively disjointed and episodic in comparison to the more carefully plotted New Comedy. But Aristotle's notion of comedy assigns more decisive importance to the sheer presence of plot than does ours. His periodization of comedy (in chapter 5 of the *Poetics*) accordingly collapses the distinctions we draw between Old and New Comedy, placing a major dividing line much earlier, between those comedies in an "iambic form" and those with

drama. Harris shows that litigants were considerably more restrained than the characters of tragedy, as a matter of strategy. While litigants might suggest that the *judges* should have an emotional response to the events of a case, Harris points out that litigants themselves very rarely, if ever, called attention to their own emotions in presenting the particulars of their arguments (Harris 2017: esp. 226–29). Harris discusses Aristotle's *Rhetoric* 3.2 at 239.

36. Menander's *Epitrepontes* has a plot parallel to that of Euripides' *Alope* (= Hyginus 187), and its characters refer to Sophokles' *Tyro* as the paradigm of their own situation (*Epitr.* 325–33). The mere word *skaphos*, cradle, is sufficient to recall the entire plot of the *Tyro* (Ar., *Lys.* 138–39; Arist., *Poet.* 16.54b25). One of the stranger instances of the Whose Baby? group on the Classical stage was Euripides' *Kretans*, which dealt with the infant Minotaur: see illustrations 5–9 in B. Cantarella 1964.

plots and arguments (*logous kai muthous*, 5.49b8–9).[37] In Aristotle's view, the decisive event was the emplotment of comedy, which he takes to be an invention of Epikharmos and Phormis in Sicily, and which (he says) was first introduced at Athens by Krates (c. 450–430). Aristotle's conception of all known comedy, then, including both what we call Old Comedy and New Comedy, is that of a plotted drama. Comedy, as Aristotle defines the entire genre, has *muthos* just like tragedy.[38]

Leaving Krates out of it, we can see from the mere juxtaposition of, say, the *Kokalos* and the *Ion* how structural correspondences between comic and tragic plots could spell particular trouble for Aristotle's efforts to differentiate comedy from tragedy. The task of distinguishing between comedy and tragedy on the basis of their plots, as opposed to their *look* in production (which was, of course, unmistakably different), would have posed significant difficulties to any theoretician of the later fourth century, such as Aristotle, who accorded so much importance to plot for the purposes of literary classification.

But Aristotle was in a special fix of his own devising. For by specifying a certain complex plot-structure (a *muthos*) featuring Recognitions and Reversals as the element that distinguishes an excellent *tragōidia* from mediocre ones, Aristotle created a definition whose terms might, without further specification, also include the dramatic narrative of a comedy like the *Kokalos* or indeed the narratives of any comedies with mistaken identities, any comedies of errors. Since one of the underlying concerns of Aristotle's social analysis of drama is to keep comedy at a proper distance while he is describing the best type of tragedy, he must take particular pains to ensure that his definition of the best type of tragedy does not unwittingly include some examples of comedy. This requires some fancy intellectual footwork, and it is primarily accomplished in chapters 11–13 of the *Poetics*.

First, to forestall the conceivable misapplication of his plot-driven analysis of the best type of tragedy, Aristotle specifies a third element of the best tragic *muthos*: "Reversal and Recognition are two parts of the plot, the third is a dire event [*pathos*]. . . . A *pathos* is a destructive or painful deed, such as deaths in the open and extreme anguish and wounds and the like" (11.52b9–13). When Aristotle describes this third element of a serious plot as "destructive or painful" (*phthartikē ē odunēra*), he is actually making a direct allusion to his definition of comedy, for in his view it is the very absence of destruction and pain

37. Aristotle does also refer to "old comedies" and "new comedies" (*Eth. Nik.* 4.8.1128a22–24), distinguished respectively by *aiskhrologia* ("foul language") and *mallon hē huponoia* ("insinuation"). It is possible, however, that he is contrasting here not what we call Old and Middle Comedy, but rather the earliest comedies of the fifth century and those of Aristophanes' time, the latter being obscene more by innuendo, by verbal wit and cleverness.

38. Heath 1987: 44, similarly, argues that "the unifying element in Aristophanic comedy is—perhaps surprisingly—the plot." See 43–54.

that makes certain (comic) difficulties amusing. In chapter 5 the ridiculousness (*to geloion*) of comedy is defined as "a mistake or shamefulness which is *non-painful* and *non-destructive*" (*hamartēma ti kai aiskhos anōdunon kai ou phthartikon*, 5.49a35). To say that the best tragic plot should contain an event that is painful or destructive is precisely to say (in Aristotle's vocabulary) that it is to be distinct from the plot of a comedy.

At first glance, it might seem that this implied reference to comedy in Aristotle's characterization of *pathos* as painful or destructive in chapter 11 is only a passing one, briefly raised and quickly dropped. But since the next section of the text, chapter 12, has for several centuries been regarded as intrusive (whether it is Aristotle's intrusion or another's is immaterial), we are entitled to read chapter 13 as a direct continuation of the argument concerning the boundary between tragedy and comedy at the end of chapter 11. If the material of chapter 13 is removed from that context, it seems to be about social class, personal character, and unhappy endings. This is the chapter, after all, where Aristotle specifies the kind of person, neither too good nor too bad, who is the appropriate subject of tragedy. But when chapter 13 is read as a continuation of chapter 11, as I read it, we can see that what motivates Aristotle's formalist-seeming rules for plot construction, along with his specification of the social rank of tragic protagonists, is the pressure he feels to answer the question, "What makes a complex plot sometimes serious, as in the *OT* or *IT*, and sometimes comic, as in the *Kokalos* or any comedy of errors?"

His answer in chapter 13 is twofold. First, the central characters must belong to the more decent and responsible strata of society;[39] they must be *spoudaioi*, men and women whose problems we can take seriously, rather than *phauloi* and *mokhthēroi*, the good-for-nothings who inhabit the universe of comedy.[40] Second, the conflict must be such that it truly could turn out disastrously for the characters with whom we sympathize; that is, their difficulties and the dire events they face must appear to them and to us as potentially disastrous. Let's take up each of these criteria in turn.

39. Aristotle's famous remarks on the middling protagonist should be glossed by his description of the middling type of citizen in *Politics* 4.11.1295a26 and following. In all cities there are three parts of the population: the exceedingly rich, the exceedingly poor, and those in between. The superrich tend to be unjust *di' hubrin* ("through insolence").

40. To hit the tragic bull's-eye (*stokhazesthai*, 13.52b28) and avoid the outer rings of comedy and the nontragic in general, Aristotle rules out the shiftless, irresponsible, anything-for-a-laugh characters (*mokhthēroi, sphodra ponēroi*) who are the natural subjects of comedy. There remains as an appropriate subject of a serious plot a person not so superlative that he could never make a mistake (like, say, Solon or other embodiments of wisdom and correct behavior, 13.53a8), but rather a person whose *pathos* or awful event occurs not through being mean or unprincipled (*mokhthēria*) but through a significant mistake, and preferably a person of social importance such as the members of the old royal families. Note that Aristotle is talking not about character *per se* but still about plot.

How do we know whether a play's complications of plot are funny or serious? In comedy the very look of the characters marks them as *phauloi*, what we might call cartoon people: because they are padded, they can be paddled. When they are hit or persecuted, we laugh rather than worry. To anyone watching an Athenian performance it would be instantly obvious from the costuming of the characters whether any given play was a comedy or a tragedy, hence obvious whether we are meant to take its characters' desperate straits seriously or for laughs.[41] But a narratological analysis is indifferent to the look of the characters. It therefore runs the risk of lowering the categorial barriers that should keep the *spoudaioi* cordoned off from the *phauloi*.[42] The unintentionally amusing quality that we may find in the *Kresphontes* and *Khryses* is greater in the retelling than in performance. So it is Aristotle's very focus on the narrative line that raises the awkward possibility that tragedies may seem comic and that the same narratological definition might apply to both tragedies and comedies. The difference between *spoudaioi* and *phauloi* characters helps to preserve the distinction between comedy and tragedy, but, to fortify that distinction, Aristotle must revert momentarily to an emphasis on formal or structural differences of plot.

Hence, Aristotle's second way of distinguishing between tragic and comic plots, which makes the same point in different but related terms. If a complex plot is to be taken seriously, we should feel that the characters are heading toward disaster, *eis dustukhian* (13.53a2). That is not the case in stories that are typical of comedy. Comedy's very plot contains a generic guarantee that no matter how difficult or hostile or nerve-wracking the situation becomes, the dénouement will not contain death or unresolved enmity: "[I]n that genre, the fiercest enemies in traditional stories, such as Orestes and Aigisthos, finally walk off the stage arm in arm as friends, and no one is killed by anyone" (13.53a36–39). Both this and the double ending typical of comedy, wherein good people are rewarded and bad people punished (as in the *Odyssey*), provide "a pleasure which is not that of *tragōidia* but is instead the appropriate pleasure of comedy" (13.53a35–36). Some tragedies may also have happy endings, but only so long as the audience never feels any assurance that the main characters are safe from impending catastrophe. The possibility and imminence of terrible misfortune are therefore crucial—not crucial to tragedy as such, that is, but crucial to distinguishing complex plots that are tragic from those that are comic.[43]

41. By Aristotle's day, the performers of comedy had begun to stop wearing the exaggerated padded costumes discussed in chapter 2.

42. Compare Aristotle's disdain for the *phortikoi* (*Eth. Nik.* 4.8.1128a5; *Pol.* 8.5.1340a14–b19).

43. Of this distinction Euripides is offered in proof, for the majority of his plays end (*teleutōsin*) in disaster rather than rescue, and in actual performance such plays are truly, undeniably tragedic (*tragikōtatai*, 13.53a27).

That may sound like a quibble, but scholars have cracked their heads for centuries over the apparent contradiction between chapter 13, which seems to recommend an unhappy ending as the proper culmination of a tragic plot, and chapter 14, which clearly sets out the merits of happy endings that allow the protagonists to survive their peril. Aristotle's preference for happy endings, which is independent of his other premises and convictions, makes it all the more imperative that he explain what makes the *kindunos* plot sometimes tragic and sometimes comic.

Here is where the social criteria we have been examining fit in. We can now understand why Aristotle accords so much classificatory importance to distinctions between better and worse sorts of social actors. For it is the social and moral class of the characters that determines, in effect, why some *kindunos* plots court disaster while others do not. In the case of comedy, the low social status of the characters provides us with a visible guarantee that the complications they face are funny, not frightening. The implication is that comic characters are not really in danger, not really at serious risk, because the stakes they play for are relatively trivial. And this implication is made explicit by Theophrastos, who defines comedy as "a non-dangerous [*akindunos*] concatenation of events involving persons in private life" (*kōmōidia estin idiotikōn pragmatōn akindunos periokhē*).[44] In other words, although Aristotle's definition of comedy and his differentiation of it from tragedy may seem to rely at times on a distinctive formal or structural feature of comedy's plot (such as the absence from the story line of a decisive *pathos* or an imminent *dustukhia*), what makes a comic plot comic is primarily the social class of the characters—a quality that is made visible by staging conventions—as well as the comparatively low-risk context of ordinary, humdrum private life.[45]

Aristotle's attention to social meanings rather than to merely formalist elements in plot construction is also clear in his discussion of Recognition. Dorothy Sayers once argued, in a very charming fashion, that Aristotle's *Poetics* was the first analysis of mystery novels, since he favored plots where someone's identity must be uncovered, often a person who has committed or is about to commit a criminal act.[46] But Aristotle is not thinking in terms of objective law and order, of crime in society and its punishment. What is Recognized, according to him, is not a person's identity but rather the social meaning of a person's identity—namely, that he or she is either your ally or your enemy, and further

44. In Diomedes, *Ars Grammatica* 3.9a (the text can be found in R. Cantarella 1949: 19–21). Diomedes does not mention Theophrastos' name at this point, but the parallelism with his Greek definition of tragedy at 3.8.1, attributed to Theophrastos, all but guarantees the source.

45. See the comments of Halliwell 1986: 153–54.

46. In her *Unpopular Opinions* (Sayers 1946: 178–90, reprinted in Winks 1980: 25–34). [Winkler 1994 [1982] proposed that the *Poetics* was a theory of the ancient Greek novel.]

that that Recognition of common interests or common enmity has implications for the life and property of all concerned (11.52a29–32, 52b2).

In this context—a context that is social through and through—the portended event of violence would have no great significance if it grew out of a conflict between established enemies: that would be no more than ordinary Greek life anyway. According to the same logic, a conflict between total strangers who mean nothing to each other is equally without social significance (14.53b17–19). When the young Oidipous came to fatal blows with an older, unyielding chariot-rider at the crossroads, that was not in itself a remarkable or troubling event. The plot that can best grip a Greek audience and move them seriously must feature a conflict between people who have a common bond but who do not realize it and who, as a consequence, end up being implicated together in an act of violence that—had they known one another's identities and what those identities signified—they would have done everything possible to avoid.[47] Belated Recognition, then, is not just a formal or structural feature of tragic plot: it is the stuff of frightening social calamity. While *kindunos* plots may be unusual in the theater of daily life, the issues they embody of betrayal and allegiance in a high-stakes game of zero-sum competition spoke directly to the hearts and minds of Classical Athenians in the context of their society.

The Best Tragedy

Let me illustrate that contention and bring both this chapter and its argument to a close with two final stories. One is far and away the best drama in Hyginus (190), at least by Aristotelian criteria. It is not attributed to any particular playwright, but the material is undoubtedly "tragic." It involves the family of Kalkhas, the mythological prophet. Kalkhas himself does not figure in the play, which concerns members of his family who are otherwise unknown to myth-history. We should probably take this as an example of a tragedy in which most of the names are made up, as Aristotle remarks was the case with Agathon's *Antheus* (9.51b21). Kalkhas had a father named Thestor and two sisters named Theonoe and Leukippe. Theonoe is kidnapped by pirates one day while playing on the beach and sold into slavery in Karia, where the king buys her and installs her as his mistress; in the course of occupying that position, she becomes a woman of some power and influence. Thestor goes in search of his daughter, is shipwrecked off the coast of Karia, and put to work as a slave in the quarries. Leukippe, now that both her sister and her father are missing, travels to Delphi to ask the god where they are. He replies that if she travels about in the guise of a priest of Apollo, she will find her family. So she cuts her hair short and disguises herself as a young priest of that god.

47. Gudeman 1934: 257–58 gives a well-organized chart of *philoi* who kill or almost kill each other.

Arriving in Karia in the king's absence, Leukippe, still disguised, has an interview with the king's mistress, who finds the stranger very attractive and asks "him" to sleep with her, not realizing that the fake priest is actually a woman and in fact her own sister. Leukippe refuses, and in a rage Theonoe orders the priest to be locked up; she then sends for a slave from the quarry to do a job for her. Thestor (her own father) is sent to her and she, not recognizing him, commands him to kill the priest. While Thestor is standing over the young man's bed with a sword, unaware that "the priest" is in reality his daughter, he exclaims, "To think that I, Thestor, having lost both my daughters Theonoe and Leukippe, should now be forced to commit this heinous crime." He turns the sword against himself and is about to drive it into his breast when Leukippe, hearing the name of her father, grabs the sword from him. Recognition ensues. Now father and daughter, reunited at last, plot to enter Theonoe's room and kill her for what she has done to them. But Theonoe too hears Thestor's name in time to identify herself and prevent that *pathos*. Finally, the king of Karia sends them all home with presents, and presumably with congratulations for a record number of *pathē* averted (two family murders and one lesbian incest) and for the narrative ingenuity that went into devising the whole elaborate scenario.[48]

Plots like that of the *Theonoe* (or *Leukippe*, as the play might well have been called) lead us to remark that the fundamental credibility of events is, like humor, notoriously mutable from era to era and from culture to culture. Modern taste may find the tragedy of Kalkhas' family preposterous, yet I maintain that there was a time when such a story would have made for a gripping drama and an important and "serious" performance. Since the authorship and date of the *Theonoe* are completely unknown, I do not cite this play-summary in order to argue that the majority of pre-Aristotelian tragedies were like that. Rather, given that some tragedies at least from the time of Euripides' *Kresphontes* (425) were indeed like that, the *Theonoe* is of interest insofar as it displays an extreme and remarkable instance of the type.

More locatable in literary history is an extraordinary play by Sophokles. In chapter 13 of the *Poetics*, Aristotle mentions Thyestes along with Oidipous in the context of *hamartia* (tragic error). In fact, Aristotle may be referring, as many have plausibly suggested, not to the notorious banquet where Thyestes made the mistake of dining unwittingly on his own children, served up to him by his malicious brother Atreus, but to another egregious error that figures in a different portion of the myth.[49] That error consisted in Thyestes' incest

48. For a more elaborate, though entirely hypothetical, reconstruction of this tragedy, see the detailed synopsis by Martin Cropp in Slater and Cropp 2009: 78–82.

49. Stinton 1975: 226–27 argues that we do not know what horrifying act Aristotle refers to here, and suggests Thyestes' unwitting seduction of his own daughter as one possibility. Stinton is followed by Moles 1979: 79.

with his daughter Pelopia, from which union Aigisthos was born.[50] The play is Sophokles' *Thyestes in Sikyon* and its plot is as follows.[51]

After his terrible banquet, Thyestes fled Mykenai and happened to pass through the territory of Sikyon. Years before, he had sent his daughter Pelopia to the king of Sikyon for safekeeping. In Sikyon Thyestes comes upon a maiden at the riverside alone in the middle of the night, partly undressed and washing her clothes. Unbeknownst to him, it is his own daughter Pelopia, who had been leading a chorus of maidens during a nocturnal festival in honor of Athena and who had slipped in the blood of a sacrificed animal and stained her priestly robe. It is this blood that she is washing out when Thyestes comes upon her and decides to rape her. He veils his face so that he will not be recognized, but during the rape Pelopia manages to slip his dagger from its sheath and keeps it to identify him. He departs quickly, however, and Pelopia's hopes of identifying her attacker are frustrated, for the moment.

Atreus soon arrives from Mykenai looking for Thyestes, since the land of his kingdom is beset with a curse of sterility and, according to the oracle, only the return of Thyestes will restore things to normal (or as normal as things there get). Atreus sees Pelopia, who is very beautiful, and thinking her to be the king's daughter asks for her hand in marriage. The king consents, not knowing that she is already pregnant by Thyestes. (Presumably the king keeps her identity—the fact that she is Atreus's niece—a secret, because he does not want to reveal to Atreus that he has given aid to Thyestes.) When Pelopia's child is born, she tries to get rid of it, knowing that it is illegitimate—though not just how illegitimate. Herdsmen find the baby being nursed by a she-goat, from which fact Aigisthos acquires his name. Atreus, however, learns that the baby has been exposed and institutes a search for his missing son, as he supposes, whereupon Aigisthos is returned to him.

Years pass. As the drama opens, Atreus has sent his sons Agamemnon and Menelaos to Delphi for information as to the whereabouts of Thyestes, and they arrive there on the very same day that Thyestes himself has come to consult the oracle about how to get revenge on his brother. The oracle tells him that if he begets a child by his own daughter he will have the revenge he seeks. Agamemnon and Menelaos take hold of Thyestes and bring him back to Atreus, who puts him in a locked room. Atreus then tells his son Aigisthos to go kill Thyestes. As Aigisthos is about to strike the fatal blow against his real father with a dagger, Thyestes recognizes the dagger as the one he lost years ago in Sikyon. He asks Aigisthos where he got the dagger and Aigisthos

50. Plato refers to the *tragōidiai* of Oidipous and of Thyestes together when speaking of incest in the *Laws* (8.838C).

51. See Lloyd-Jones 1996: 106–7 and Pearson 1917: vol. 1, pp. 185–87 for a brief summary and discussion. The ancient sources for this drama are Hyginus 88 and Apollodorus 2.14.

says that his mother lent it to him. Pelopia is then summoned and she confirms their awful suspicions. Pretending to look more closely at the dagger, she takes it and stabs herself in the heart. This emotionally complex moment of Recognition averts one *pathos* (son slaying father), is the occasion for another (mother/daughter kills herself), and causes yet a third. Aigisthos' family interests are now realigned so as to be for Thyestes and against Atreus. He takes the bloody dagger and shows it to Atreus as proof that he has killed Thyestes. Atreus celebrates a joyful sacrifice by the seashore and in the midst of it Aigisthos cuts him down.

The marvelous construction of this plot produces contradictory feelings almost simultaneously: the shocking realization of Pelopia's past shame, intensified by her suicide, an act of honor and also a disturbing return to the night of her rape, as she plunges her father's dagger into her body. This is countered—but not cancelled—by the joy of father and son finally united and the revenge against their common enemy, which their reunion now makes possible.

These are strong feelings, but they are not exploited for their own sake, since they arise from the events themselves, *auta ta pragmata* (to reprise Aristotle's formula from his *Rhetoric*). Melodramatic as they seem, they are firmly grounded in the actual character of Greek social life, with its organization into households, its habitual dramatization in public gossip and storytelling of the rise and fall of people's fortunes, and its strong sense of the precariousness of anyone's success in that agonistic environment. Aristotle, too, had a finely tuned sense of the issues, issues written into the social scripts of real life, and his dissection of what makes the best tragedies work gives us a sort of X-ray of the Athenian heart and mind, the fears and sympathies that animated men and women in that corner of the ancient Mediterranean.

So, far from being a purely formalist or structural analysis of tragic plot, Aristotle's *Poetics* reveals how people actually felt and acted in a society whose dramas have later been selectively appropriated for the needs of quite different societies. The point is not that we should cease rethinking Attic plays in terms relevant to our own quite different cultures—the *Gospel at Colonus*, for example, does this very well.[52] But we should certainly be more aware, and more wary, of the distorting effects of our long and complex traditions, so that when we appeal to the authority of Greek drama, we know what we are invoking.

We may find Oidipous more tragic than Iphigeneia. But it was she who walked away with the Oscar.

52. Compare van Weyenbergh 2013, Budelmann 2004, and Wetmore 2002, who survey various adaptations of Greek tragedy in African theater. On recent politicized productions of Greek plays in the United States, see Powers 2018.

APPENDIX I

Tragōidoi

THE GREEK WORD *tragōidoi* seems obviously to mean "billy goat singers"—not just "goat singers." Connections between Dionysos and generic goats, which can be found for example in the famous antipathy between the goat and the grapevine,[1] should not be relevant to the specifically masculine term *tragōidoi*.[2] The etymology is as patent as its significance is obscure.[3] Given the habits of sophistic playfulness[4] and the reluctance of ancient scholars ever to doubt that the path of least resistance to an explanation was correct, it would be amazing if someone had not conjectured that a billy goat was the prize awarded to the chorus that won the tragic competition. This conjecture is indeed found in a document of the third century BCE—a chronology of famous events in Greek history with a special emphasis on data of literary interest.[5] The notion became dogma and was repeated numerous times by later ancient writers, though other possibilities long continued to be entertained. It may even be true, but it can hardly be anything else than a good guess. The exhaustive inquiry of Burkert 1966 finds goats from earliest times in the pictorial and literary entourage of Dionysos, but no explicit evidence of a goat prize or (what would be in this context the same thing) a goat sacrifice. Burkert nevertheless believes that a goat was sacrificed to Dionysos and that *tragōidoi* were named from this.[6]

1. Paus. 2.13.6

2. The paradoxical term *tragaina*, "female billy goat," is used by Aristotle of a hermaphrodite goat (*Gen. Anim.* 4.4.770b35).

3. For fun, one may cite Harrison 1902, who proposes, by emending Stephanos, s.v. *tragos*, that tragedy is a beer-song.

4. Plato, *Kratylos* 408C–D is the earliest association of tragedy with goats—because of their rough (*trakh-*) hides.

5. A long marble inscription found on the island of Paros, hence known as the *Marmor Parium*; *FGrHist* 239.

6. My reservations about Burkert's magisterial treatment have to do not with whatever doubts I have about the existence of a goat prize but rather with his insistence on

As it happens, there is a hitherto-unnoticed billy goat sacrifice on *Elaphēboliōn* 10, the first day of the City Dionysia—not in Athens proper, but in the Marathonian Tetrapolis (*IG* II^2 1358 B 17–18). Surely this could be regarded as the smoking gun that Burkert was searching for in order to confirm his theory. But no sooner does the evidence for it appear in all its propitiousness than it confounds us with its generosity. For on that sacred calendar, the billy goat victim is specified as one that is "all black" (*pammelas*). This is just as surely a confirmation of the ephebic symbolism of the Dionysian black goatskin, which Vidal-Naquet described (for the details, see chapter 1). Were *tragōidoi* so called because they sang at the sacrifice of a billy goat? Or was an all-black billy goat sacrificed in a northern region of Attika in solidarity with the ephebic celebration going on in Athens at the Dionysia?

The ephebic hypothesis makes possible another interpretation of *tragōidoi*, one that does not entail the denial of a goat prize/sacrifice but may stand independently beside the theory that would derive tragedy from it. It goes like this. In dealing with the social institution of the Athenian ephebate, we should try to give equal weight to the practical discipline that exercises young men in doing what men are to do (march in file and be honorable and prudent) and to the symbolic inversions that variously inform that liminal period. Such inversions also have their practical side. For instance, just as still happens in modern military training, the young men are degraded in order to be upgraded. That is, they are insulted as sissies, girls, and crybabies in order to promote their decisive rejection of all boyishness. The army, as we say, turns boys into men. So said the ancients as well: "[A]nd they were not allowed to return to the city until they had become men."[7] Here we must briefly allude to the well-known distinction between physical puberty and social puberty. A rite of passage to manhood is symbolically a puberty rite, but it may take place years after a boy's body has begun to undergo the physical changes of adolescence.

With this in mind, I will simply mention that, among the meanings of *tragos* ("billy goat"), only one has any *prima facie* connection to the human voice or to

---

interpreting tragedy as a cultural performance on sacrificial themes, despite the fact that the City Dionysia is one festival for which a sacrificial prize is least attested. If tragedy as such was mainly and originally about issues of sacrifice, it might as well have developed at any of the numerous animal slaughters of ancient Greece. Further, that it should have grown from the sacrifice of a goat rather than, say, a bull seems to me faintly ludicrous: can we imagine Aiskhylos saying of great Agamemnon that he was cut down like a goat at the manger? In reply, however, it might be possible to hold that it was precisely because there was *not* a literal enactment of an animal sacrifice (or only a slightly ludicrous one) that a choral meditation on sacrifice developed at the Dionysia. A billy goat is sacrificed for a city foundation in Aristophanes, *Birds* 902, 959, 1056–57, but that, of course, may be some sort of joke.

7. Justin 3.3 on the Spartan *krypteia*.

singing (*-ōidos*). Aristotle, once in a discussion of puberty and again in a discussion of voice-pitch, uses the word *tragizein* to mean the breaking or changing of the voice that adolescent boys experience.[8] The word continued in use: see Porphyry on Ptolemy's *Harmony* 253A; Alexander of Aphrodisias' *Problemata* 1.125.[9] Aristotle attaches *ho kalousi* to *tragizein*, which results in "what they call *tragizein*," thereby indicating that adolescent voice-change is not the primary referent of the root *trag-*; rather, the word acquires that meaning in some special circumstance that Aristotle's reader might need reminding of. An analogy would be our use of "frog" in the phrase "a frog in one's throat": the word "frog" alone does not make one think of a person with a hoarse voice. The usage also occurs in [Aristotle] *De audibilibus* 804a17 and in later writers. The term at Hippokrates' *Epidemics* 6.3.14 may refer to voice-breaking, or it may be a generalized expression for those undergoing puberty: *epēn aphrodisiazein arxōntai ē tragizein*, "whenever they begin to be sexually active or to *tragizein*." When used to refer to the adolescent boy's voice, *tragizein* may simply mean "bleat," but the word's implications are probably wider. It may, in the Greek folk-system, also be a way of saying that a boy's change of voice is a warning sign of the onset of other goat-like qualities, such as rank smell and indiscriminate lust. Like ephebes, goats are noticeably wayward and must be controlled.[10]

Tragizein (and *tragān*), then, might best be translated as "to go through puberty," "to show the signs of adolescence" (of which voice-change is only one). The noun *tragos* indicates another such change when it occurs in a cryptic Hippokratic saying at *Epidemics* 6.4.21 about the swelling of a boy's testicles at puberty: *tragos, hokoteros an phanēi exō orkhis, dexios, arsen, euōnumos, thēlu* ("billy goat, whichever testicle appears outside, right-side male, left-side female").[11] Galen commented on this passage.[12] Martial 3.24

8. Arist., *Hist. Anim.* 7.1; *Gen. Anim.* 5.7.787b32–788a2.

9. Hesykhios, s.v. *tragizein*.

10. Plutarch remarks that dogs and billy goats exemplify lack of self-control and proneness to pleasure: *Conj. Praec.* 139B; cf. *Qu. Rom.* 11 (290A); Aelian, *Nat. Anim.* 7.19; Adamantius Judaeus, *Physiognōmonika* 2.2.14. On the malodor of billy goats, see Herodotos 3.112 (*dusodmotatōi*); Horace, *Satires* 1.2.27; Seneca, *Epistles* 86.13; *tragion* is the name of a plant that stinks like a billy goat in the fall, according to Dioskorides 4.50. See Eyben 1972: esp. 688–91 on the voice and smell of teenage boys.

11. Cf. *Epidemics* 2.5.1. Latin has an analogous usage of *hirquitallus* from *hircus*, "goat," for boys becoming men. See Paulus, *Festus* 101M; 105M: *hirquitalli pueri primum ad virilitatem accedentes: a libidine [sc. hircorum] dicti* ("'hirquitalli': boys when they first approach manhood, so named after [goats'] lust"). Censorinus, *De die natali* 5 brings this Latin expression into conjunction with the Greek and mentions the connection with voice rather than lust: *in secunda hebdomade, vel incipiente tertia, vocem crassiorem et inaequabilem fieri quod appellat [tragizein], antiqui nostri hirquitallire* ("in the second seven-year period of life, or at the beginning of the third, the voice becomes coarser and more uneven: that's what's called [*tragizein*], *hirquitallire* by our forebears").

12. *De usu partium* 14.7 (4.172–74 Kühn); Galen's *Commentary on* Epidemics 6 (17.B.211 ff. Kühn). See also *De semine* 2.5 (4.633 Kühn).

associates the billy goat's foul smell specifically with its testicles, which are cut off at the moment of sacrifice. Burkert deduces from this that "the procedure was the same at every he-goat sacrifice."[13]

Aristotle explains the connection between testicular and vocal change in terms of mechanics. The increased tension caused by heavier testes on the channels that lead from the scrotum through the heart to the vocal chords causes the voice to drop lower. Aristotle compares the effect to that of loom weights.[14] Two activities affect this natural process: sexual activity accelerates it; the voice exercises of boys who take frequent part in choruses retard it.[15]

I propose that *tragōidoi* began as a slightly jocular designation of ephebic singers, not because their voices were breaking (that was long past and anyway no one can sing well whose voice is breaking), but because they were identified as those undergoing social puberty.[16] More accurately, they were *representative* of those undergoing social puberty: only a select group of the best ephebic singer-dancers could actually perform.[17] Given the low repute of goats, not to mention goatherds, the name must be regarded—perhaps paradoxically to us—as a somewhat comic formation.[18]

13. Burkert 1983: 68.

14. Arist., *Gen. Anim.* 5.7.787b20–788a7.

15. Arist., *Hist. Anim.* 7.1.581a21–27.

16. There may be a more literal aspect that reinforced the metaphorical dimension and made *tragizein* an appropriate designation for ephebic singing. Margoliouth 1911: 61–62 brought adolescent voice-breaking into relation with tragedy on the basis of the mournful and *uneven* nature of the singing, as described by [Aristotle], *Problems* 19.6: "[F]or in great misfortune or grief the uneven [*anōmales*] is expressive [*pathētikon*], while the even is less mournful." The same language is found in Aristotle's discussion of voice-change during puberty: *Hist. Anim.* 7.1 (*anōmalestron, homalē*, 581a18–19); *Gen. Anim.* 5.7 (*anōmalos*, 788a1).

17. Because of this fact I have not stressed what will seem to many the most obvious connection between *rites de passage* and the ephebes' tragic chorus—their sometime dressing as women. The ephebes as a group had just as important a role to play in the festival by being in the audience (where they did not dress as women) as their representative best dancers and singers did by being in the orchestra. Further, the key ephebic issues are family and political authority, responsibility to the gods and the dead, and a young man's maximizing of personal *timē* ("honor") without insulting his peers or betters. Gender is a key item in the system, but it is a dependent rather than an independent variable. Finally, even as choristers, ephebes did not always dress as women; sometimes they even dressed as ephebes (see chapter 1, page 48).

18. As was held by the ancient scholar reported in the *Etym. Mag.* who said that tragedy is so called "because the choruses were mainly comprised of satyrs, whom they jokingly [*skōptontes*] called billy goats" (*Etym. Mag.* 764, ad. Τραγῳδία). Available online here: https://archive.org/stream/etymologikontome00etymuoft#page/n365/mode/2up.

We seem to have in the *tragos* word-group a coherent and rather interesting view of puberty as a complex of new smells, sounds, attitudes, and bodily changes summed up in the emblem of the goat.[19]

19. Professor Evelyn B. Harrison draws my attention to Plutarch, who recounts that Theseus, just before he set sail for Krete (the last and greatest of his ephebic exploits), was sacrificing a she-goat by the seaside and it suddenly turned into a he-goat (*Theseus* 18). This story illustrates not only the dramatic change of state that ephebes were thought to go through, but also the complex involvement of several divinities and social classes. Theseus' sacrifice is directed to Aphrodite, and the story is tied to a procession of Athenian maidens to the temple of Apollo Delphinios in Athens.

APPENDIX II

Phluakes

THE COMIC SCENES painted on South Italian vases are usually thought to depict *phluakes*, a word used to refer to the authors, the actors, and the scripts alike of a kind of play or theatrical presentation.[1] The only near-solid justification for so naming these performances is a passage from Sosibios the Spartan, a Hellenistic writer of uncertain date, cited by Athenaios: "Amongst the Spartans there was an olden style of comic playfulness, not very dignified [*spoudaios*], inasmuch as in these matters, too, Sparta aimed at restraint [*to liton*]; someone would imitate in plain [*eutelei*] speech some thieves stealing fruit or a foreign doctor speaking like the passage from Alexis' *Mandragorizomenē* [II 348 Kock, omitted here]. Those who pursued such playfulness were called in Sparta *dikēlistai* ["showmen"], as if one were to call them makers of equipment [*skeuopoious*] and imitators [*mimētas*]. There are many terms, differing by region, for the class of *dikēlistai*: the Sikyonians call them *phallophoroi* ["phallos-carriers" or "phallos-wearers"]; others call them *autokabdaloi*; some, such as the Italians, call them *phluakes*; but most call them *sophistai*. The Thebans, who usually have a special term for anything, call them *ethelontai* ["volunteers"]."[2] This passage is followed immediately by Strattis frag. I 725 Kock on Theban jargon, and then a passage from Semos of Delos *On Paians* (*FGrHist* IV 496) describing performances by *autokabdaloi* (iamboi), *ithyphalloi*, and *phallophoroi*, not specified as belonging to any particular region.

As often in Athenaios, it is difficult to be sure where he leaves off quoting or citing his source and begins to add other material. Even if most of the material is from Sosibios, one might suspect that the citations of Alexis and Strattis

1. On the tradition of *phluakes*, see Taplin 1993: 48–53. Taplin argues that the "*phluax*" vases have no connection with a South Italian folk-comedy tradition, but rather derive from Athenian comedy. Green 1991a comes to a similar conclusion. For a more recent, nuanced, and comprehensive review of the evidence, see Favi 2017.

2. Ath. 14.621D.

are due to Athenaios rather than to Sosibios writing on matters of cult and ceremony in Lakedaimonia. It is possible that the list of regional names for comparable performers is also due to Athenaios rather than Sosibios, but in any case, we have some Hellenistic or imperial Greek scholar's assertion that Greeks in southern Italy used the term *phluakes* (singular *phluax*) for an old and undignified type of playfulness.

Of the two principal authors who are said to have written *phluakes*, Rhinthon lived in the time of Ptolemy Soter (early third century BCE) and was associated with the town of Tarentum, nestled in the heel of Italy, a center of production for the numerous Apulian vases with comic scenes.[3] The other, Sopatros, was born on Paphos and lived in Alexandria from the time of Alexander to Ptolemy II (late fourth to mid-third century).

The evidence that *phluax* was the name that Greek actors in southern Italy would have used of themselves is not strong, but I will continue to refer to them as such, on the strength of Sosibios' remark that *phluax* was the regional name in South Italy for that sort of performance and also because etymological considerations suggest that it is a particularly appropriate name for padded performers (anywhere). Radermacher, in an analysis of classic brevity, first broke the word down into its root *phlu-* with a suffix *-ax*.[4] The Greek suffix *-ax* is similar to English *-ster*, which is added to nouns and adjectives to produce a slightly derogatory or distancing designation for persons identified in terms of one quality or activity, such as "youngster," "oldster," "gangster," "mobster," "trickster," "songster," "spinster," and the like. In Greek, *-ax* words are attested mainly in comedy: *neax* ("youngster"), *ploutax* ("rich guy"), *kelex* ("racer"), *kōmax* ("funster"), *khleuax* ("jokester"), *thalamax* ("low-deck oarsman"), *khaskax* and *khaunax* ("big mouth"). *Epidaurax* and *Rhodax* mean not "Epidaurian" and "Rhodian" but "an Epidaurian/Rhodian type of person." It is plausible enough that *ruax* ("lava stream"), the only other u-stem in the *-ax* group, is a semipersonification with the same distancing function, as if the lava were a somewhat obnoxious agent that just insisted on flowing.

3. Steph. Byz., *Rhinthōn Tarantinos, phluax, ta tragika metarruthmizōn es to geloion* ("Rhinthon of Tarentum, a *phluax*, who refashioned the tragic so as to make it funny"); Souda, *Rhinthōn Tarantinos, kōmikos, arkhēgos tēs kaloumenēs hilarotragōidas, ho esti phluakographia* ("Rhinthon of Tarentum, a comic poet, originator of the so-called hilarotragedy, that is *phluax* literature"). Nossis, herself from Epizephyrian Lokroi at the toe of Italy and a contemporary of Rhinthon, wrote an imaginary epitaph for him (*Anth. Pal.* 7.414), in which he laughingly tells a passerby that he was born in Syracuse, a little nightingale of the Muses, who has plucked his ivy from "tragic *phluakes*." On the dramas of Rhinthon, see Taplin 1993: 49–52. Taplin argues that Rhinthon's dramas have nothing to do with the *phluax* vases; among other things, the vases have been shown to date from before Rhinthon began producing his own plays (see esp. 51–52). Perhaps the vases reflect Athenian comedy, as Taplin argues, or perhaps they testify to the existence of *phluax* performances antedating Rhinthon.

4. Radermacher 1924: 1–10.

The three related forms *rheō* ("I flow"), *rhoos* ("stream"), and *ruax* ("lava flow") are matched by *phleō, phloos, phluax*. Chantraine's analysis of *phleō* and *phluō* shows that they cover the same interestingly broad range of meanings: A. "grow abundantly" (of plants), B. "teem" (of flocks) and "overflow" (of water), C. "chatter" or "spit out" (of words). Chantraine therefore assigns them to a common root that fluctuates between *phleϝ-* and *phlu*. Most commentators on the word *phluax*, including the ancient ones such as Pollux (9.149) and Hesykhios, have connected it with the notion of silly chatter (*phluaria*) or, since Körte, with Dionysos as "vegetation demon." But at least as strong a case can be made for associating the word with the most distinctive, ever-present feature of these persons' appearance, the stuffing in their torso. The earliest surviving use of *phle-* is "be abundant" in Aiskhylos, *Agamemnon* 377, 1416, Empedokles 80 D-K, and Antimakhos frag. 36 Kinkel (both of the latter discussed by Plut., *Qu. Conv.* 5.8.2: 683D–F), which shows up in Hesykhios' glosses as *phlei = gemei* ("be full"). Trendall noted the possibility: "If φλύαξ [*phluax*] is thus to be associated with φλέω [*phleō*], the sense of 'tumid' or 'swelling' would not be inappropriate as applied to the phlyax actors in their well-padded costumes, which recall those of the padded dancers who figure so frequently upon Corinthian vases."[5]

We should not feel compelled to choose between the two possibilities, which we might neologize as "gabster" and "flabster," since in the playfulness of comic discourse either one would sooner or later summon the other into existence and since, harking back to Stronger Speech's code for the male physique, both a flapping tongue and a flabby body are equally signs of the undesirably slack.[6]

5. Trendall 1967: 9. *Contra* Favi 2017.
6. See Ar., *Clouds* 963–83.

AFTERWORD

A Note on the Text of This Book

Kirk Ormand

IN EDITING JACK WINKLER'S last book for publication thirty years after Jack had done all he could with the manuscript, David Halperin and I were faced with some difficult choices. Jack's knowledge of nineteenth- and twentieth-century scholarship in the areas where he was working was impeccable, and the text as he left it was a testament to his rigorous standards and inquisitive habits of mind. But it was clear from a glance at Jack's discussions of a wide range of topics that, in some areas at least, scholarship had advanced significantly since he died. Part of that progress was due directly to Jack's influence: earlier versions of chapters 1 and 2 of this book had appeared in his lifetime or shortly after his death, and they served as a catalyst for later developments. Some advances in scholarship, however, were entirely independent of his work, and a few either contested it or had the effect of calling some of Jack's hypotheses into question. If Jack's book was not to be published as a kind of historical artifact, then, it was necessary to bring the scholarship up to date.

That has proved a daunting task, not least because Jack's project was so broadly conceived and because it incorporated evidence from so many specialties and subspecialties of classical scholarship. I have tried wherever possible to bring in references from the past thirty years in areas where important work has appeared. These include Athenian manhood, the ephebate, the tragic theater and rituals surrounding it, the social dimensions of the dramatic festivals, vase evidence for theatrical practices, cockfighting, and Aristotle's theories of tragedy. Work on the tragic theater, its shape, its place in the civic institutions of Classical Athens, and in particular on evidence for theatrical practice beyond Athens and beyond the fifth century has been especially fruitful in the last twenty years. It is one of my great regrets that Jack did not survive to see and interact with the recent work of Eric Csapo, Peter Wilson, Sarah Price, Luca Giuliani, D. M. Carter, and many others. Because work in these areas has been so prolific, however, the reader must assume that additional, updated references are meant to be representative, not exhaustive. Where I have missed important work, I offer apologies to the scholars I have overlooked.

It has been a pleasure to discover the extent to which Jack actually anticipated the results of recent research. Some of his most original and pioneering ideas, based on an alert and minute survey of shreds of evidence, have been confirmed. In particular, Jack argued for the rectangular shape of early Greek theaters, relying on the incomplete and speculative information that he had at the time. Since then, improved archaeological data and careful investigation into epigraphical evidence have confirmed Jack's argument. Again, I have indicated representative works of scholarship that vindicate his instincts.

At the same time, I have not shied away from subsequent developments that present challenges to Jack's interpretations or that raise questions about them that he did not and could not anticipate. One of the most memorable and characteristic features of Jack's scholarly temperament was the constant delight with which he greeted each new piece of evidence or any new argument he discovered that required him to rethink, reimagine, or reconceive his work. Jack was the least dogmatic scholar imaginable: he always welcomed new approaches and was hardly hostile to the play of interpretations. He certainly would have found ways to qualify some of his assertions in the light of new evidence, either to bolster his thesis on a different basis or to sacrifice one aspect of it so as to expand it in a new direction. While we cannot rewrite his manuscript to engage, for example, in a dialogue with Csapo's challenges to the generally accepted story of the origins of Greek tragedy, we have not hesitated to record those challenges and to point out where they might cause trouble for Jack's interpretation or require him to rethink his positions. We have tried, in other words, to make Jack's text contemporary: wherever possible we have preserved Jack's own words (though sometimes we have reordered whole sections of the argument), while highlighting the moments when Jack would undoubtedly have needed to engage with new and emerging scholarship.

Though Jack's work on Athenian drama has been widely read and noted, and though it has had some influence in a number of domains, much of it remains as fresh, as startling, as original, and as unique to him as it was when he wrote this book. That is because Jack's novel and striking reinterpretation of the social meanings of Greek drama has not been taken much further; some of this book's central concerns have simply gone unaddressed in the intervening thirty years. A few scholars have elaborated his insights, but—despite Jack's hopes at the time he had to abandon work on the project—no one has taken up the task of completing his work and filling in the gaps in its argument as a whole. So the book remains almost as innovative now as it was when it was composed. And while some aspects of Jack's central thesis have been challenged in various ways, the core of that thesis—the idea that the Athenian tragic theater was one of a set of institutions that informally functioned to train young men on the verge of adulthood in the necessary modes of being a man and to represent the drama of early manhood as a central problem in Athenian society and culture—has neither been expanded nor refuted. It has not, in short, been superseded. It remains, in our opinion, a major contribution to the understanding of Athenian drama.

One last detail. While trying to preserve many of the quirks of Jack's manuscript, we have had to confront one that presented us with an impossible dilemma. Jack had a principled opposition to perpetuating the convention of Latinizing Greek names, which had the effect of transforming, in the eyes of modern readers, a strange and distant culture into a quaint and deceptively familiar Victorian facsimile. Accordingly, Jack preferred Sophokles and Aiskhulos to their Latin cousins, and he insisted that Psappho not lose the fizzy Ps- at the start of her name. (He once told a class, with a characteristically light touch, that "Psappho" was "more butch than Sappho.") Even Jack, however, could not apply his principles consistently, which led to wild variation in the transliteration of Greek words and names in the manuscript. In particular, neither Jack nor we could come up with a consistent rule for transliterating upsilons (y or u?). We tried at first to correct Jack's practice and to systematize completely all transliteration of Greek words and names according to his principles. But that led to some results—for example, Mukenai for Mycenae or Loukianos for Lucian—that, we thought, would create problems of comprehension for the book's audience (which will include, most probably, many nonspecialists—at least, that is what Jack hoped and it is what we hope as well). Not only did we have to acknowledge that we found such spellings grotesque (if, admittedly, refreshing); we also had to deal with the fact that Jack himself never went so far in his zeal as to insert them. In the end, we have had to accept a certain inconsistency, which we have tried to make uniform as much as we could. For example, we retained Lucian but compromised on Mykenai and Aiskhylos. We have tended to preserve y for upsilon in proper names and also in the names of vases or clothes or dances (thus, pyxis or khlamys or *gymnopaidikē* and *pyrrhikē*), which would otherwise become meaningless and opaque, whereas we have tended to use u for upsilon in most Greek words, following Jack's occasional usage (*kindunos*, *hupokritēs*), though we have retained *thyrsos* (since the word is familiar), in the form of *thyrsoi*, as well as *syn-* compounds, about which Jack himself was inconsistent. We have tolerated the contradictory imperatives in Jack's unswerving transliteration and anglicization of the word *symposion*. Even Jack consistently wrote Achilles in place of Akhilleus, and we have followed his practice there, while trying to preserve the Greekness of most transliterated names.

It has been an inexpressible pleasure for me to work with Jack's manuscript, to track down references to aspects of Greek antiquity that Jack knew but did not have the time and energy to document fully, and to bring certain aspects of his work up to date. In the process, I have been constantly impressed by the breadth and depth of Jack's knowledge, all the more humbling when I reflect that I am now a decade and a half older than Jack was when he died. It has also been a great pleasure to work with David Halperin on this book. I have known David for more than thirty-five years now, and he has been a treasured mentor and friend throughout our long acquaintance. It is not too much to say that I will be a bit heartbroken to put this project to rest. But I hope that it will stand, at long last, as an important part of Jack's legacy as well as an enduring monument of classical scholarship.

ABBREVIATIONS OF CLASSICAL SOURCES

Aelian		
	Nat. Anim.	*On the Nature of Animals*
	Var. Hist.	*Various History*
Aiskh.		Aeschines
	Anth. Pal.	*Palatine Anthology*
Ar.		Aristophanes
	Akh.	*Acharnians*
	Ekkl.	*Ecclesiazusae*
	Thesm.	*Thesmophoriazusae*
	Lys.	*Lysistrata*
Arist.		Aristotle
	Ath. Pol.	*Constitution of the Athenians*
	EE	*Eudemian Ethics*
	Eth. Nik.	*Nicomachean Ethics*
	Gen. Anim.	*On the Generation of Animals*
	Hist. Anim.	*History of Animals*
	Kret. Pol.	*Constitution of the Cretans*
	Poet.	*Poetics*
	Pol.	*Politics*
	Rhet.	*Rhetoric*
Ath.		Athenaeus
	Com. Adesp.	*Comica Adespota*
Dem.		Demosthenes
	Etym. Mag.	*Etymologicum Magnum*
Eur.		Euripides
Homer		
	Od.	*Odyssey*
	IG	*Corpus of Greek Inscriptions*
Isok.		Isocrates
	Ad. Demon.	*To Demonicus*
	Antid.	*Antidosis*

Lys.		Lysias
Paus.		Pausanias
Plato		
	Prot.	*Protagoras*
	Symp.	*Symposium*
Plut.		Plutarch
	Alkib.	*Life of Alcibiades*
	Conj. Praec.	*Conjugal Precepts*
	Inst. Lac.	*Customs of the Spartans*
	Lyk.	*Life of Lycurgus*
	Qu. Gr.	*Greek Questions*
	Qu. Rom.	*Roman Questions*
	Qu. Conv.	*Sympotic Questions*
	Thes.	*Life of Theseus*
Sextus Empiricus		
	Adv. Math.	*Against the Mathematicians*
Soph.		Sophocles
	Ant.	*Antigone*
	OC	*Oedipus at Colonus*
	Tr.	*Women of Trachis*
Steph. Byz.		Stephanus of Byzantium
Them.		Themistius
	Or.	*Orations*
Thouk.		Thucydides
Xen.		Xenophon
	Ath. Pol.	*Constitution of the Athenians*
	Hell.	*Hellenica*
	Kyr.	*Cyropaedia*
	Lak.	*Constitution of the Spartans*
	Mem.	*Memorabilia*
	Symp.	*Symposium*

ABBREVIATIONS OF JOURNALS AND BOOKS

AA *Archäologischer Anzeiger*

AC *L'Antiquité Classique*

AJA *American Journal of Archaeology*

AK *Antike Kunst*

AR *Archaeological Reports*

ARV[2] Beazley, J. D. 1963. *Attic Red-Figure Vase-Painters*, 2nd ed., 3 vols. (Oxford: Clarendon Press).

BCH *Bulletin de correspondance hellénique*

BSA *Annual of the British School at Athens*

ClAnt *Classical Antiquity*

CP *Classical Philology*

CQ *Classical Quarterly*

CR *Classical Review*

DFA Pickard-Cambridge, Arthur W. 1968. *The Dramatic Festivals of Athens*, 2nd ed., revised by John Gould and David M. Lewis (Oxford: Clarendon Press).

FGrHist *Die Fragmente der griechischen Historiker*, ed. F. Jacoby (Leiden, 1957–).

G&R *Greece and Rome*

GRBS *Greek, Roman and Byzantine Studies*

HSCP *Harvard Studies in Classical Philology*

IC *Inscriptiones Creticae: Opera et Consilio Friderici Halbherr Collectae*, ed. Margarita Guarducci (Rome: La Libreria Dello Stato, 1935).

IGD Webster, T. B. L., and A.D. Trendall. 1971. *Illustrations of Greek Drama* (London: Phaidon).

JdAI *Jahrbuch des deutschen Archäologischen Instituts*

JHS *Journal of Hellenic Studies*

Kock Kock, Theodore. 1888. *Comicorum Atticorum Fragmenta* (Leipzig: Teubner).

MDAI *Mitteilungen des deutschen Archäologischen Instituts*

MH *Museum Helveticum*

PCG *Poetae Comicae Graecae*, ed. R. Kassel and C. Austin (Berlin: de Gruyter, 1983–).

PCPS *Proceedings of the Cambridge Philological Society*

PMG *Poetae Melici Graeci*, ed. Denys Page (Oxford: Clarendon Press, 1962).

P&P *Past and Present*

PP *Parola del Passato*

REA *Revue des Études Anciennes*

REG *Revue des Études Grecques*

TAPA *Transactions of the American Philological Association*

TRI *Theatre Research International*

ZPE *Zeitschrift für Papyrologie und Epigraphik*

BIBLIOGRAPHY

Aeneas Tacticus, Asclepiodotus, and Onasander. 1928. *Aeneas Tacticus, Asclepiodotus, and Onasander*, trans. Illinois Greek Club, Loeb Classical Library (Cambridge, MA: Harvard University Press).

Anderson, John K. 1970. *Military Theory and Practice in the Age of Xenophon* (Berkeley: University of California Press).

Andrewes, M. 1924. "Euripides and Menander," *CQ* 18: 1–10.

Arias, Paolo E. 1934. "Alcune osservazioni sul teatro del Pireo in Attica e su quello di Tera," *Dionisio* 4: 93–99.

———. 1962. *A History of Greek Vase Painting*, trans. and revised by Brian B. Shefton (London: Thames and Hudson).

Ashby, C. 1988. "The Case for the Rectangular/Trapezoidal Orchestra," *TRI* 13: 1–20.

Austin, Colin. 1968. *Nova Fragmenta Euripidea in Papyris Reperta*, Kleine Texte für Vorlesungen und Übungen 187 (Berlin: de Gruyter).

Austin, Colin, and S. Douglas Olson (eds.). 2004. *Aristophanes* Thesmophoriazusae (Oxford: Oxford University Press).

Barker, Andrew. 1984. *Greek Musical Writings*, vol. 1. (Cambridge: Cambridge University Press).

Barrett, W. S. (ed.). 1964. *Euripides Hippolytos* (Oxford: Clarendon Press).

Barringer, Judith. 2001. *The Hunt in Ancient Greece* (Baltimore: Johns Hopkins University Press).

Bassi, Karen. 2003. "The Semantics of Manliness in Ancient Greece," in Ralph M. Rosen and Ineke Sluiter (eds.), *Andreia: Studies in Manliness and Courage in Classical Antiquity* (Leiden: Brill), 25–58.

Beazley, J. D. 1955. "Hydria Fragments in Corinth," *Hesperia* 24: 304–19.

Belfiore, Elizabeth. 1992. "Aristotle and Iphigenia," in Amélie Oksenberg Rorty (ed.), *Essays on Aristotle's Poetics* (Princeton, NJ: Princeton University Press), 359–78.

Belpassi, Loris. 1988. "L'Oreste 'Taurico' e l'efebia. Alcune considerazioni sui vv. 67–122 della *I.T.* di Euripide," *Quaderni Urbinati di Cultura Classica*, n.s. 30.3 (1988): 117–21.

Bieber, Margarete. 1961. *The History of the Greek and Roman Theater*, 2nd ed. (Princeton, NJ: Princeton University Press).

Blass, Fridericus. 1908. *Antiphontis Orationes et Fragmenta, adiunctis Gorgiae Antisthenis Alcidamantis Declamationibus*, 2nd ed. (Leipzig: Teubner).

Boardman, J. 1963. "Artemis Orthia and Chronology," *BSA* 58: 1–7.

Boegehold, A. 1965. "An Archaic Corinthian Inscription," *AJA* 69: 259–62.

Borthwick, E. K. 1968. "Notes on the Plutarch De Musica and the Cheiron of Pherecrates," *Hermes* 96: 60–73.

———. 1970. "Two Scenes of Combat in Euripides," *JHS* 90: 15–21.

Bourdieu, P. 1977. *Outline of a Theory of Practice* (Cambridge: Cambridge University Press).

Brelich, Angelo. 1961. *Guerre, Agoni e Culti nella Grecia Arcaica*, Antiquitas, ser. 1, vol. 7 (Bonn: R. Habelt).

Brommer, Frank. 1959. *Satyrspiele: Bilder griechischer Vasen*, 2nd ed. (Berlin: de Gruyter).

———. 1964. "Zum Deutung der Pronomosvase," *AA* (Heft 1): 109–14.

Bruneau, P. 1965. "Le motif des coqs affrontés dans l'imagerie antique," *BCH* 89: 112–13.

Bryant, Arthur A. 1907. "Boyhood and Youth in the Days of Aristophanes," *HSCP* 18: 73–122.

Budelmann, Felix. 2004. "Greek Tragedies in West African Adaptations," *PCPS* 50: 1–28.

Burian, Peter. 2011. "Athenian Tragedy as Democratic Discourse," in D. M. Carter (ed.), *Why Athens? A Reappraisal of Tragic Politics* (Oxford: Oxford University Press), 95–118.

Burkert, Walter. 1966. "Greek Tragedy and Sacrificial Ritual," *GRBS* 7: 87–121.

———. 1983. *Homo Necans: The Anthropology of Ancient Greek Sacrificial Ritual and Myth* (Berkeley: University of California Press).

Burnett, Anne Pippin. 1971. *Catastrophe Survived: Euripides' Plays of Mixed Reversal* (Oxford: Clarendon Press).

———. 1985. *The Art of Bacchylides* (Cambridge, MA: Harvard University Press).

Buschor, Ernst. 1928. "Ein choregisches Denkmal," *MDAI* 53: 96–108.

Campbell, David A. 1982. *Greek Lyric*, Loeb Classical Library (Cambridge, MA: Harvard University Press).

Campbell, John. 1964. *Honour, Family and Patronage* (Oxford: Oxford University Press).

Cantarella, B. 1964. *Euripide, I Cretesi* (Milan: Istituto Editoriale Italiano).

Cantarella, Raffaele. 1949. *Aristofane, Le Commedie*, vol I. (Milan: Istituto Editoriale Italiano).

Capps, Edward. 1904. "The Introduction of Comedy into the City Dionysia," *Decennial Publications of the University of Chicago*, first series, vol. 6, no. 11: 259–88.

———. 1943. "A New Fragment of the List of Victors at the City Dionysia," *Hesperia* 12: 1–11.

Carpenter, Thomas. 2007. "Introduction," in Eric Csapo and Margaret Miller (eds.), *The Origins of Theater in Ancient Greece and Beyond: From Ritual to Drama* (Cambridge: Cambridge University Press), 41–47.

Carter, D. M. 2008. *The Politics of Greek Tragedy* (Liverpool: Liverpool University Press).

———. 2011a. "Plato, Drama, and Rhetoric," in D. M. Carter (ed.), *Why Athens? A Reappraisal of Tragic Politics* (Oxford: Oxford University Press), 45–67.

——— (ed). 2011b. *Why Athens? A Reappraisal of Tragic Politics* (Oxford: Oxford University Press).

Carter, Jane Burr. 1987. "The Masks of Ortheia," *AJA* 91: 355–83.

Carter, L. B. 1986. *The Quiet Athenian* (Oxford: Clarendon Press).

Cartledge, Paul. 1977. "Hoplites and Heresies: Sparta's Contribution to the Technique of Ancient Warfare," *JHS* 97: 11–27.

Catling, H. W. 1977. "Excavations at the Menelaion, Sparta, 1973–1976," *AR* 23: 42.

Ceccarelli, Paola. 1998. *La pirrica nell'antichità greco romana: Studi sulla danza armata* (Pisa: Istituti Editoriali e Poligrafici Internazionali).

Ceccarelli, Paola, and Silvia Milanezi. 2007. "Dithyramb, Tragedy—and Cyrene," in Peter Wilson (ed.), *The Greek Theatre and Festivals: Documentary Evidence* (Oxford: Oxford University Press), 185–214.

Chandler, L. 1926. "The North-West Frontier of Attica," *JHS* 46: 1–21.

Chaniotis, Angelos. 1996. *Die Verträge zwischen kretischen Poleis in der hellenistischen Zeit*, Heidelberger althistorische Beiträge und epigraphische Studien 24 (Stuttgart: Steiner Verlag).

———. 2007. "Theatre Rituals," in Peter Wilson (ed.), *The Greek Theatre and Festivals: Documentary Studies* (Oxford: Oxford University Press), 48–66.

Coles, R. A. 1974. *A New Oxyrhynchus Papyrus: The Hypothesis of Euripides' Alexandros*, *Bulletin of the Institute of Classical Studies*, supplement 32 (London: Institute of Classical Studies).

Collard, Christopher, and Martin Cropp (eds. and trans.). 2008. *Euripides: Fragments Aegeus-Meleager*, Loeb Classical Library (Cambridge, MA: Harvard University Press).

Connor, W. R. 1988. "Early Greek Land Warfare as Symbolic Expression," *P&P* 119: 3–29.

Coppola, Alessandra, Caterina Barone, and Monica Salvadori (eds.). 2016. *Gli oggetti sulla scena teatrale ateniese: Funzione, rappresentazione, comunicazione* (Padua: CLEUP).

Crome, J. F. 1935–36. "*Hipparcheioi Hermai*," *Athenische Mitteilungen (Abteilung des Deutschen Archäologischen Instituts)* 60–61: 300–14, plates 101–8.

Crosby, Margaret. 1955. "Five Comic Scenes from Athens," *Hesperia* 24: 76–84, plates 34–37.

Csapo, Eric. 1986. "A Note on the Würzburg Bell Crater H5697 ('Telephus Travestitus')," *Phoenix* 40.4: 379–92.

———. 1993a. "Deep Ambivalence: Notes on a Greek Cockfight (Part I)," *Phoenix* 47.1:1–28.

———. 1993b. "Deep Ambivalence: Notes on a Greek Cockfight (Parts II–IV)," *Phoenix* 47.2: 115–24.

———. 2006. "Cockfights, Contradictions, and the Mythopoetics of Ancient Greek Culture," *Arts* 28: 9–41.

———. 2006–7. "The Cultural Poetics of the Greek Cockfight," *AAIA Bulletin* 4: 20–37.

———. 2007. "The Men Who Built the Theatres: *Theatropolai*, *Theatronai*, and *Arkhitektones*," in Peter Wilson (ed.), *The Greek Theatre and Festivals: Documentary Studies* (Oxford: Oxford University Press), 87–121.

———. 2010. "The Context of Choregic Dedications," in Oliver Taplin and Rosie Wyles (eds.), *The Pronomos Vase and Its Context* (Oxford: Oxford University Press), 79–130.

———. 2015. "The Earliest Phase of 'Comic' Choral Entertainments in Athens: The Dionysian Pompe and the 'Birth' of Comedy," in Stylianos Chronopoulos and Christian Orth (eds.), *Fragmente einer Geschichte der griechischen Komödie/Fragmentary History of Greek Comedy* (Heidelberg: Verlag Antike), 66–108.

Csapo, Eric, and Margaret Miller (eds.). 2007. *The Origins of Theater in Ancient Greece and Beyond: From Ritual to Drama* (Cambridge: Cambridge University Press).

Csapo, Eric, and William J. Slater. 1994. *The Context of Ancient Drama* (Ann Arbor, MI: University of Michigan Press).

Daux, G. 1971. "Le serment des éphèbes athéniens," *REG* 84: 370–83.

Davidson, James. 2007. *The Greeks and Greek Love: A Bold New Exploration of the Ancient World* (New York: Random House).

Davies, J. K. 1971. *Athenian Propertied Families: 600–300 B.C.* (Oxford: Clarendon Press).

Dawe, R. D. 1968. "Some Reflections on Ate and Hamartia," *HSCP* 72: 89–123.

Dawkins, R. M. (ed.). 1929. *The Sanctuary of Artemis Orthia at Sparta*, *JHS*, supplement 5 (London: Macmillan).

Dayton, John. 2006. *The Athletes of War: An Evaluation of the Agonistic Elements in Greek Warfare* (Toronto: Edgar Kent).

Delavaud-Roux, Marie-Hélène. 1993. *Les Danses armées en Grèce antique* (Aix-en-Provence: Publications de l'Université de Provence).

Detienne, Marcel. 1968. "La Phalange: Problèmes et controverses," in *Problèmes de la guerre en Grèce ancienne*, ed. Jean-Pierre Vernant (Paris: La Haye Mouton), 119–42.

Deubner, Ludwig. 1932. *Attische Feste* (Berlin: H. Keller).

Diels, Hermann, and Walther Kranz (eds.). 1954. *Die Fragmente der Vorsokratiker*, 7th ed. (Berlin: Weidmann).

Diggle, J. 1970. *Euripides Phaethon* (Cambridge: Cambridge University Press).

Dilke, O.A.W. 1948. "The Greek Theatre Cavea," *BSA* 43: 125–92, plates 51–54.

———. 1950. "Details and Chronology of the Greek Theatre," *BSA* 45: 21–62, plates 1–5.

Dinsmoor, W. B. 1951. "The Athenian Theater of the Fifth Century," in *Studies Presented to David Moore Robinson on His Seventieth Birthday*, vol. 1 (St. Louis: Washington University), 309–30.

Downes, W.E.D. 1904. "The Offensive Weapon in the Pyrrhic," *CR* 18: 101–6.

Duncan, Anne. 2011. "Nothing to Do with Athens? Tragedians at the Courts of Tyrants," in D. M. Carter (ed.), *Why Athens: A Reappraisal of Tragic Politics* (Oxford: Oxford University Press), 69–84.

Duplouy, Alain. 2006. *Le Prestige des élites: Recherches sur les modes de reconnaissance sociale en Grèce entre les xe et ve siècles avant J.-C.* (Paris: Les Belles Lettres).

Edmondson, Colin N. 1982. "Onesippos' Herm," in *Studies in Attic Epigraphy History and Topography Presented to Eugene Vanderpool, Hesperia,* supplement 19 (Princeton, NJ: American School of Classical Studies at Athens), 48–50.

Else, Gerald F. 1957. *Aristotle's Poetics: The Argument* (Cambridge, MA: Harvard University Press).

Eyben, E. 1972. "Antiquity's View of Puberty," *Latomus* 31: 678–97.

Favi, Federico. 2017. *Fliaci testimonianze e frammenti,* Studia comica 7 (Heidelberg: Verlag Antike).

Foley, Helene P. 1988. "Tragedy and Politics in Aristophanes' *Acharnians*," *JHS* 108: 33–47.

———. 2000. "The Comic Body in Greek Art and Drama," in Beth Cohen (ed.), *Not the Classical Ideal: Athens and the Construction of the Other in Greek Art* (Leiden: Brill), 275–312.

———. 2001. *Female Acts in Greek Tragedy,* Martin Classical Lectures (Princeton, NJ: Princeton University Press).

Fouchard, Alain. 2010. "Comment reconnaître les élites en Grèce ancienne?," in Laurent Capdetrey and Yves Lafond (eds.), *La Cité et ses élites: Pratiques et représentation des forms de domination et de contrôle social dans les cités grecques* (Bordeaux: Ausonius), 359–78.

Friedrich, Wolf H. 1953. *Euripides und Diphilos,* Zetemata 5 (Munich: C. H. Beck).

Froning, Heide. 1971. *Dithyrambos und Vasenmalerei in Athen,* Beiträge zur Archäologie 2 (Würzburg: Triltsch).

Frontisi-Ducroux, Françoise, and François Lissarrague. 1990. "From Ambiguity to Ambivalence: A Dionysiac Excursion through the 'Anakreontic' Vases," in David M. Halperin, John J. Winkler, and Froma I. Zeitlin (eds.), *Before Sexuality: The Construction of Erotic Experience in the Ancient Greek World* (Princeton, NJ: Princeton University Press), 211–56.

Furtwängler, Adolf, and Karl Reichhold. 1904–32. *Griechische Vasenmalerei,* 3 vols. (Munich: F. Bruckmann A-G).

Garner, Richard. 1987. *Law and Society in Classical Athens* (London: Croom Helm).

Garvie, A. F. 1978. "Aeschylus' Simple Plots," in R. D. Dawe, J. Diggle, and P. E. Easterling (eds.), *Dionysiaca* (Cambridge: Published by The Editors, Classical Faculty Library, Cambridge), 63–86.

Gauthier, Philippe. 1976. *Un Commentaire historique des "Poroi" de Xénophon* (Geneva: Droz).

Gebhardt, Elizabeth. 1974. "The Form of the Orchestra in the Early Greek Theater," *Hesperia* 43: 428–40, plate 89.

Ghiron-Bistagne, Paulette. 1976. *Recherches sur les acteurs dans la Grèce antique* (Paris: Les Belles Lettres).

Gilmore, David D. (ed.). 1987. *Honor and Shame and the Unity of the Mediterranean* (Washington, DC: American Anthropological Association).

Giuliani, Luca. 1996. "Rhesus between Dream and Death: On the Relation of Image to Literature in Apulian Vase-Painting," *Bulletin of the Institute of Classical Studies* 41: 71–86.

———. 2010. "Rhesos: On the Production of Images and the Reading of Texts," in E. Walter-Karydi (ed.), *Myths, Texts, Images: Homeric Epics and Ancient Greek Art* (Ithaca: Centre for Odyssean Studies), 239–56.

Gleason, Maud. 1990. "The Semiotics of Gender: Physiognomy and Self-Fashioning in the Second Century C.E.," in David M. Halperin, John J. Winkler, and Froma I. Zeitlin (eds.), *Before Sexuality: The Construction of Erotic Experience in the Ancient Greek World* (Princeton, NJ: Princeton University Press), 389–416.

Goette, H. R. 2007. "An Archaeological Appendix," in Peter Wilson (ed.), *The Greek Theatre and Festivals: Documentary Studies* (Oxford: Oxford University Press), 116–21.

Golden, Leon. 1992. *Aristotle on Tragic and Comic Mimesis*, American Philological Association, American Classical Studies 29 (Atlanta: Scholars Press).

Golden, Mark. 1979. "Demosthenes and the Age of Majority at Athens," *Phoenix* 33.1: 25–38.

Goldhill, Simon. 1990. "The Great Dionysia and Civic Ideology," in John J. Winkler and Froma I. Zeitlin (eds.), *Nothing to Do with Dionysos? Athenian Drama in Its Social Context* (Princeton, NJ: Princeton University Press), 97–129.

———. 1994. "Representing Democracy: Women at the Great Dionysia," in R. Osborne and S. Hornblower (eds.), *Ritual, Finance, Politics: Athenian Democratic Accounts Presented to D. M. Lewis* (Oxford: Clarendon Press), 347–69.

Gomme, A. W., A. Andrewes, and K. J. Dover (eds.). 1945–81. *Historical Commentary on Thucydides*, 5 vols. (Oxford: Clarendon Press).

Goulaki-Voutira, Alexandra. 1996. "Pyrrhic Dance and Female Pyrrhic Dancers," *RIdIM/RCMI Newsletter* 21.1: 3–12.

Gouldner, Alvin W. 1965. *Enter Plato: Classical Greece and the Origins of Social Theory* (New York: Basic Books).

Graham, A. J. 1964. *Colony and Mother City in Ancient Greece* (Manchester: University Press).

Gray, V. J. 1985. "Xenophon's *Cynegeticus*," *Hermes* 113: 156–72.

Green, J. R. 1985. "A Representation of the *Birds* of Aristophanes," in Jifi Frel and Sandra Knudsen Morgan (eds.), *Greek Vases in the J. Paul Getty Museum* (Malibu, CA: The J. Paul Getty Museum), 2: 95–118.

———. 1991a. "Notes on Phlyax Vases," *Numismatica e Antichità Classiche. Quaderni Ticinesi* 20: 49–56.

———. 1991b. "On Seeing and Depicting the Theatre in Classical Athens," *GRBS* 32: 15–50.

———. 2007. "Let's Hear It for the Fat Man: Padded Dancers and the Prehistory of Drama," in Eric Csapo and Margaret Miller (eds.), *The Origins of Theater in Ancient Greece and Beyond: From Ritual to Drama* (Cambridge: Cambridge University Press), 96–107.

Green, J. R., and Beryl Rawson. 1981. *Antiquities: A Description of the Classics Department Museum in the Australian National University, Canberra* (Canberra: Faculty of Arts, Australian National University).

Greenhalgh, P.A.L. 1973. *Early Greek Warfare: Horsemen and Chariots in the Homeric and Archaic Ages* (Cambridge: Cambridge University Press).

Griffith, Mark. 1995. "Brilliant Dynasts: Power and Politics in the *Oresteia*," *ClAnt* 14: 62–129.

———. 2010. "Satyr Play and Tragedy, Face to Face," in Oliver Taplin and Rosie Wyles (eds.), *The Pronomos Vase and Its Context* (Oxford: Oxford University Press), 47–63.

———. 2011. "Extended Families, Marriage, and Inter-city Relations in (Later) Athenian Tragedy," in D. M. Carter (ed.), *Why Athens? A Reappraisal of Tragic Politics* (Oxford: Oxford University Press), 175–208.

Gudeman, A. 1934. *Aristoteles Poetik* (Berlin: de Gruyter).

Haigh, A. E. 1907. *The Attic Theater*, 3rd ed., revised by A. Pickard-Cambridge (Oxford: Clarendon Press).

Hall, Edith. 2010. "Tragic Theatre: Demetrios' Rolls and Dionysos' Other Woman," in Oliver Taplin and Rosie Wyles (eds.), *The Pronomos Vase and Its Context* (Oxford: Oxford University Press), 159–79.

Halliday, W. R. 1926. "Xanthos and Melanthos and the Origin of Tragedy," *CR* 40: 179–81.

Halliwell, Stephen. 1986. *Aristotle's Poetics* (London: Duckworth).

Halperin, David M. 1990a. "The Democratic Body: Prostitution and Citizenship in Classical Athens," in David Konstan and Martha Nussbaum (eds.), *Greek and Roman Sexuality* = *differences*, 2.1: 1–28.

———. 1990b. *One Hundred Years of Homosexuality and Other Essays on Greek Love* (New York: Routledge).

Halperin, David M., John J. Winkler, and Froma I. Zeitlin (eds.). 1990. *Before Sexuality: The Construction of Erotic Experience in the Ancient Greek World* (Princeton, NJ: Princeton University Press).

Hammond, N.G.L. 1972. "The Conditions of Dramatic Production to the Death of Aeschylus," *GRBS* 13: 387–450.

Hansen, M. H. 1977. "How Did the Athenian *Ecclesia* Vote?," *GRBS* 18: 135–36.

———. 1982. "The Athenian *Ecclesia* and the Pnyx," *GRBS* 23: 244–49.

Harder, Annette. 1985. *Euripides'* Kresphontes *and* Archelaos*: Introduction, Text and Commentary*, *Mnemosyne*, supplement 87 (Leiden: Brill).

Harris, Edward M. 1988. "When Was Aeschines Born?," *CP* 83: 211–14.

———. 2017. "How to 'Act' in an Athenian Court," in S. Pappaioannou, A. Serafim, and B. de Vela (eds.), *The Theater of Justice: Aspects of Performance in Greco-Roman Oratory and Rhetoric*, *Mnemosyne*, supplement 403 (Leiden: Brill), 223–42.

Harris, Edward M., Delfim F. Leão, and P. J. Rhodes (eds.). 2010. *Law and Drama in Ancient Greece* (London: Duckworth).

Harrison, J. E. 1902. "Is Tragedy the Goat-Song?," *CR* 16: 331–32.

Heath, Malcolm. 1987. *Political Comedy in Aristophanes*, *Hypomnemata*, supplement 87 (Göttingen: Vandenhoeck & Ruprecht).

Henderson, Jeffrey. 1991. "Women and the Athenian Dramatic Festivals," *TAPA* 121: 133–47.

Hercher, Rudolf. 1873. *Epistolographi Graeci* (Paris: Firmin Didot).

Herzfeld, Michael. 1986. *The Poetics of Manhood: Contest and Identity in a Cretan Mountain Village* (Princeton, NJ: Princeton University Press).

Hondius, J.J.E., and A. M. Woodward. 1919–21. "Inscriptions," *BSA* 24: 88–119.

Hubbard, Thomas (ed.). 2003. *Homosexuality in Greece and Rome: A Sourcebook of Basic Documents* (Berkeley: University of California Press).

Humphries, S. C. 1985. "Lycurgus of Butadae: An Athenian Aristocrat," in John W. Eadie and Josiah Ober (eds.), *The Craft of the Ancient Historian: Essays in Honor of Chester G. Starr* (Latham, MD: University Press of America), 199–252.

Isler-Kerényi, Cornelia. 2007. "Komasts, Mythic Imaginary, and Ritual," in Eric Csapo and Margaret Miller (eds.), *The Origins of Theater in Ancient Greece and Beyond: From Ritual to Drama* (Cambridge: Cambridge University Press), 77–95.

Jameson, Michael H. 1980. "Apollo Lykeios in Athens," *Archaiognosia* 1: 213–35.

Jeanmaire, Henri. 1913. "La Cryptie Lacédémonienne," *REG* 26: 121–50.

Jentoft-Nilsen, Marit. 1982. "Some Objects Relating to the Theatre," *J. P. Getty Museum Journal* 10: 159–64.

Johansen, K. Friis. 1959. *Eine Dithyrambosaufführung*, Arkaeologisk-kunsthistoriske Meddelelser udgivet af Det Kongelige Danske Videnshabcrnes Selskab, Bind 4, nr. 2 (Copenhagen: Munksgaard).

Jones, John. 1962. *On Aristotle and Greek Tragedy* (London: Chatto and Windus).

Jucker, H., and E. Risch. 1979. "Orthia oder Ortheia? Zum Namen der Göttin *Orthia*," *Hefte des Archäologischen Seminars der Universität Bern* 5: 27–32.

Junker, Klaus. 2010. "The Transformation of Athenian Theatre Culture around 400 BC," in Oliver Taplin and Rosie Wyles (eds.), *The Pronomos Vase and Its Context* (Oxford: Oxford University Press), 131–48.

Karouzou, S. P. 1946. "Choes," *AJA* 50: 122–39.

Katsouris, A. G. 1975. *Tragic Patterns in Menander* (Athens: Hellenic Society for Humanistic Studies).

Kistler, Erich. 2004. "'Kampf der Mentalitäten': Ian Morris' 'Elitist-' versus 'Middling-Ideology,'" in Robert Rollinger and Christoph Ulf (eds.), *Griechische Archaik: Interne Entwicklungen—Externe Impulse* (Berlin: Akademie Verlag), 145–76.

Kitto, H.D.F. 1955. "The Dance in Greek Tragedy," *JHS* 75: 36–41.

———. 1966. "Aristotle and Fourth Century Tragedy," in Maurice Kelly (ed.), *For Service to Classical Studies: Essays in Honour of Francis Letters* (Melbourne: F. W. Cheshire), 113–29.

Kolb, Frank. 1981. *Agora und Theater, Volks- und Festversammlung*, Archäologische Forschungen 9 (Berlin: Mann Verlag).

Konstan, David. 2013. "Propping Up Greek Tragedy: The Right Use of *Opsis*," in George W. M. Harrison and Vayos Liapis (eds.), *Performance in Greek and Roman Theatre*, *Mnemosyne*, supplement 353 (Leiden: Brill), 63–76.

Kowalzig, Barbara, and Peter Wilson, eds. 2013. *Dithyramb in Context* (Oxford: Oxford University Press).

Krentz, P. 1985. "The Nature of Hoplite Battle," *ClAnt* 4: 50–62.

———. 2000. "Deception in Archaic and Classical Greek Warfare," in H. van Wees (ed.), *War and Violence in Ancient Greece* (Swansea: Classical Press of Wales), 167–200.

———. 2002. "Fighting by the Rules: The Invention of the Hoplite Agon," *Hesperia* 71: 23–39.

Kunisch, Norbert. 1974. "Parthenopaios," *AK* 17: 39–41.

Kurke, Leslie. 1999. *Coins, Bodies, Games, and Gold: The Politics of Meaning in Archaic Greece* (Princeton, NJ: Princeton University Press).

———. 2007. "Visualizing the Choral: Epichoric Poetry, Ritual and Elite Negotiation in Fifth-Century Thebes," in Chris Kraus, Simon Goldhill, Helene P. Foley, and Jaś Elsner (eds.), *Visualizing the Tragic: Drama, Myth, and Ritual in Greek Art and Literature* (Oxford: Oxford University Press), 63–101.

———. 2011. *Aesopic Conversations: Popular Tradition, Cultural Dialogue, and the Invention of Greek Prose* (Princeton, NJ: Princeton University Press).

Labarbe, Jules. 1953. "L'âge correspondant au sacrifice du *koureion* et les données historiques du sixième discours d'Isée," *Bulletin de la Classe des Lettres de l'Académie Royale de Belgique*, 5th ser., no. 39: 358–94.

Latacz, Joachim. 1977. *Kampfparänese, Kampfdarstellung und Kampfwirklichkeit in der Ilias, bei Kallinos und Tyrtaios*, Zetemata 66 (Munich: C.H. Beck).

Lattimore, Richmond. 1958. *The Poetry of Greek Tragedy* (Baltimore: Johns Hopkins University Press).

———. 1964. *Story Patterns in Greek Tragedy* (Ann Arbor, MI: University of Michigan Press).

Lawler, Lillian B. 1964. *The Dance of the Ancient Greek Theatre* (Iowa City: University of Iowa Press).

Lear, Andrew, and Eva Cantarella. 2008. *Images of Greek Pederasty: Boys Were Their Gods* (New York: Routledge).

Lech, Marcel Lysgaard. 2009a. "Marching Choruses? Choral Performance in Athens," *GRBS* 49.3: 343–61.

———. 2009b. "The Shape of the Athenian Theatron in the Fifth Century: Overlooked Evidence," *GRBS* 49.2: 223–26.

Lewis, D. M. 1958. "When Was Aeschines Born?" *CR*, n.s. 8: 108.

———. 1973. "Attic Ephebic Inscriptions," *CR*, n.s. 23: 254–55.

Lippold, G. 1937. "Zu den Imagines Illustrium," *MDAI (Römische Abteilung)* 52: 44–47.

Lissarrague, François. 1990. "Why Satyrs Are Good to Represent," in John J. Winkler and Froma I. Zeitlin (eds.), *Nothing to Do with Dionysos? Athenian Drama in Its Social Context* (Princeton, NJ: Princeton University Press), 228–36.

Lloyd-Jones, Hugh (ed., trans., and comm.). 1996. *Sophocles: Fragments*, Loeb Classical Library (Cambridge, MA: Harvard University Press).

Lofberg, John O. 1925. "The Date of the Athenian *Ephebeia*," *CP* 20: 330–35.

Lonsdale, Steven. 1993. *Dance and Ritual Play in Greek Religion* (Baltimore: Johns Hopkins University Press).

Loraux, Nicole. 1986. *The Invention of Athens*, trans. Alan Sheridan (Cambridge, MA: Harvard University Press).

Lorimer, Hilda L. 1947. "The Hoplite Phalanx," *BSA* 42: 76–138.

Lucas, D. W. (ed. with comm.). 1981. *Aristotle:* Poetics (Oxford: Clarendon Press).

Luce, Stephen Bleecker. 1930. "Attic Red-Figured Vases and Fragments at Corinth," *AJA* 34: 334–43.

Luppe, W. 1972. "Die Zahl der Konkurrenten an den komischen Agonen zur Zeit des Peloponnesischen Krieges," *Philologus* 116: 53–75.

Ma, John. 1994. "Black Hunter Variations," *PCPS* 40: 49–80.

——. 2008. "The Black Hunter Revisited," *Cambridge Classical Journal* 54: 188–208.

Maass, Michael. 1972. *Die Prohedrie des Dionysostheaters in Athen*, Vestigia 15 (Munich: C.H. Beck).

McCoskey, Denise Eileen, and Emily Zakin (eds). 2009. *Bound by the City: Greek Tragedy, Sexual Difference, and the Formation of the* Polis (Albany: State University of New York Press).

McCulloch, H. Y., and H. D. Cameron. 1980. "Septem 12–13 and the Athenian Ephēbia," *Illinois Classical Studies* 5: 1–14.

McDonald, W. A. 1943. *The Political Meeting Places of the Greeks*, Johns Hopkins University Studies in Archaeology 34 (Baltimore: Johns Hopkins Press).

Margoliouth, David S. 1911. *The Poetics of Aristotle* (London: Hodder and Stoughton).

Marshall, C. W. 2014. *The Structure and Performance of Euripides'* Helen (Cambridge: Cambridge University Press).

Marx, William. 2012. *Le Tombeau d'Oedipe. Pour une tragédie sans tragique* (Paris: Éditions de Minuit).

Maxwell-Stuart, P. G. 1970. "Remarks on the Black Coats of the Ephebes," *PCPS* 196, n.s. 16: 113–16.

Meier, Christian. 1993. *The Political Art of Greek Tragedy*, trans. Andrew Webber (Baltimore: Johns Hopkins University Press).

Merkelbach, R. 1972. "Aglauros, die Religion der Epheben," *ZPE* 9: 277–83.

——. 1973. "Der Theseus des Bakchilides (Gedicht für ein attisches Ephebenfest)," *ZPE* 12: 56–62.

Mette, H. J. 1982. "Von der Jugend," *Hermes* 110: 257–68.

Miller, M.C. 1999. "Reexamining Transvestism in Archaic and Classical Athens: The Zewadski Stamnos," *AJA* 103: 223–53.

Mingazzini, Paolino. 1969. *Greek Pottery Painting* (London: Hamlyn).

Mitchel, F. W. 1964. "Derkylos of Hagnous and the Date of *IG*[2] II 1187," *Hesperia* 33: 337–51.

——. 1975. "The So-Called Earliest Ephebic Inscription," *ZPE* 19: 233–43.

Mitchell, Lynette G., and P. J. Rhodes (eds.). 1997. *The Development of the* Polis *in Archaic Greece* (New York: Routledge).

Mitchell-Boyask, Robin. 1999. "Euripides' *Hippolytus* and the Trials of Manhood (The Ephebia?)," in Mark W. Padilla (ed.), *Rites of Passage in Ancient Greece: Literature, Religion, Society* (Lewisburg, PA: Bucknell University Press), 42–66.

Mitsos, M. 1965. "Χορηγικὴ ἐπιγραφὴ ἐκ Βαρκίζης," *Archaiologikē Ephēmeris* 104: 163–67.

Moles, John. 1979. "Notes on Aristotle, *Poetics* 13 and 14," *CQ* 29: 77–94.

Moreau, Jacques. 1954. "Sur les *Saisons* d'Aristophane," *La Nouvelle Clio* 6: 327–44.

Morris, Ian. 1996. "The Strong Principle of Equality and the Archaic Origins of Greek Democracy," in Josiah Ober and Charles Hedrick (eds.), *Demokratia: A Conversation on Democracies, Ancient and Modern* (Princeton, NJ: Princeton University Press), 19–48.

Munn, Mark. 1996. "First Excavations at Panakton on the Attic-Boiotian Frontier," *Boeotia Antiqua* 6: 47–58.

———. 2010. "Panakton and Drymos: A Disputed Frontier," in Hans Lohmann and Torsten Mattern (eds.), *Attika: Archäologie einer "zentralen" Kulturlandschaft* (Wiesbaden: Harrassowitz Verlag), 189–200.

Musso, Olimpio. 1974. *Euripide / Cresfonte: Introduzione, testo critico dei frammenti e commento*, Testi e documenti per lo studio dell'antichità 47 (Milan: Istituto editoriale cisalpino—La goliardica).

Nauck, Augustus. rpr. 1964. *Tragicorum Graecorum Fragmenta*, 2nd ed. (Hildesheim: Olms).

Nimis, S. 1984. "Fussnoten: Das Fundament der Wissenschaft," *Arethusa* 17: 105–34.

Ober, Josiah. 1985. *Fortress Attica: Defense of the Athenian Land Frontier, 404–322 B.C.*, *Mnemosyne*, supplement 84 (Leiden: Brill).

———. 1989. *Mass and Elite in Democratic Athens* (Princeton, NJ: Princeton University Press).

———. 2008. *Democracy and Knowledge: Innovation and Learning in Classical Athens* (Princeton, NJ: Princeton University Press).

Ormand, Kirk (ed.). 2012. *A Companion to Sophocles* (Malden, MA: Wiley-Blackwell).

———. 2014. *The Hesiodic* Catalogue of Women *and Archaic Greece* (New York: Cambridge University Press).

Osborne, Robin. 1985. "The Erection and Mutilation of the Hermai," *PCPS* 31: 47–73.

———. 1987. *Classical Landscape with Figures: The Ancient Greek City and Its Countryside* (London: George Philip).

———. 2010. "Who's Who on the Pronomos Vase?," in Oliver Taplin and Rosie Wyles (eds.), *The Pronomos Vase and Its Context* (Oxford: Oxford University Press), 149–58.

Padilla, Mark W. (ed.). 1999. *Rites of Passage in Ancient Greece: Literature, Religion, Society* (Lewisburg, PA: Bucknell University Press).

Page, Denys L. 1934. *Actors' Interpolations in Greek Tragedy* (Oxford: Clarendon Press).

——— (ed.). 1962. *Poetae Melici Graeci* (Oxford: Clarendon Press).

——— (ed.). 1972. *Aeschyli septem quae supersunt tragoedias* (Oxford: Clarendon Press).

Parke, Herbert W. 1977. *Festivals of the Athenians* (Ithaca, NY: Cornell University Press).

Parker, Holt. 2015. "Vaseworld," in Ruby Blondell and Kirk Ormand (eds.), *Ancient Sex: New Essays* (Columbus, OH: Ohio State University Press), 23–142.

Patterson, C. 1987. "*Hai Attikai*: The Other Athenians," in Marilyn Skinner (ed.), *Rescuing Creusa: New Methodological Approaches to Women in Antiquity*, special issue of *Helios*, n.s. 13.2: 49–67.

Pearson, A. C. 1917. *The Fragments of Sophocles*, 3. vols. (Cambridge: Cambridge University Press).

Pelagatti, Paola. 1957. "La ceramica Laconica del museo di Taranto," *Annuario della Scuola archeologica di Atene e delle missioni italiane in Oriente* (Istituto Poligrafico dello Stato): 7–44.

Pélékidis, Chrysis. 1962. *Histoire de l'éphébie attique des origines à 31 avant Jésus-Christ* (Paris: E. de Boccard).

Pickard-Cambridge, Arthur W. 1946. *The Theatre of Dionysus in Athens* (Oxford: Clarendon Press).

———. 1962. *Dithyramb Tragedy and Comedy*, 2nd ed., rev. T.B.L. Webster (Oxford: Clarendon Press).

Pleket, H. W. 1965. Review of Ch. Pélékidis, *Histoire de l'éphébie attique des origines à 31 avant Jésus-Christ* (Paris, E. de Boccard, 1962), *Mnemosyne* ser. 4, 18: 441–46.

Pöhlmann, E. 1981. "Die Proedrie des Dionysostheaters im 5. Jahrhundert und das Bühnenspiel der Klassik," *MH* 38: 129–46.

Poppelreuter, Josephus. 1893. *De comoediae atticae primordiis particulae duae* (Berlin: Ullstein).

Porter, J. R. 1990. "Tiptoeing through the Corpses: Euripides' *Electra*, Apollonius, and the Bouphonia," *GRBS* 31: 255–80.

Poursat, J.-C. 1967. "Une vase signée du Musée National d'Athènes: Pyrrhicistes victorieux," *BCH* 91: 102–10.

———. 1968. "Les représentations de danse armée dans la céramique attique," *BCH* 92: 550–615.

Powers, Melinda. 2018. *Diversifying Greek Tragedy on the Contemporary US Stage* (Oxford: Oxford University Press).

Price, Sarah. 1990. "Anacreontic Vases Reconsidered," *GRBS* 31: 133–75.

Pritchett, William K. 1974. *The Greek State at War, Part II* (Berkeley: University of California Press).

Quinn, Josephine Crawley. 2007. "Herms, Kouroi, and the Political Anatomy of Athens," *G&R* 54.1: 82–105.

Raaflaub, Kurt. 1993. "Homer to Solon: The Rise of the Polis. The Written Sources," in M. H. Hansen (ed.), *The Ancient Greek City-State: Symposium on the Occasion of the 250th Anniversary of The Royal Danish Academy of Sciences and Letters, July 1–4, 1992*, Historisk-filosofiske Meddelelser 67 (Copenhagen: Munksgaard), 41–105.

———. 1997. "Soldiers, Citizens, and the Evolution of the Early Greek *Polis*," in Lynette G. Mitchell and P. J. Rhodes (eds.), *The Development of the* Polis *in Archaic Greece* (New York: Routledge), 49–59.

Radermacher, L. 1924. *Zur Geschichte der griechischen Komödie* (Vienna and Leipzig: Hölder-Pichler-Tempsky).

Radt, S. L. 1976. "Zum 13. Kapitel von Aristotles' *Poetik*," in J. M. Bremer, S. L. Radt, and C. J. Ruijgh (eds.), *Miscellanea Tragica in honorem J. C. Kamerbeek* (Amsterdam: Hakkert), 271–84.

Rees, B. R. 1972. "*Pathos* in the *Poetics* of Aristotle," *G&R* ser. 2, 19: 1–11.

Reinmuth, O. 1952. "The Genesis of the Athenian Ephebia," *TAPA* 83: 34–50.

———. 1971. *The Ephebic Inscriptions of the Fourth Century B.C.*, *Mnemosyne*, supplement 14 (Leiden: Brill).

Revermann, Martin. 2006. *Comic Business: Theatricality, Dramatic Technique, and Performance Contexts of Aristophanic Comedy* (Oxford: Oxford University Press).

Rhodes, Peter J. 1972. *The Athenian Boule* (Oxford: Clarendon Press).

———. 1980. "Ephebi, Bouleutae and the Population of Athens," *ZPE* 38: 191–97.

———. 1981. *A Commentary on the Aristotelian* Athenaion Politeia (Oxford: Clarendon Press).

Rhodes, Peter J., and Robin Osborne. 2004. *Greek Historical Inscriptions, 404–323 BC* (Oxford: Oxford University Press).

Richter, G. 1942. "Another Archaic Greek Mirror," *AJA* 46: 319–24.

Ridley, P. T. 1979. "The Hoplite as Citizen: Athenian Military Institutions in Their Social Context," *AC* 48: 508–48.

Risom, S. 1913. "Le siège du prêtre de Dionysos Eleuthereus au théâtre d'Athènes," in *Mélanges Holleaux. Recueil de mémoires concernant l'antiquité grecque offert à Maurice Holleaux en souvenir de ses années de direction à l'École française d'Athènes (1904–1912)* (Paris: A. Picard), 257–63.

Robertson, Bruce. 2000. "The Scrutiny of New Citizens at Athens," in Virginia J. Hunter and J. C. Edmondson (eds.), *Law and Social Status in Classical Athens* (Oxford: Oxford University Press), 149–74.

Roos, Ervin. 1951. *Die tragische Orchestik im Zerrbild der altattischen Komödie* (Lund: Gleerup).

Rorty, Amélie Oksenberg (ed.). 1992. *Essays on Aristotle's Poetics* (Princeton, NJ: Princeton University Press).

Rose, Herbert Jennings (ed.). 1933. *Hygini Fabulae* (Leiden: A.W. Sijthoff).

Rosen, Ralph, and Ineke Sluiter (eds.). 2003. *Andreia: Studies in Manliness and Courage in Classical Antiquity* (Leiden: Brill).

Rosenmeyer, Thomas G. 1985. "Ancient Literary Genres: A Mirage?" *Yearbook of Comparative and General Literature* 34: 74–84.

Rothwell, Kenneth S., Jr. 2007. *Nature, Culture, and the Origins of Greek Comedy: A Study of Animal Choruses* (Cambridge: Cambridge University Press).

Roussel, Pierre. 1941. "Les Chlamydes noires des éphèbes athéniens," *REA* 43: 163–65.

——. 1942. *Étude sur le principe de l'ancienneté dans le monde hellénique*, Académie des inscriptions et belles-lettres, Mémoires de l'Institut national de France, vol. 43, part 2 (Paris: Imprimerie Nationale).

Ruschenbusch, E. 1979. "Die soziale Herkunft der Epheben um 330," *ZPE* 35: 173–76.

——. 1981. "Epheben, Bouleuten und die Bürgerzahl von Athen um 330 v. Chr.," *ZPE* 41: 103–5.

Rusten, Jeffrey. 1982. "Dicaearchus and the *Tales from Euripides*," *GRBS* 23: 357–67.

Sackey, Albert A. 2010. "The Hamartia of Aristotle," *Legon* 21: 77–99.

Salmon, J. 1977. "Political Hoplites?" *JHS* 97: 84–101.

Samsell, Lennie, Michael Regier, Cheryl Walton, and Lesley Cottrell. 2014. "Importance of Android/Gynoid Fat Ratio in Predicting Metabolic and Cardiovascular Disease Risk in Normal Weight as Well as Overweight and Obese Children," *Journal of Obesity* 2014, Article ID 846578, 7 pages, https://doi.org/10.1155/2014/846578.

Sayers, Dorothy. 1946. *Unpopular Opinions* (London: Gollancz).

Scarpi, Paolo. 1979. "La pyrrichè o le armi della persuasione," *Dialoghi di Archeologia*, n.s. 1: 78–97.

Schmidt, Margot. 1967. "Dionysien," *AK* 19: 70–81.

Schneider-Hermann, G. 1982. "Two Apulian Red-Figured Vases," in M. L. Gualandi, L. Massei, and S. Settis (eds.), *Aparchai: Nuove ricerche e studi sulla Magna Grecia e sulla Sicilia antica in onore di Paolo Enrico Arias* (Pisa: Giardini), 501–4, plates 140–41.

Schwartz, Adam. 2009. *Reinstating the Hoplite: Arms, Armour and Phalanx Fighting in Archaic and Classical Greece, Historia* Einzelschriften 207 (Stuttgart: Steiner Verlag).

Scott, Gregory L. 2018. *Aristotle's Favorite Tragedy:* Oedipus *or* Cresphontes*?*, 2nd ed. (New York: ExistencePS Press).

Shapiro, H. A. 1981. *Art, Myth, and Culture: Greek Vases from Southern Collections* (New Orleans: New Orleans Museum of Art, in conjunction with Tulane University).

Shüler, Will. 2017. "The Greek Tragic Chorus and Its Training for War: Movement, Music and Harmony in Theatrical and Military Performance," in *War and Theatrical Innovation*, ed. Victor Emeljanow (London: Palgrave Macmillan), 3–21.

Siewert, Peter. 1977. "The Ephebic Oath in Fifth-Century Athens," *JHS* 97: 102–11.

——. 1982. *Die Trittyen Attikas und die Heeresreform des Kleisthenes*, Vestigia 33 (Munich: C. H. Beck).

Sifakis, Gregory M. 1967. *Studies in the History of Hellenistic Drama* (London: Athlone Press).

Simon, Erika. 1968. "Tereus. Zur Deutung der Würzburger Satyrspieler-Scherbe," *Festschrift des Kronberg-Gymnasiums* (Aschaffenburg), 155–67.

——. 1971. "Die 'Omphale' des Demetrios: Zur Satyrspielvase in Neapel," *AA* 86: 199–206.

——. 1982 [1972]. *The Ancient Theatre*, trans. C. E. Vafopoulou-Richardson (London: Methuen).

——. 1983. *The Festivals of Attica: An Archaeological Commentary* (Madison, WI: University of Wisconsin Press).

Skinner, Marilyn. 2013 [2005]. *Sexuality in Greek and Roman Culture*, 2nd ed. (Malden, MA: Wiley-Blackwell).

Slater, William J., and Martin Cropp. 2009. "Leukippe as Tragedy," *Philologus* 153.1: 63–85.

Smith, Cecil H. 1881. "Actors with Bird-Masks on Vases," *JHS* 2: 309–14.

Smith, Tyler Jo. 2007. "The Corpus of Komast Vases: From Identity to Exegesis," in Eric Csapo and Margaret Miller (eds.), *The Origins of Theater in Ancient Greece and Beyond: From Ritual to Drama* (Cambridge: Cambridge University Press), 48–76.

——. 2010. *Komast Dancers in Archaic Greek Art* (Oxford: Oxford University Press).

Snodgrass, Anthony. 1965. "The Hoplite Reform and History," *JHS* 85: 110–22.

——. 1980. *Archaic Greece: The Age of Experiment* (Berkeley: University of California Press).

——. 1993a. "The 'Hoplite Reform' Revisited," *Dialogues d'histoire ancienne*, 19: 47–61.

——. 1993b. "The Rise of the *Polis*: The Archaeological Evidence," in M. H. Hansen (ed.), *The Ancient Greek City-State: Symposium on the Occasion of the 250th Anniversary of The Royal Danish Academy of Sciences and Letters, July 1–4, 1992*, Historisk-filosofiske Meddelelser 67 (Copenhagen: Munksgaard), 30–40.

Sommerstein, Alan. 2010. "Adolescence, ephebeia, and Athenian Drama," in *The Tangled Ways of Zeus and Other Studies in and around Greek Tragedy* (Oxford: Oxford University Press), 48–60.

Stanton, G. R., and P. J. Bicknell. 1987. "Voting in Tribal Groups in the Athenian Assembly," *GRBS* 28: 51–92.

Staveley, E. S. 1972. *Greek and Roman Voting and Elections* (London: Thames & Hudson).

Stewart, Edmund. 2017. *Greek Tragedy on the Move: The Birth of a Panhellenic Art Form c. 500–300 BC* (Oxford: Oxford University Press).

Stinton, T.C.W. 1975. "*Hamartia* in Aristotle and Greek Tragedy," *CQ* 25: 221–54.

Stone, Laura M. 1981. *Costume in Aristophanic Comedy* (New York: Arno Press).

Szemerényi, O. 1971. Review of Pierre Chantraine, *Dictionnaire Étymologique de la langue grecque* 1–2, *Gnomon* 43: 641–75.

Taplin, Oliver. 1987. "Phallology, *Phylakes*, Iconography and Aristophanes," *PCPS*, n.s. 33: 92–104.

——. 1993. *Comic Angels and Other Approaches to Greek Drama through Vase Painting* (Oxford: Clarendon).

Taplin, Oliver, and Rosie Wyles (eds.). 2010. *The Pronomos Vase and Its Context* (Oxford: Oxford University Press).

Tölle, Renate. 1964. *Frühgriechische Reigentänze* (Waldsassen: Stiftland-Verlag).

Trendall, A. D. n.d. *Greek Vases in University House* (Canberra).

——. 1967. *Phlyax Vases, Bulletin of the Institute of Classical Studies*, supplement 19 (London: University of London, Institute of Classical Studies).

Tronchetti, Carlo. 1983. *Ceramica Attica a figure nere: grandi vasi, anfore, pelikai, crateri*, Materiali del Museo Archeologico Nazionale di Tarquinia 6 (Rome: G. Bretschneider).

Van Gennep, Arnold. 1960. *The Rites of Passage*, trans. M. B. Vizedom and G. L. Caffee (Chicago: University of Chicago Press).

Van Hoorn, G. 1951. *Choes and Anthesteria* (Leiden: Brill).

Van Looy, Herman. 1963. "Les fragments d'Euripide," *AC* 32:162–99, 607–8.

Van Weyenberg, Astrid. 2013. *The Politics of Adaptation: Contemporary African Drama and Greek Tragedy* (Amsterdam and New York: Rodopi).

Vernant, Jean-Pierre. 1991. *Mortals and Immortals: Collected Essays*, ed. Froma I. Zeitlin (Princeton, NJ: Princeton University Press).

Vickers, Brian. 1973. *Towards Greek Tragedy: Drama, Myth, Society* (London: Longman).

Vickers, Michael. 1978. *Greek Vases* (Oxford: Ashmolean Museum).

Vidal-Naquet, Pierre. 1981. "The Black Hunter and the Origin of the Athenian *Ephebeia*," in R. L. Gordon (ed.), *Myth, Religion and Society: Structuralist Essays by M. Detienne, L. Gernet, J.-P. Vernant & P. Vidal-Naquet* (Cambridge: Cambridge University Press), 147–62.

———. 1986a. *The Black Hunter: Forms of Thought and Forms of Society in the Greek World*, trans. Andrew Szegedy-Maszak (Baltimore: Johns Hopkins University Press).

———. 1986b. "The Black Hunter Revisited," *PCPS*, n.s. 32: 126–44.

Webster, Thomas B. L. 1948. "South Italian Vases and Attic Drama," *CQ* 42: 15–27.

———. 1954. "Fourth Century Tragedy and the Poetics," *Hermes* 82: 294–308.

———. 1956. *Greek Theater Production* (London: Methuen).

———. 1960. "Greek Dramatic Monuments from the Agora and Pnyx," *Hesperia* 29.3: 254–84, plates 65–68.

———. 1962. *Monuments Illustrating Tragedy and Satyr Play, Bulletin of the Institute of Classical Studies*, supplement 14 (London: University of London, Institute of Classical Studies).

———. 1967. *The Tragedies of Euripides* (London: Methuen).

———. 1970. *The Greek Chorus* (London: Methuen).

Wehrli, Fritz. 1976 [1931]. *Lathe Biōsas. Studien zur ältesten Ethik bei den Griechen* (Stuttgart: Teubner).

Wetmore, Kevin. 2002. *The Athenian Sun in an African Sky: Modern African Adaptations of Classical Greek Tragedy* (Jefferson, NC: McFarland).

Wheeler, E. L. 1982. "*Hoplomachia* and Greek Dances in Arms," *GRBS* 23: 225–29.

White, Stephen. 1992. "Aristotle's Favorite Tragedies," in Amélie Oksenberg Rorty (ed.), *Essays on Aristotle's Poetics* (Princeton, NJ: Princeton University Press), 221–40.

———. 1995. "Thrasymachus the Diplomat," *CP* 90: 307–27.

Wide, S. 1898. *Lakonische Kulte* (Leipzig: Teubner).

Wilamowitz-Moellendorf, U. von. 1883. "Die Beiden Elektren," *Hermes* 18: 214–63.

———. 1893. *Aristoteles und Athen* (Berlin: Weidmann).

Wiles, David. 1997. *Tragedy in Athens: Performance Space and Theatrical Meaning* (Cambridge: Cambridge University Press).

Wilson, Peter. 2000. *The Athenian Institution of the* Khoregia: *The Chorus, the City and the Stage* (Cambridge: Cambridge University Press).

——— (ed.). 2007a. *The Greek Theatre and Festivals: Documentary Studies* (Oxford: Oxford University Press).

———. 2007b. "Performance in the *Pythion*: The Athenian Thargelia," in Peter Wilson (ed.), *The Greek Theatre and Festivals: Documentary Studies* (Oxford: Oxford University Press), 150–82.

———. 2011. "The Glue of Democracy? Tragedy, Structure, and Finance," in D. M. Carter (ed.), *Why Athens: A Reappraisal of Tragic Politics* (Oxford: Oxford University Press), 19–44.

Winkler, Jack. 1981. "Gardens of Nymphs: Public and Private in Sappho's Lyrics," *Women's Studies: An Inter-Disciplinary Journal* 8.1–2: 65–91.

Winkler, John J. 1994 [1982]. "The Invention of Romance," in J. Tatum (ed.), *The Search for the Ancient Novel* (Baltimore: Johns Hopkins University Press), 23–38.

———. 1985. "The Ephebes' Song: *Tragôidia* and *Polis*," *Representations* 11: 26–62.

———. 1989. "Women in Armor Men in Drag: The Poetics of Manhood in Athenian Drama," *Stanford Humanities Review*, 1.1 (Spring): 6–24.

———. 1990a. *The Constraints of Desire: The Anthropology of Sex and Gender in Ancient Greece* (New York: Routledge).

———. 1990b. "The Ephebes' Song: *Tragōidia* and *Polis*," in John J. Winkler and Froma I. Zeitlin (eds.), *Nothing to Do with Dionysos? Athenian Drama in Its Social Context* (Princeton, NJ: Princeton University Press, 1990), 20–62.

———. 1990c. "Phallos Politikos: Representing the Body Politic in Athens," in David Konstan and Martha Nussbaum (eds.), *Greek and Roman Sexuality*=*differences*, 2.1: 29–45.

Winks, Robin W. 1980. *Detective Fiction: A Collection of Critical Essays* (Englewood Cliffs, NJ: Prentice-Hall).

Wohl, Victoria. 1998. *Intimate Commerce: Exchange, Gender, and Subjectivity in Greek Tragedy* (Austin, TX: University of Texas Press).

Wolff, Christian. 1992. "Euripides' *Iphigenia among the Taurians*: Aetiology, Ritual, and Myth," *ClAnt* 11.2: 308–34.

Worman, Nancy. 2015. "What Is 'Greek Sex' For?," in Ruby Blondell and Kirk Ormand (eds.), *Ancient Sex: New Essays* (Columbus, OH: Ohio State University Press), 208–30.

Worthington, I. 1985. "KINDUNEUEIN: To Be on Trial," *PP* 40: 38–39.

Wurster, Wolfgang W. 1979. "Die neuen Untersuchungen am Dionysostheater in Athen," *Architectura* 9: 58–76.

Wyles, Rosie. 2010. "The Tragic Costumes," in Oliver Taplin and Rosie Wyles (eds.), *The Pronomos Vase and Its Context* (Oxford: Oxford University Press), 231–53.

Yatromanolakis, Dimitrios. 2008. *Sappho in the Making: The Early Reception* (Washington, DC: Center for Hellenic Studies).

———. 2001. "Visualizing Poetry: An Early Representation of Sappho," *CP* 96: 159–68.

Zeitlin, Froma I. 1996. *Playing the Other: Gender and Society in Classical Greek Literature* (Chicago: University of Chicago Press).

Zuntz, G. 1965. *An Inquiry into the Transmission of the Plays of Euripides* (Cambridge: Cambridge University Press).

INDEX LOCORUM

GENERAL INDEX

Page numbers in *italics* denote figures.

A NOTE ON THE AUTHOR

JOHN J. WINKLER WAS born on August 11, 1943, and died on April 25, 1990, at the age of forty-six. His publishing career lasted barely a decade, but in that time he wrote three books and nineteen articles, coedited or coauthored four other books, and translated into English a late Greek novel, *Leucippe and Clitophon*, by Achilles Tatius. He was one of the most talented and original classical scholars of his generation.

Winkler specialized in popular, marginal, and noncanonical literature, such as folk narratives, melodramas, magical spells, and dream-books. When he came to treat more dignified literary forms, he emphasized their playfulness as well as the divergent meanings they held for different groups within the local communities that produced them. He sidestepped the history of ideas in favor of an anthropologically grounded analysis of social practices. His work transformed several fields of classical studies, promoted a variety of feminist, anthropological, narratological, and theoretical approaches to the study of Greek and Latin texts, and contributed to both lesbian and gay male studies.

Winkler was born in St. Louis, Missouri. He attended St. Louis University from 1960 to 1963, where he produced a text and translation of the *Carmen de Algorismo* from a study of five Vatican Library manuscripts. Upon graduation, he declined a Woodrow Wilson Fellowship to join the Benedictine order. He trained at St. Lawrence's Abbey in Ampleforth, England, until 1966, returning to teach at the St. Louis Priory until 1970. In that year, he left the Benedictines and entered the doctoral program in Classics at the University of Texas at Austin. He received a PhD in 1974 for a dissertation entitled "In Pursuit of Nymphs: Comedy and Sex in Nonnos' Tales of Dionysos."

Winkler taught at Yale and at Stanford, was a Mellon Fellow at the University of Southern California, and held fellowships from the National Endowment for the Humanities, the American Council of Learned Societies, and the Guggenheim Foundation; he was the first Stanford faculty member to hold two Internal Fellowships at the Stanford Humanities Center. He received the Goodwin Award of Merit from the American Philological Association for his book *Auctor & Actor: A Narratological Reading of Apuleius's* The Golden Ass (Berkeley: University of California Press, 1985). His first book, *Later Greek Literature,* was a coedited collection of essays for the Yale Classical Studies series that appeared in 1982. He coedited three books with Princeton University Press: *Nothing to Do with Dionysos? Athenian Drama in Its Social Context* (1990), *Before Sexuality: The Construction of Erotic Experience in the Ancient Greek World* (1990), and *Ancient Greek Novels: The Fragments* (1995). A final book, *The Constraints of Desire: The Anthropology of Sex and Gender in Ancient Greece* (New York: Routledge, 1990), brings together a number of his essays on female agency and male bravado in the ancient Mediterranean world.

Winkler was not only a scholar. He was also a tireless, intrepid, and effective political activist, especially for feminist, gay, and minority causes within the academy. While an assistant professor at Yale, he helped to found a women's studies program at the university, and in 1977 he was one of the chief organizers (and the only faculty organizer) of Gay Rights Week, one of the first initiatives to address lesbian and gay concerns on a college campus. He continued to work for a variety of women's and minority interests while at Stanford. When he was diagnosed with AIDS, he used his own case to educate the Stanford community about the pandemic. In accordance with his final wishes, the proceeds from the sale of this volume will contribute to funding The John J. Winkler Memorial Prize that, since 1991, has been awarded annually to the author of the best undergraduate or graduate paper in a risky or marginal field of classical studies.